SLEUTHS, INC.

Also by HUGH EAMES
WINNER LOSE ALL: DR. COOK
AND THE THEFT OF THE NORTH POLE

SLEUTHS, INC.

Studies of Problem Solvers
**DOYLE
SIMENON
HAMMETT
AMBLER
CHANDLER**

HUGH EAMES

J. B. LIPPINCOTT COMPANY

Philadelphia and New York

Grateful acknowledgment is made to the following for permission to quote the excerpts described:

Atheneum Publishers: From Eric Ambler's *The Intercom Conspiracy,* copyright © 1969 by Eric Ambler; *The Levanter,* copyright © 1972 by Eric Ambler; and *Dr. Frigo,* copyright © 1974 by Eric Ambler.

Jonathan Cape and John Murray: From Eric Ambler's Introduction to *The Adventures of Sherlock Holmes* by Arthur Conan Doyle, copyright © 1974 by Eric Ambler.

Delacorte Press: From the book *The Choirboys* by Joseph Wambaugh. Copyright © 1975 by Joseph Wambaugh. Reprinted by permission of Delacorte Press.

E. P. Dutton: From *The Life of Raymond Chandler* by Frank MacShane. Copyright © 1976 by Frank MacShane. Reprinted by permission of the publishers, E. P. Dutton.

Harvard University Press: From *The Molly Maguires* by Wayne G. Broehl, Jr., copyright © 1964 by the President and Fellows of Harvard College.

Houghton Mifflin Company: From *The Simple Art of Murder* by Raymond Chandler, copyright © 1950 by Raymond Chandler, and *The Long Goodbye* by Raymond Chandler, copyright © 1953 by Raymond Chandler; and from *Raymond Chandler Speaking* by Dorothy Gardiner and Katherine Sorley Walker, copyright © 1962 by Mrs. Helga Greene.

John Houseman: From the essay "Lost Fortnight," copyright © 1965 by *Harper's Magazine.*

Alfred A. Knopf, Inc.: For permission to quote from the copyrighted works of Dashiell Hammett, Eric Ambler, and Raymond Chandler.

Little, Brown and Company: From *An Unfinished Woman* by Lillian Hellman, copyright © 1969 by Lillian Hellman, and *Scoundrel Time* by Lillian Hellman, copyright © 1976 by Lillian Hellman.

G. P. Putnam's Sons: From *A Life in My Hands* by J. W. Ehrlich, copyright © 1965 by J. W. Ehrlich.

Georges Simenon: From *Maigret and the Dead Girl, Maigret and the Headless Corpse, Maigret and the Old Lady,* and *Maigret's Memoirs.*

U.S. Library of Congress Cataloging in Publication Data

Eames, Hugh.
　Sleuths, Inc.: studies of problem solvers,
Doyle, Simenon, Hammett, Ambler, Chandler.

　Bibliography: p.
　1. Detective and mystery stories—History and criticism. 2. Detectives. 3. Problem solving.
I. Title.
PN3448.D4E2　　809.3'872　　78–15990
ISBN–0–397–01294–2

CONTENTS

Acknowledgments
7

SHERLOCK HOLMES—Arthur Conan Doyle
9

JULES MAIGRET—Georges Simenon
48

SAM SPADE—Dashiell Hammett
98

A Note on PAT GARRETT
141

ERIC AMBLER
148

PHILIP MARLOWE—Raymond Chandler
185

NOTES
222

SELECTED BIBLIOGRAPHY
224

ACKNOWLEDGMENTS

On July 24, 1976, a Dashiell Hammett conference took place in San Francisco. I want to thank the staff at University Extension, University of California, Berkeley, for creating this event; and I want to acknowledge my debt to David Fechheimer, Joe Gores, and William F. Nolan for the information which they presented there.

I would also like to thank Jehanne Biétry-Salinger Carlson for her translation of Simenon's *Paris-Soir* series on Stavisky.

— SHERLOCK HOLMES —
Arthur Conan Doyle

*My life is spent in one long effort to escape from
the commonplaces of existence.*
"The Red-headed League"

I

THAT SOME PROBLEMS seem unsolvable by Man is a proposition
agreed upon by problem solvers of many sorts and sizes, including
the master, Sherlock Holmes.

At the end of the adventure known as "The Cardboard Box,"
the great sleuth, disturbed by certain events included in the problem, turned to Watson and said, "What is the meaning of it,
Watson? What object is served by this circle of misery and violence and fear? It must tend to some end, or else our universe is
ruled by chance, which is unthinkable. But what end? There is the
great standing perennial problem to which human reason is as far
from an answer as ever."

Most of the problems to be examined here are problems that
have been solved. Some of them come from fiction, some from
fact, and all have at least one thing in common; they are problems
of a criminal nature. This is so because there is as much interest
in problem solvers as in problems solved, and because the best-
known problem solvers are fictional characters who exist for one
reason only, the apprehension of criminals.

Why is it that the manly, gentlemanly art of problem solving, the natural territory of Phi Beta Kappas, scientists, and PhDs, has been taken over, in the public mind, by a dubiously educated crew of junkies and boozers popularly known as sleuths, shamuses, and private eyes?

The answer, it seems, lies with Edgar Allan Poe, who believed that man's finest quality was his ability to reason. "Man's chief idiosyncracy being reason," he wrote, "it follows that . . . the more he reasons, the nearer he approaches the position to which this chief idiosyncracy irresistibly impels him."

Believing this, Poe invented a man of thought and genius— Auguste Dupin—and involved him, deliberately, in the solution of problems that were criminal. Poe did so because, as the poet Daniel Hoffman has pointed out, he believed that police officials were bureaucrats, that bureaucracy operated to the prejudice of gifted individuals, and that, just as society's enemy was the criminal, so was bureaucracy's enemy the man of thought.

"Police work, like all civil service, is by nature a bureaucracy, an arm and extension of the social establishment," Hoffman wrote in *Poe*. . . . "In every bureaucracy success is achieved through the practice of bureaucratic virtues: at their lower levels these include coming to work punctually, showing deference to one's superiors, and the like. The higher bureaucratic virtues . . . include dedication to one's duty and the application of an approved method to its performance."

Hoffman then pointed out that in "The Purloined Letter" the *préfet de police* of Paris is "a first-rate bureaucrat, the finest flower which the system that produced him can produce. That even his talents are unavailing to recover the purloined letter Poe intends as an indictment not merely of the man but of the system: the bureaucracy."[1]*

And so it is: Sherlock Holmes and his fellow problem solvers are restricted to criminal problems rather than problems in more respectable fields, because Poe placed originality in opposition to

*Sources for all numbered quotations are given in the Notes section at the back of the book.

social control and, as he did so, created the archetypal problem solver, the genius who is smarter than the cops.

———

Aside from their special abilities in intricate affairs, problem solvers are like normal people: complex, and with troubles of their own.

Consider Holmes. If he is to be comprehended in the round he must be studied not only at his most tremendous but also at his most pitiful.

The troubles of Holmes are caused by one of his most remarkable traits, his refusal to associate himself with "any investigation which does not tend towards the unusual and even the fantastic." As he once told Watson, "My dear fellow, Life is infinitely stranger than anything which the mind of man could invent. We would not dare to conceive the things that are really commonplace."

Normally, Holmes lives "in the very centre of five millions of people, with his filaments stretching out and running through them, responsive to every little rumor or suspicion of unsolved crime."

His personal problems begin when, as in the dog days of August, the great criminals are absent, the lesser thieves are lying low, and no interesting cases are available. It is then that the reader learns of the miseries of being Holmes. The great man becomes as flustered as a child denied its candy. His perspective vanishes, he misrepresents, he loses his bearings entirely.

"The days of the great criminal cases are past," he moans. "Man, at least criminal man, has lost all enterprise and originality. As to my own little practice, it seems to be generating into an agency for the recovery of lost lead pencils."

For relief, he turns to drugs, most often cocaine.

"Sherlock Holmes took his bottle from the corner of the mantelpiece, and his hypodermic syringe from its neat morocco case," Watson observed in *Sign of the Four.* "With his long, white, nervous fingers he adjusted the delicate needle and rolled back his left shirt cuff. For some time his eyes rested thoughtfully upon the sinewy forearm and wrist, all dotted and scarred with innumerable puncture marks. Finally, he thrust the sharp point home, pressed down the tiny piston, and sank back into the velvet-lined armchair with a long sigh of satisfaction."

Watson is apologetic and evasive. "He only turned to the drug as a protest against the monotony of existence when cases were scanty and the papers uninteresting."

Holmes is much more specific. "My mind rebels at stagnation. Give me problems, give me work, give me the most obtuse cryptogram, or the most intricate analysis, and I am in my proper atmosphere. I can then dispense with artificial stimulants. But I abhor the dull routine of existence. I crave for mental exaltation."

After Holmes has kicked the habit, the boredom problem remains. Matters reach a point where it is necessary for him to collect his pistol and a hundred bullets, then perch on a living-room chair and absorb himself in adorning "the opposite wall with a patriotic V R done in bullet-pocks." Gradually Holmes learns to solace himself by playing his violin, so that fairly often when, unknown to Holmes, a troubled citizen is hastening toward Baker Street, the mournful sounds of a violin are floating in the air outside 221B.

In a sense, Sherlock Holmes can be thought of as a truth junkie, a man with an extraordinary need to know. Anthony Storr saw him as a "personified intellect freed from any accompanying emotion other than a passion for truth." W. H. Auden was also impressed by Holmes's "love of the neutral truth" and described him as "a genius in whom scientific curiosity is raised to the status of heroic passion."

Holmes cannot know the truth about the most tremendous questions, but he can absorb himself in criminal puzzles, and as he approaches each individual solution, he can get a whiff of those delights, those profounder realities, deputies for the sublime, that so exalted him—"something transcendently stimulating and clarifying"—when he doped.

———

There were at least two false starts: Sherrington Hope, Sherringford Holmes. When the superb connection occurred, the first name came from the Irish village of Sherlockstown, and the last was borrowed from the author's favorite American, Oliver Wendell Holmes.*

In the beginning Sherlock Holmes was so lean that he seemed even taller than he actually was—over six feet. He had a "thin, razorlike face, a great hawksbill of a nose, and two small eyes set close together on either side of it."

Then the magazine illustrators seized him, made him less ugly, and went to work on his double-billed deerstalker hat, Inverness cloak, magnifying glass, and violin: articles as characteristic of him as his phrases, "deep water, Watson" and "you know my methods."

As for the rest, the great problem solver is as he is because of several men. Poe, the first, was followed by Dr. Joseph Bell, a Scottish surgeon who contributed the methods Holmes used to solve his cases. "My methods," Holmes usually called them, although he could pump the phrase up to "those faculties of deduction and logical synthesis which I have made my special province."

Dr. Bell was one of Doyle's instructors at medical school in Edinburgh. There this splendid rationalist, backed by his students and dressers, would glance at each patient, then diagnose for his students' benefit. He once inquired of a new patient:

"Well, my man, you've served in the army?"

"Aye, sir."

"Not long discharged?"

"No, sir."

"A Highland regiment?"

"Aye, sir."

"A non-com officer?"

"Aye, sir."

"Stationed in Barbados?"

"Aye, sir."

Dr. Bell then turned to his students and explained, "You see,

*The above explanation is taken from Pierre Nordon's authoritative biography of Doyle. For additional information about Doyle's conscious selection of the name Sherlock, see the more recent *The Adventures of Conan Doyle,* by Charles Higham.

gentlemen, the man was respectful but did not remove his hat. They do not in the army, but he would have learned civilian ways had he been long discharged. He has an air of authority and he is obviously Scottish. As to Barbados, his complaint is Elephantiasis, which is West Indian and not British."

Sherlock Holmes was born when Conan Doyle, as a young doctor with a slow practice, amused himself daily by writing stories. One afternoon the idea of creating a detective somewhat like Poe's Dupin came to Doyle. Remembering Dr. Bell, he decided that if that surgeon was a sleuth, he would reduce detection to an exact science.

"The precise and intelligent recognition and appreciation of minor differences is the real essential factor in all successful medical diagnosis," Dr. Bell had declared at one lecture. "Eyes and ears which can see and hear, memory to record at once and to recall at pleasure the impressions of the senses, and an imagination capable of weaving a theory or piercing together a broken chain or unraveling a tangled clue, such are the implements of his trade to the successful diagnostician."

And so it is that Sherlock Holmes, not having seen Watson for three months, can arrive at his friend's home and astonish him by observing, "I perceive that you have been unwell lately. Summer colds are always a little trying."

When the flabbergasted Watson asks Holmes how he did it, Holmes points to Watson's patent-leather slippers.

"Your slippers are new," he says. "You have not had them more than a few weeks. The soles which you are at this moment presenting to me are slightly scorched. For a moment I thought they might have got wet and had been burned in the drying. But near the instep is a small circular wafer of paper with the shopman's hieroglyphics upon it. Damp water would of course have removed it. You have been sitting with your feet outstretched to the fire, which a man would hardly do even in so wet a June as this if he were in his full health."

But Dr. Bell was not the only man of science to contribute to Sherlock Holmes and his methods of deduction.

———

The art of deductive reasoning, of drawing rational conclusions from observed correlations of observed facts, was discovered in embryo by the Greeks and inherited by Europe. But century after century passed before deductive methods made much impression on mankind.

During these centuries the comfortable teaching that God had created man in his own image was taken for granted, and the standard of proof, throughout the Western world, was the Bible and its sacred tales, themselves the products of a succession of venerable ancients tuned in to divine voices. The Judeo-Christian idea of creation was so firmly established that, in 1650, a British student of the Old Testament and its numerology announced that creation had occurred in 4004 B.C. Other scholars then pinpointed the event at precisely 9:00 P.M. on October 23 of that year.

Literature's first deductive reasoner appears to have been invented by Voltaire in 1748. As Theodore Besterman wrote of Voltaire, "Sherlock Holmes must have read attentively the third chapter in *Zadig.*"

There Zadig, a pleasant young man, observes to himself, "No one is happier than a philosopher who reads in this great book that God has placed before our eyes." Moments later Zadig's study of footprints and other bits of evidence left by passing animals enables him to correctly identify a lost dog as a small spaniel bitch that had recently had puppies, was long-eared, and had a lame foot. He is also able to determine that a missing horse was very fast, stood fifteen hands high, and had small hooves and a tail three and a half feet long.

Poe wrote his first Dupin tale in 1842, at a time when the public had not developed much sense of what constitutes proof. In *The Energies of Art* Jacques Barzun wrote, "What Poe's original idea needed in order to blossom was a wider indoctrination of the method of science, so that the taste for reading 'The Book of Life' [Sherlock Holmes's phrase] should be general and addressed to physical fact. This came with the great Darwinian controversy which filled the monthly magazines. . . . It was in 1880, seven years before Conan Doyle's epoch-making *Study in Scarlet,* that Huxley addressed a London Working Men's College 'On the Method of

Zadig' and then published his lecture: 'In no distant future,' he concludes, 'the method of Zadig . . . will enable the biologist to reconstruct the scheme of life from its beginning.' In other words, the theory of Evolution is the greatest detective story ever."

The belief that nature was the result of a process of organic evolution and natural selection, rather than of divine intelligence, was separately developed by Charles Darwin and Alfred Wallace around the middle of the nineteenth century. Darwin's *The Origin of Species by Means of Natural Selection* was published on November 24, 1859. The first printing, 1,250 copies, sold out in one day, and the great debate began: a handful of evolutionists opposed by the whole of the Christian bureaucracy.

Like Holmes, Darwin was a gifted amateur. The marvels that he noticed while examining his beetle collection, assembled with an almost total lack of curiosity, transformed him from a young and ardent snipe shooter into a friend of scientists and an enthusiast for truth.

"I worked on true Baconian principles," Darwin wrote, "and . . . collected facts on a wholesale basis."

Mere ideas did not interest him. The power of ascent, he insisted, must be founded on rational arguments and physical evidence.

One biographer wrote of him as prying "with sober detective cunning" into "some of nature's most genial ingenuities of dog-eat-dog." His paper, "The Various Contrivances by Which Orchids Are Fertilized by Insects," has been described as "a study of nature's trap doors and spring mechanisms."

Darwin spent much of his time investigating problems that most people would consider excessively humble.

One was barnacles. They absorbed him for eight years, after which he published a study of their taxonomy and natural history.

He was an authority on earthworms and was particularly interested in the manner in which stones are buried by the earthworms' castings.

He was a student of the history of the commonest domestic animals, an authority on matters such as the presence of cats in ancient Egypt and lap dogs in imperial Rome.

In 1871 he published *The Descent of Man.* Only then did he fit human beings into the great scheme of evolution, describing them as descended from ape stock. Man, it seemed, was not so much a fallen angel as a risen ape.

As a problem solver the great Holmes has much in common with the greater Darwin.

He too is a devotee of the humbler sort of fact and has published studies of minutiae. These include: a study of cigar ashes, a study of tattoos, two monographs on the variability of human ears, one paper on the influence of trade upon the form of the human hand, and another paper on the tracking of footprints and their preservation in plaster of paris.

About these and other trifles, Holmes is the world's supreme authority, but about the Copernican theory he knows nothing. As he tells Watson, "It is of the highest importance . . . not to have useless facts elbowing out the useful ones."

"But the Solar System!" Watson protests.

"What the deuce is it to me? . . . You say we go round the sun. If we went round the moon it would not make a pennyworth of difference to me or my work."

It is the tiny details—what Dr. Bell called "the precise and intelligent recognition and appreciation of minor differences"—that interest Holmes, and to a degree that must have given Conan Doyle great joy at the moment of invention.

"Never trust to general impressions, my boy," Watson is advised. "My first glance is always at a woman's sleeve. In a man it is perhaps better first to take the knees of the trousers."

Pipes, watches, and bootlaces are almost as important. The reader is charmed to learn that in one instance it was of immense value to the great sleuth to note "the depth to which the parsley had sunk into the butter on a hot day."

Darwin was much the same sort of man. He made no attempt to solve the larger problems, such as the dilemma between design and chance. A dog, it seemed, might as well speculate on the mind of man, as man on the mind of the Creator.

Self-identity has never been one of Holmes's problems. "I'm a consulting detective, if you can understand what that is," he advises Watson, early in the game. "Here in London we have lots of government detectives and lots of private ones. When these forces are at fault, they come to me, and I manage to put them on the right scent. They lay all the evidence before me, and I am generally able, by the help of my knowledge of the history of crime, to set them straight."

Later Holmes puts it more forcefully. "I am generally recognized, by both the public and by the official force, as being the final court of appeal in doubtful cases."

Nor does Watson have any doubts about the kind of person Holmes is. Emotions, he once reported, "were abhorrent to his cold, precise, but admirably balanced mind." At another time Watson declared, "Grit in a sensitive instrument would not be more disturbing than a strong emotion in a nature such as his."

But in the field Holmes becomes a different man. "His face flushed and darkened," Watson observed. "His brows were drawn into two hard, black lines, while his eyes shone down from beneath them in a steely glitter. His face was bent downwards, his shoulders bowed, his lips compressed, and the veins stood out like whipcord in his long, sinewy neck. His nostrils seemed to dilate with a purely human lust for the chase."

Those who have commented on Holmes have frequently used the word "tracker." "He is a tracker," Pierre Nordon wrote, "a hunter-down, a combination of bloodhound, pointer, and bulldog, who runs people to earth as the foxhound does the fox; in fact, a sleuth."

Anthropologists who write of Man the hunter assert that agricultural and industrial civilizations have added nothing to what they call the basic wiring of the human animal. "We are wired for hunting—for the emotions, the excitement, the curiosities ... that were needed to survive in the hunting way of life. And we are wired basically on a primate model."[2]

Watson identified Holmes as "the most perfect reasoning and observing machine that the world has ever known." Today it seems reasonable to inquire if Holmes could not just as properly be identified as, like the rest of us, a hunter and a seeker.

———

Sherlock Holmes solved, by his personal estimate, "Five hundred cases of capital importance." Of these, Watson "wrote up" sixty-four or so, most of which possessed that quality so necessary to Holmes, the ability to involve him in possibilities profounder and more rewarding than those contained in the reality known to the man on the street.

The sensationalism of some of these cases has never been equaled by any other writer of criminal fiction. It is a quality that literary critics dislike but which medical men, such as Conan Doyle, accept as an authentic part of life. Heraclitus said, "Because it sometimes seems so unbelievable, the truth often escapes being known." Doyle would surely agree.

It is time, now, to examine one or two problems that were particularly satisfactory to the great sleuth.

———

In "The Adventure of the Bruce-Partington Plans" the corpse of a young man is found alongside the tracks of the London underground railway.

The victim is Cadogan West, a clerk in the naval arsenal. His skull is crushed, and his pockets contain papers relating to the extremely secret Bruce-Partington submarine.

Holmes is called into the case by his brother Mycroft, an important figure in the Foreign Office. Three papers relating to the submarine are still missing, Mycroft explains. Their recovery is essential.

Inspector Lestrade of Scotland Yard, also on the case, has decided that Cadogan West stole the plans, then rendezvoused with a spy who refused to pay West's price. Afterwards, Lestrade maintains, the spy followed West aboard the underground train, murdered him, seized the missing documents, and threw the corpse off the train.

Such reasoning Holmes ignores. As he begins his investigation, he is puzzled by the fact that the police search of the victim's clothing failed to turn up a ticket to the Underground.

When Holmes examines the area where the corpse was discovered, his interest rises. "I saw on his keen, alert face that tightening of the lips," Watson comments, "that quiver of the nostrils, and concentration of the heavy, tufted brows, which I knew so well."

Leaving the scene, Holmes is in a splendid mood. He confides to Watson, "There is material here. There is scope." The fact is, Holmes has already come to certain specific conclusions: (1) that West was not killed in the vicinity of the spot where his body was found; (2) that the corpse fell, not from the car, but from the roof of the car; and (3) that the corpse fell where it did because that spot was just beyond a complicated junction point where the subway cars regularly rock, pitch, and sway.

Back at Baker Street, Holmes asks his brother for the names and addresses of the most important international spies in London.

After this information has been supplied, Holmes studies a map of the underground system and discovers that the most important spy of all, Hugo Oberstein, lives in a building that abuts the underground tracks at a point where the trains emerge from a tunnel. Holmes also learns that because of a nearby intersection of major lines, the underground trains are often forced to halt directly under Oberstein's rear window.

Holmes and Watson break into Oberstein's flat and find that the distance from the ledge of Oberstein's rear window to the roofs of the halted cars is a drop of only four feet. Watson is ecstatic. "You have never risen to a greater height," he tells Holmes.

Now it is only a matter of time. As it turns out, Colonel Valentine Walter, the younger brother of the director of the arsenal, has lost a large sum of money on the stock market. Hugo Oberstein, aware of this, has tempted the colonel by offering him £5,000 for the submarine plans. West is murdered because he has caught Colonel Walter stealing these plans. The Colonel and Oberstein then take the corpse to Oberstein's and drop it out the window onto the roof of a train.

After the plans have been returned to the arsenal, Holmes spends an afternoon at Windsor Castle. There a "remarkably fine emerald tie-pin" is presented to him by, it is implied, Queen Victoria.

———

"Silver Blaze" provides another exceptionally gratifying demonstration of Holmes's genius as a problem solver. As the story begins, John Straker, trainer of Silver Blaze, the three-to-one favorite in the Wessex Cup, is murdered a few days before the race, and the great horse vanishes. With these events the main topic of talk throughout England, Holmes is called into the case by Colonel Ross, the owner of Silver Blaze and Straker's employer. On the way to the stable at King's Pyland in Devonshire, Holmes reviews the case for Watson's benefit.

John Straker's skull was shattered by a blow from a sharp weapon.

On the night before the murder, the stable boy who regularly slept in the horse's stall ate a supper of curried mutton to which someone had added opium.

Those who ate the same curried mutton at Straker's table felt no ill effects.

When Holmes and Watson arrive at the village nearest King's Pyland, they are met by a carriage containing Colonel Ross and Inspector Gregory. The Inspector, straight from Scotland Yard, informs Holmes that he has arrested a bookmaker named Simpson, who has been hanging around King's Pyland.

"Simpson . . . had a great interest in the disappearance of the favorite," the Inspector explains; "he lies under the suspicion of having poisoned the stable boy . . . he was armed with a heavy stick, and his cravat was found in the dead man's hand. I really think we have enough to go before a jury."

As soon as the carriage reaches King's Pyland, Watson, Colonel Ross, and Inspector Gregory descend. Holmes, however, remains seated, and Watson realizes that his friend has tumbled onto something big. "There was a gleam in his eyes, and a suppressed excitement in his manner," Watson reports, "which convinced me, used as I was to his ways, that his hand was upon a clue."

And indeed, Holmes has recognized the "immense significance of the curried mutton." Powdered opium, he reasons, has a definite taste, a taste that curry could disguise. It is not possible that the arrested bookmaker, Simpson, a stranger to the trainer's household, could have dictated the menu on the fatal evening. "Therefore Simpson becomes eliminated from the case," Holmes explains, "and our attention centers upon Straker and his wife, the only people who could have chosen curried mutton for supper that night. The opium was added after the dish was set aside for the stable boy."

Holmes soon comes up with a second clue. Silver Blaze was guarded not only by one stable boy and a dog that shared his stall; two more stable boys slept in the loft above the stall. And on the night when the horse vanished, the dog did not bark, a point proven by the fact that the boys in the loft were not awakened. This suggests that the dog must have known the person who entered the stall.

For Holmes, the problem from here on is child's play. After studying the tracks on the moor, he traces Silver Blaze to a rival stable a mile or so from King's Pyland. There he questions the trainer, an old horse faker who soon acknowledges that he found the great horse wandering nearby, painted out his identifying marks, and hid him in a stall.

Back at King's Pyland, Holmes clears up everything. John Straker had a mistress who cost him too much money. He tried to recoup by betting against Silver Blaze. Then, while Straker was trying to lame the horse by nicking its tendons with a knife, the frightened animal reared and accidentally struck and killed its attacker with a sharp hoof.

The adventure ends with Silver Blaze pounding to victory in the Wessex Cup.

———

Cases such as these provide Holmes with splendid problems, but the villains are amateurs, criminals by circumstance rather than profession, and not really worthy of the great sleuth. It is a situation which has troubled him for years, the principal reason for his lack of interest in the personalities of the wrongdoers.

Holmes does know, however, that from somewhere in the

criminal world of London, he is being opposed by an intriguing opponent. "For years," he tells Watson, "I have continually been conscious of . . . some deep organizing power which forever stands in the way of the law and throws its shield over the wrongdoer."

Eventually Holmes identifies the mastermind as Professor James Moriarty, one of the world's foremost abstract thinkers. Moriarty's treatise on the binomial theorem written when he was twenty-one brought him to the attention of Europe and won him the mathematical chair at one of the smaller English universities.

Unfortunately, the blood of this powerful thinker is infected by a wild and overpowering criminal strain. When unpleasant events occur in the vicinity of his university, Moriarty's name becomes connected with them. He resigns, goes to London, and establishes a tutorial school for army officers. Behind such a front his criminality thrives. Holmes calls him "the Napoleon of Crime . . . one of the great brains of the century."

Moriarty does not appear in many of Holmes's adventures. Nevertheless, he is there behind the scenes. Indeed, there is a historical basis for the presence, in London, of such an imposing criminal character. As Holmes asks one police official, "Have you ever read of Jonathan Wild?"

II

ACCOUNTS OF HEROES such as Holmes demand exceptional villains. Balance is required; the criminal must be worthy of the sleuth. Indeed, criminals can be problem solvers too.

The trouble with Moriarty is that very little is known about him. He provides a melodramatic hint, but not much more, of what historical London stocks in villains.

But about Jonathan Wild there is an abundance of information, more than enough to show that, like Holmes, he too had his "methods." Crime lord of London through ten flamboyant years,

1716–1725, he was the first criminal to become a celebrity—as much of a presence in the London of his time as Holmes was in the late Victorian era.

———

Jonathan Wild was a stocky man with a double share of animal magnetism. Even before he became famous, women fought over him. In his prime, he was accompanied by up to six bodyguards when he moved about London. He wore armor under his clothes and a turban over his head. The armor was needed because despite his bodyguards he had been wounded seventeen times. The turban was required because two of these wounds were skull fractures that had been mortised with plates of polished silver.

Wild was born in Wolverhampton in 1682, educated in its schools, and trained to be a buckle maker. In 1710, for unknown reasons, he abandoned everything—job, wife, and child—and slipped away to London. His criminal education then began. Arrested for a small debt, he was imprisoned in the Wood Street Compter and for the next two years associated with every type of criminal.

"It is said that a woman introduced him to crime, or at least to the London 'street scene' as a way of life," the authors of a recent study, Duncan Chappell and Marilyn Walsh, wrote. "More likely is that the corruption of . . . jailers and magistrates convinced him that crime was a most lucrative field."[3]

The lady in question, Mary Milliner, was a stand-up whore whom Wild had met in prison. Her specialty was picking pockets during the act. They teamed up after his release and soon had enough money to buy a tavern.

Most of their customers were thieves, and Wild fenced whatever was offered. But instead of trotting to the traditional receivers, he returned to the victims and presented himself as an honest man who, on a basis of "no questions asked," was helping to restore stolen property to its rightful owners. The victims were delighted.

His success was noted by a man named Hitchens, officially the Under Marshal of London, who was unofficially its leading fence.* Hitchens offered Wild a job, and Wild accepted, mainly because he was interested in learning the mechanics of "thief-taking."

In that era, when the establishment of a regular police force was regarded by the British, for reasons to be noted presently, as a cure worse than the disease, thief-taking—the process of finding, arresting, and securing the conviction of thieves—was an established profession and a sophisticated one. The thief-takers were regarded by the public as men who did their dangerous work out of a sense of duty. But many of them were also thieves.

This condition became more so in 1692 when the government, hoping to reduce crime, created a Parliamentary Reward System that encouraged deceit. The reward for capturing and securing the conviction of a thief was raised to forty pounds (in 1974, roughly $2,000), and a Royal pardon was awarded to anyone who turned in, and secured the conviction of, two thieves.

It was a system that swiftly created fresh squads of professional informers, perjurers, blackmailers, and false witnesses. As Wild's most authoritative biographer, Gerald Howson, observed, "To the thief-takers, who had plenty of people working for them already, these new measures must have seemed like manna from heaven. The statute gave them virtual power of life and death over thieves."[4]

At the end of one year, Wild left the Under Marshal and went back into business for himself.

The Under Marshal had regarded receiving as a protection racket. He had pressured the thieves to sell him their loot at a

---

*Throughout most of the seventeenth and eighteenth centuries in England, the line separating criminal activities from commercial ones was indistinct. In London the sale of public office was routine, and the posts of City Marshal and Under Marshal were at the Lord Mayor's disposal to defray the expenses of office.

At the time, some 10,000 to 12,000 thieves earned a living in London. Most of them were victims of the industrial revolution, craftsmen from the shires who, having lost their jobs, had streamed into the capital city in search of work that did not exist.

Meanwhile, Moll Cutpurse, a woman who liked cigars, had turned the trade in stolen goods into a properly organized business. In *The Professional Fence*, Carl Klockars wrote that Moll's operation was based on "controlling thieves under the threat of informing on them, running a central clearing house for stolen property, tutoring thieves, and currying the favor of the judiciary." She died in 1659.

fraction of its potential value. Wild, however, saw receiving as a business in which the basic idea was to keep everybody happy. When he interviewed the victims, he asked how much they were willing to pay. Whatever sum they named, he returned their property for a little less. He also offered the thieves more than other fences, as much as 50 percent.

The result was that all London flocked to him. He organized the Office of Lost and Stolen Property, and while he himself was developing an extraordinary image as a gentleman, a friend of the victimized, his Office turned into a national institution. But Jonathan Wild's sensational success had also created an enormous problem. The logic of his position demanded that he be in complete control of criminal London.

In their study, Chappell and Walsh point out, "He knew that the key to his complex . . . structure was control . . . for example, the existence of gangs of thieves who were not under his control posed the possibility of thefts from which he could not 'recover' the property. This in turn might damage his reputation and make him vulnerable to suspicion and attack. . . ."[5]

———

Let us follow Jonathan Wild as he attacks the problem of bringing order to the turbulence of criminal London.

He divides the metropolis into districts and assigns gangs to them, each led by a transported criminal who has returned to London illegally, so that Wild has a grip on him.

He sets up a bookkeeping system that tells him which thieves are still outside his control and which thieves there is enough evidence against to bring the forty-pound reward.

London thieves had once stolen only when they needed money. Now, victims of an organizational genius, they steal when Wild tells them to. "The thief-takers are now our complete masters," one thief complained; ". . . and they send us into several Wards and Situations (as a Corporal sends soldiers to stand Sentinel) . . . and if we refuse they'll have us committed for some former crime."

Wild next reduces the thieves' share of the plunder. Those who rebel are framed and hung. Wild pockets each forty pounds.

Some of his thieves prey on churches, some on the House of Parliament, some on fairs. One ancient account relates that his " 'Spruce Prigs' went to Court on Birth-Nites, to Balls, Operas, Plays, and Assemblies, for which purpose they were furnished with handsome Equipages, such as Chariots, with Footmen in Liveries, and also Valets-de-Chambres, the Servants all being Thieves like the Master."

Sometimes Wild pays an instructor to teach his thieves to dance.

Although he will always be a fence, since that is his main source of income, Wild now goes into thief-taking on a large scale. He becomes, Howson wrote, "an extremely skillful and courageous hunter-down of criminals and breaker of gangs." Thus, while he is on his way to becoming criminal boss of London, he is at the same time providing the city with much of its law and order.

And he does not limit himself to London. His hunting posses of thief-takers ride throughout England. Unlike the parish constables, Wild's men can travel freely. "This, the first thing that in any way resembled a CID or 'crime squad' in English history," Howson noted, "was something unheard of before."

He employs agents to keep tabs on criminals who have been transported to the colonies. If any return to England prematurely, his men bag them and Jonathan pockets the forty pounds. His control of criminal London becomes tighter and tighter. Virtually nothing escapes him. He reaches for it all. Between 1721 and 1723, Howson reports, Wild "destroyed four large gangs in London that comprised the hard core of the underworld and for the next two years the highwaymen gave London a wide berth."

———

He is now several times a millionaire, possesses numerous warehouses stuffed with stolen goods, and is the admiral of a one-ship navy that smuggles between England and the continent.

Long ago the government, aware of what he was doing, made a show of putting him out of business by passing a law so obviously aimed at him that it became known as the Jonathan Wild Act. But he nullified it by adjusting certain procedures.

With crime continuing to rise, the government ponders the problem of reducing it. Since Wild is in control of virtually all information about theft, he is consulted and recommends that the reward for taking a thief be increased by one hundred pounds. This suggestion is adopted.

"It is certain that the greatest part of his dark Proceedings would still have continued a Secret of the World," his original biographer wrote, "had it not been, that in his Gay hours, when his heart was open, he took Pleasure in recounting his past Roguries, and with a great deal of Humor, Bragg's of his biting the world; often hinting, not without Vanity, at the poor understanding of the greatest Part of Mankind, and his own superior Cunning."

But his situation was never perfect, there was one constant weakness. Everything depended on his image, which he had enlarged. In addition to being the friend of the victimized, the celebrated proprieter of the Office of Lost and Stolen Property, he had assumed the role of Thief-Taker General of Britain and Ireland. As such, on hanging days, he carried a silver baton and rode ahead of the carts of the victims, zestfully proclaiming that his children were coming.

In 1724 he arrested a minor folk hero, Jack Sheppard, whose reputation was based on his having broken into jail to rescue his mistress. Now, while awaiting trial, Sheppard himself escaped; he was recaptured and returned to prison, where he was strapped into assorted leg irons and handcuffs. Once again, Jack Sheppard escaped. By the time Wild's thief-takers recaptured him, he was England's most celebrated criminal.

"Hundreds of visitors came to see him in his cell," Carl Klockars wrote in *The Professional Thief,* "and the daily press reported all he had to say . . . he railed against Jonathan Wild. Almost overnight, Wild's image withered. The anger that the people normally felt for thieves was turned on Wild . . . for bringing down the dapper Jack Sheppard."

From then on Wild was in trouble. His career ended abruptly when he was forty-three. He had made an enemy of some powerful person and was destroyed by Sir William Thompson, a judge with a particularly devious reputation, who had written the Jonathan Wild Act.

Just as Capone was imprisoned for failure to pay his income taxes in 1935, so was Wild, in 1725, charged and found guilty of accepting ten guineas from a blind woman who ran a drapery store. This he did, the charge read, "without discovering, apprehending, or causing to be apprehended the felon who had stolen the lace . . ."—a crime specifically defined in the Jonathan Wild Act.

On the night before he was hung, Wild drank poison, but the dose was too heavy and he vomited it up.

———

When it came to establishing a professional police force, the English were astonishingly tardy.

In Wild's era the population of London was approximately 500,000. A century later it had increased to 1,670,000, and while the disorder in the streets had risen proportionately, the government had nothing to rely on except those institutions that had already proven so inadequate.

There was an enfeebled body of night watchmen, many of whom were in league with the thieves. There were the thief-takers, thieves themselves. There was also the ponderous army, with its volley fire and saber charges. These troops, in the case of mob riots, could not legally be called out until property had been damaged.

And finally, there were a number of small bands of investigators and bounty hunters employed by various magistrates. The most important, the Bow Street Runners, was the offspring of citizens' patrols organized in 1748 by Henry Fielding, the novelist and magistrate. They have been described, by Sir Leon Radzinowicz, as "a closely knit caste of speculators in the detection of crime, self-seeking and unscrupulous, but also daring and efficient." These men, bounty hunters, were the first Englishmen to make a serious study of the art of apprehending criminals. In their way, they were the predecessors of Sherlock Holmes. They can be regarded as official private investigators available for hire by institutions and wealthy individuals.

Aside from such forces, crime in London was unopposed, and the disorder in the streets, fed by an uprooted, unproductive, gin-swacked population, was astonishing. At various times toward the end of the eighteenth century, the Prince of Wales, the Duke of York, and the Lord Mayor of London had been separately mugged, while the Great Seal of England had been stolen and melted down for silver. Horace Walpole claimed going out in public was like going into battle.

Meanwhile, virtually nothing was being done to control the tumult. The reason for this, most historians agree, was the English evaluation of the situation in France.

For years Englishmen had been telling each other the tyrannical, despotic deeds of the French police. And when Napoleon turned the gendarmes over to Fouché, who established a notorious network of spies and *agents provocateurs,* "an example was provided across the channel," police historian Charles Reith wrote, "which killed all power of reasoning in the minds of most people in England, and ended all argument regarding the need and value of police."[6]

In London things did not begin to change until 1820, when a battalion of Scots Guards refused an order to fire on a rioting mob. The Duke of Wellington, alarmed, urged the formation of a police force. Robert Peel, who had organized the Royal Irish Constabulary, was brought over from Dublin to become Home Secretary, with the specific task of creating a police force. His first proposal, made in 1822, was rejected by the parliamentary committee, which supported the traditional argument: the establishment of a police force would lead to espionage, tyranny, and the total loss of individual liberty.

In the next few years Peel educated where he could. "I want to teach people," he wrote Wellington, "that liberty does not consist of having your house robbed by organized gangs of thieves, and in leaving the principal streets of London in the nightly possession of drunken women and vagabonds."

In 1828 Peel again proposed that Parliament authorize the formation of a central police force in London. "One individual out of every twenty in London is a criminal," he told Parliament. As for the rest of the nation, he read aloud a letter from a county magistrate. "In every county throughout England, crime has so rapidly and fearfully increased as to shake all confidence in either public or private security."

Crime in England, he advised Parliament, was "without parallel in the annals of any other civilized country." This time the membership of the reporting committee had been carefully chosen, and its report favored the formation of a central police force in London.

"I require a man," Peel wrote a friend, "of great energy, great activity both of body and mind, accustomed to strict discipline and with the power of enforcing it, and taking an interest in the duty to be assigned to him. Then he must be a gentleman and entirely trustworthy. . . . With the soldier I would unite a sensible lawyer as the other magistrate."

The required "man of great energy" was Charles Rowan, a former lieutenant-colonel under Wellington, who had retired to Ireland and become a magistrate. The "sensible lawyer" was Richard Mayne, a graduate of Dublin and Cambridge, and a barrister with an excellent mind.

Neither Rowan nor Mayne knew each other before their appointment as Joint Commissioners of the Metropolitan Police, but both were dedicated to the police idea and soon formed a close partnership, with Mayne, who was fourteen years younger, being more willing to learn from his colleague.

Together, they established the governing principles for bringing law and order to the world's most brutal metropolis. Rowan handled most of this and did the job in twelve weeks. Thirteen of the first seventeen division superintendents were drawn from the list of recently retired army sergeant-majors, and their influence was important.

The selection of individual policemen was as thorough as possible. Candidates had to present letters from three employers; they also had to read and write and understand what they read. Those who passed the preliminary tests were interviewed by both commissioners.

Some of the first 825 constables chosen were ex-soldiers or marines, but most of the men had no concept of military order and discipline. They were, as the two commissioners acknowledged, the sweepings of the streets. It was raining on the day of their first assembly; and some of them stood parade with umbrellas over their heads. Others were drunk. Of the first 2,800 constables, 2,238 were soon dismissed, mostly for drinking.

Uniforms of scarlet and gold had been the original idea, but Rowan and Mayne insisted on dress entirely disassociated from the military. They created a uniform consisting of a top hat, a blue civilian tailcoat, and dark trousers. For armament each constable had nothing but a short wooden baton.

From the start, Peel, Rowan, and Mayne had recognized that everything depended on public approval. The Metropolitan Police were to be a service rather than a force, preventive rather than oppressive. That was why the constables carried no guns. As one police historian wrote, "The police . . . should become respected rather than feared by the populace. It is difficult to overestimate the significance of a police force that relies not on the weapons of war to support its authority, but on winning popular support for its function."

They hit the streets on September 29, 1829. Opposing them was every element that had profited from the immense disorder, professional criminals, their henchmen, and political agitators of every variety.

It was a battle. The daily reports could be sickening. Policemen were tossed into the Thames, thrown onto spiked railings, kicked to death on the pavement.

When the police prosecuted offenders in the courts, "they had to face, alone, shameful hostility from council, juries, and judges," Reith wrote. "With absolute right on his side, it was a common experience for a policeman to lose his case on a technical point of law, of which he had too little knowledge. . . . The columns of the daily press carried lies, mockery, and vilification in connection with nearly every action of the Commissioners and their men which came to the notice of journalists."[7]

By the end of the first year, representatives of every class in the metropolis were demanding that the police be disbanded. Hostility was publicly expressed by magistrates, judges, cabinet ministers, and the King himself. In the heat of events, Rowan and Mayne patiently drilled noncommissioned officers in the rules for improving the discipline of the individual constable:

He shall be civil and obliging to all people of every rank and class.

He must remember that there is no qualification so indispensable to a police officer as a perfect command of temper.

If he do his duty in a quiet and determined manner, such conduct will probably excite the well-disposed of the by-standers to assist him.

Gradually, the visible sufferings of the constables, in their role as martyrs, appealed to the public, and the police began to receive praise. At night during the first four years, rioting mobs came close to defeating them; but the constables, armed only with their batons, won without requiring military aid. At the same time, crime visibly declined. The streets became safe to walk on at night. In 1839 and 1856 the police idea was extended to the counties.

Thus, gradually, throughout England, riotous disorder was brought under control and ceased to be a nation's problem.

———

The first British detectives, investigators employed by the magistrates, were experienced men with impressive records. Their customs, however, were such that there was no place for them in the Metropolitan Police, as created by Charles Rowan.

In *The First Detectives,* Belton Cobb wrote that "an officer was given an assignment by a magistrate and was not expected to report . . . until he brought in the results," and, "quite often he would be away . . . for ten days or more, with nobody bothering about what had become of him or being suspicious that he might be wasting his time."

At first the Metropolitan Police had no detective unit of any sort, and was entirely a preventive organization of a semimilitary nature; preventive, in the sense of putting men on the streets who possessed the legal power to enforce laws and the support of higher authority. Constables answered sergeants, sergeants answered inspectors, and on and up through the bureaucratic hierarchy.

"The Metropolitan Police are efficient in the preventive part of their duties," a magistrate informed a committee in 1833. "In the detective part they are . . . deficient—from the nature of their regulations and their discipline."

The first detectives in the Metropolitan Police were sponsored by Joint Commissioner Richard Mayne. They were known, semiofficially, as "active officers," a phrase based on the idea of using "active, intelligent officers" for special work. The detective department was not officially created until 1842. It consisted of two inspectors and six sergeants. The Criminal Investigation Department was founded in 1877.

Such are the origins of Scotland Yard.

III

OVER THE YEARS, some critics have maintained that police officials in London appreciate the good life, and consider it their duty to raise their families in the finest possible manner, but in all of Holmes there is not the slightest suggestion of police corruption.

The world of Holmes reflects Poe's thinking about the conflict between originality and bureaucracy, the problem solver versus social control. For Holmes, the trouble at Scotland Yard is that its men are at best unimaginative and at worst dumb.

"He is not a bad fellow, although an absolute imbecile in his profession," Holmes says of one detective. "He has one positive virtue. He is brave as a bulldog and as tenacious as a lobster." On another occasion the great sleuth refers to a situation as "villainy with a motive so transparent that even a Scotland Yard official can see through it."

And so it is that, in the London of Conan Doyle, when

Scotland Yard is at its wit's end, the problem is passed to Holmes, whose name is seldom mentioned in the newspapers. After he has solved the case, and the business of the exposure of the villain has been handed to Scotland Yard, the great sleuth stands off to the side and, a mocking smile on his face, listens "to the general chorus of misplaced congratulations."

Yet, when all is said and done, Sherlock Holmes is very much a part of the mythology of the police, who are themselves the method which a slowly evolving, organizing society has invented to control the streets and reduce anarchy. If Holmes is superior to the cops, he nevertheless turns his results over to them, and is the brightest star in the police drama. In the theater of the downfall of evil and the triumph of the gods—the theater as Plato saw it—Sherlock Holmes is *the* brilliant, triumphant reminder that crime does *not* pay.

Conan Doyle had what C. P. Snow described as "a singularly romantic imagination . . . it simplifies and heightens. It can be benign, and give us a feeling of a desirable world . . . which most of the time he did." It was also an imagination, Snow added, in which "much of the grit of everyday life is washed away."

Other critics have made similiar points. Crime buff John Patterson has noted that the basic assumption in the Holmes adventures is "that society is basically sound, its laws admirable, and crime a wicked aberration." Ross Macdonald has pointed out that the thought and language of the Holmes stories are permeated by an air of blithe satisfaction with a social system based on privilege.

Sherlock Holmes is descended from landed gentry. He is a member of the privileged class in a nation ruled by an elite. "They have their place in the hierarchy," Snow wrote of Holmes and Watson, "and it is a respected and influential place. Although Holmes sometimes produced admirable liberal sentiments . . . they take an entirely unaffected, unenvious pleasure in their connection with the eminent, especially with miscellaneous royalty."

With the exception of Allan Pinkerton and his descendants and certain problem solvers found in the novels of Eric Ambler,

Sherlock Holmes is the only establishment figure discussed here. Jules Maigret, Sam Spade, and Philip Marlowe are aware, usually intensely so, of the economic realities of the world in which they sleuth, including the extent of what is called corruption. But not Holmes. For the most part, that private income which permits him to charge no fee—"my work is its own reward"—shields him from anything that does not titillate his scientific curiosity.

Yet he is not an innocent. He is as complex as any human being, and if he seems unaware of forces such as the will to power, he nevertheless knows that "one has to be discreet when one talks of high matters of state." He regards the press as "a most valuable institution, if you only know how to use it." He once refused to discard the idea that a British statesman might destroy certain documents harmful to himself.

Holmes enjoys helping the mighty great, but he does not fawn. In "The Adventure of the Second Stain," the Prime Minister and the Foreign Secretary are reluctant to reveal certain aspects of the problem that has brought them to Holmes. It is too much for the great sleuth. "You are two of the most busy men in the country," he says, "and in my own small way I also have a good many calls on me. I regret exceedingly that I cannot help you in this matter, and any continuation of this interview would be a waste of time."

The leaders of the British Empire capitulate.

Holmes is only slightly less forceful in "The Adventure of the Illustrious Client." Here he is approached by a middleman who expects him to accept a case without knowing the identity of the client. Holmes's reply is tart: "I am accustomed to have mystery at one end of my cases, but to have it at both ends is too confusing. I fear, Sir James, that I must decline to act."

———

Sherlockologists believe he was born about 1854. He may have attended Oxford; he may have gone to Cambridge. The problem is being negotiated, with no end in sight. Wherever he studied, he was not clubby. "I was never a very sociable fellow, Watson," he once observed, "always moping about in my rooms and working on my own little methods of thought."

He did, however, have at least one close school friend, Victor Trevor, the son of an adventurer who had found a fortune in the gold fields. One evening at Victor's home, while Victor, his father, and Holmes were at the table, Victor urged Holmes to demonstrate his methods. The results astonished the senior Trevor.

"All the detectives in fact and fiction would be children in your hands," Trevor told Holmes. "That's your line of life, sir, and you may take the word of a man who has seen something of the world."

This was, Holmes said long afterwards, "the first thing which ever made me feel that a profession might be made out of what up to that time had been the merest hobby."

He was twenty-three when he came to London. "I had rooms in Montague Street, just round the corner from the British Museum, and there I waited, filling in my too abundant leisure time by studying those branches of science which made me more efficient. Now and again cases came my way, principally through . . . old fellow students."

The third of these cases involved strange events at the estate of the Musgraves, one of the oldest families in the kingdom. There Holmes recovered what had been hidden for centuries, the ancient crown of the Kings of England. By 1881, the year he met Watson, Holmes had a sizable connection. In the next few years his reputation became international. He continued to work for no fee, but accepted presents. The finest, which some view as a bribe, came from the Duke of Holdernesse, who awarded him 6,000 pounds for solving the mysterious disappearance of the Duke's son.

In 1902 Holmes declined the offer of a knighthood, and in 1903, after twenty-three years of active service, he retired to a cottage in Sussex. There he raised bees and wrote the *magnum opus* of his later years, *Practical Handbook of Bee Culture, with some Observations upon the Segregation of the Queen.*

In 1912, after an appeal from the Prime Minister, Holmes came out of retirement to hunt down the German agent, Von Bork. It took him two years to get his man, then he went back to his bees.

———

A Study in Scarlet, Doyle's first story about Sherlock Holmes, was published in 1887. In the next few years a dozen or so more of Holmes's adventures appeared, and by 1893 the great sleuth was a celebrity.

But in the meantime Conan Doyle had become leery of his superman. "I weary of his name," he complained. And so, in the December 1893 issue of *Strand Magazine,* over the pleas of its editor, Doyle locked Holmes and Moriarty in mortal combat and sent them over a cliff in Switzerland.

The public was shocked and outraged. "Over twenty thousand people canceled their subscriptions immediately," Charles Higham wrote in *The Adventures of Conan Doyle.* " 'You beast!' one woman's letter began. Young men in the city wore black silk bands around their hats. . . . The Prince of Wales was especially dashed by the great detective's demise."

When others begged Doyle to bring Holmes back, Doyle replied, "He is at the foot of the Reichenbach Falls, and there he stays."

Seven years passed before Doyle's attitude began to change. He then wrote *The Hound of the Baskervilles.* The editor of *Strand Magazine* advised his readers that the adventure had occurred before Holmes fell from the cliff.

Years earlier, for the world rights to his first Holmes story, Doyle had received twenty-five pounds. In 1913 his agent informed him of an offer from America. If Doyle would bring Holmes back to life and explain away the problem of his reported death, a magazine publisher would pay $5,000 per story for a minimum of six stories, the $5,000 representing the American rights only.

On a postcard Doyle replied, "Very well. A.C.D."

———

Doyle had allowed his daughter to crawl about his desk while he wrote the first Holmes adventures. Now, sixteen years later, he demanded absolute silence throughout his household.

As it turned out, Holmes had not really fallen to his death, he had only arranged that it appear so. Moriarty was dead, but two of the most dangerous members of his gang were still at large.

Had Holmes returned to London, his life would have been in danger. And so he spent two years in Tibet, then operated a laboratory in France. The murder of Ronald Adair was the problem that drew him back to Baker Street.

Six months later, when this news was published, the response was tremendous. "The scenes in the railway bookstalls were worse than anything I ever saw at a bargain sale," one woman remembered.

It was an era when there were few cars, and no radios, movies, or television. Each month *Strand Magazine* sold 350,000 copies. Years later, a retired editor recalled, "Alone of all the . . . authors in . . . the beginning of the popular illustrated magazine, Conan Doyle writing Sherlock Holmes was the only one— Kipling and Wells *not* excepted—whose name on the cover as a contributor was sufficient to justify the publisher in increasing by many thousands the print run for that particular issue."

Perhaps it was as Anthony Lejeune wrote, "The Great Detective . . . was a symbol . . . he brought the ancient message of hope: that somewhere, if we could only find it, there is a rational solution, a perfect answer, to the mysteries which surround us."

IV

WE KNOW THAT HOLMES is as he is because of Edgar Allan Poe, because of Dr. Joseph Bell, and because of Charles Darwin; but their contributions are minor when compared to that of Arthur Conan Doyle. As Dr. Bell once wrote Doyle, "You are Sherlock Holmes."

When Conan Doyle was young he decided that Homo sapiens was still evolving, and that teeth, hair, even sight were on the way out. "Instinctively, when we think of the more advanced type of young man," Doyle wrote a friend, "we picture him as bald, and with double eye glasses." He added, "I am an absolute animal, myself, and my only sign of advance is that two of my back teeth are missing."

In a sense he was just that, "an absolute animal," six feet tall and weighing two hundred and fifteen pounds. He was related, on his mother's side, to an Irish fighting family, the Packs, and as a youth he rejoiced in battle. When he was twenty-one he went to the Arctic as surgeon aboard a whaler. He was so aggressive that the captain offered to make him harpooner as well as surgeon, with double pay, if Doyle would make a second voyage.

For most of his life he was exceptionally athletic. He played association football until he was forty-five, and continued at cricket for ten more years. He boxed at least once a week. He was proficient with foil, bow, and rifle; rode frequently, despite a tendency to take falls; and drove his car in one international road competition. He enjoyed golf and made it into the third round of the English amateur billiard championships. He introduced skiing at Davos in Switzerland. He did not like to fly in planes, but ballooning thrilled him.

Conan Doyle was intensely romantic. In his late twenties, having abandoned Christianity, he searched for a code to live by. The Middle Ages and the concept of knightly honor attracted him, and he wrote two novels set in the time of pennons and chivalry. For much of his life, thereafter, he conducted himself by the code championed by his fictional heroes: "Fearless to the strong, humble to the weak. Chivalry toward all women, of high or low degree. Help to the helpless, whoever shall ask for it. And to this I pledge my knightly honor."

When his son described a woman as ugly, Doyle slapped him. And when, after seven years of marriage, his first wife became tubercular and was given only a short time to live, Doyle tended her with such care that she lived on for thirteen years.

In the meantime, he fell in love with a woman named Jean Leckie. Until some months after his first wife's death, when he and Jean finally married, their relations remained platonic. His mother and sister knew about this, and so did his sister's husband, William Hornung.

Hornung, the creator of the fictional gentleman-thief, Raffles, thought Doyle attached too much importance to whether or not his relationship with Jean was platonic. "I can't see that it makes all that difference," he advised Doyle.

Doyle, furious at what he interpreted as Hornung's coarseness, replied, "It makes all the difference between innocence and guilt."

Such being Doyle's character, it is not surprising that when in real life his attention was called to large injustices committed by the law enforcement bureaucracy, he moved vigorously in opposition to official justice.

————

Great Wyrley is a rude mining village a few miles beyond Birmingham in the midlands. In 1903 the Church of England vicar there was the Rev. Sapurji Edalji, a Hindu who had married the daughter of another Church of England pastor, and had served in Great Wyrley for eighteen years, raising a family there.

Beginning about 1892 and running through 1895, the Edaljis and other families in Great Wyrley were disturbed by a series of practical jokes and anonymous letters that expressed hatred towards the Edaljis, and especially their half-caste son, George. A few of these letters were sent to the head of the nearby Walsall Grammar School, and the key to that institution was once discovered on the Edaljis' doorstep.

The police decided that the letter writer was George Edalji, who was trying, they contended, to embarrass his parents. The Chief Constable of Staffordshire, Captain the Honorable George Anson, hinted at such suspicions in a letter to Rev. Edalji. The bizarre events ceased late in 1895, and for the next eight years life in Great Wyrley was tranquil.

Then, beginning in series in February 1903, sixteen horses and cows had their stomachs sliced open, this despite the increasing watchfulness of the police. Each carcass bore a long, shallow wound that caused blood to spurt, but did not pierce the gut.

At the same time another series of anonymous letters began to circulate in the village. In them the writer gloated over the attacks on the animals, suggested that the same sort of thing might happen to young ladies, and denounced George Edalji as the leader of an organized gang of animal murderers. Each letter, for reasons unknown at the time, contained references to the sea and slanderous references to the headmaster of Walsall Grammar School.

George Edalji was, by this time, twenty-seven. He lived with his parents at the vicarage and commuted to Birmingham, where he practiced law. He was a dark-complected man, respected in his profession, and the author of a book on railway law. He was also frail and reserved, neither smoked nor drank, and did not enjoy socializing.

One morning a passer-by found a colliery pony lying in a field bleeding to death from a long slit in its belly. The police marched to the vicarage and seized a case of George's razors. They also collected a pair of his boots, stained with black mud; a pair of his trousers, mudstained along the cuffs; and a vest and jacket stained with what appeared to be blood. All of these items, the police later announced, were covered with pony hairs.

In Birmingham George was arrested, then escorted back to Great Wyrley. He denied that he had attacked the pony. He had visited various clients in the village until 9 P.M., he declared, and had then retired to the vicarage and the room where he and his father slept. He insisted that he remained in that room until morning. His father, a light sleeper, supported him.

At the trial the prosecution argued that George had left the vicarage between two and three in the morning, tramped a half-mile in the rain, evading twenty policemen, slashed the pony, then returned to the vicarage in a roundabout way.

George was found guilty, and was sentenced to seven years in jail. He was also struck off the rolls of the Law Society.

In those days a Court of Appeals did not exist in England, and the law provided no solace for its victims. Before long, however, a former Chief Justice of the Bahamas attempted to get George's case reopened. In addition, a newspaper campaigned on George's behalf, and a petition signed by 10,000 people, several hundred of whom were lawyers, was submitted to the court.

Back at Great Wyrley, the attacks on the animals continued.

The police explanation was that George's accomplices were working to make him appear innocent. Then three years later, suddenly and unexpectedly, George was released from prison. No explanation was made; no restitution was offered. He returned to society a discharged convict, unpardoned, and under surveillance, his career shattered. He wrote some articles about his case and various newspapers and magazines soon began to champion his cause.

Meanwhile, Conan Doyle's first wife had died and his life, for the most part, was empty of enthusiasms. One day, in a newspaper, he came across an article by George. "As I read it the unmistakable accent of truth forced itself to my attention," Doyle explained later, "and I realized that I was in the presence of an appalling tragedy, and that I was called upon to do what I could to set it right."

For the next eight months, Doyle gave virtually all of his attention to George's predicament. "I must admit that in ordinary life I am by no means observant," he wrote in his memoirs, "and that I have to throw myself into an artificial frame of mind before I can weigh evidence and anticipate the sequence of events." Nevertheless, he performed superbly.

He began his attack by writing to everyone connected with the case and requesting their explanations of various points. From their answers he learned:

That the razors seized by the police had been clean.

That gravy from underdone meat could have been responsible for the bloodstains on the vest and housecoat.

That the police had cut away a piece of the pony's hide, needing it for evidence, and had afterwards placed George's clothes and the piece of hide in the same sack.

That on the evening before the attack on the pony, it had rained before George got back from Birmingham and made his calls around the village, which could account for the black mud stains on the cuffs of his trousers.

That these cuffs held no trace of the sandy clay soil found in the fields surrounding the carcass of the pony.

Doyle then went to Great Wyrley. "What aroused my indignation and gave me the driving force to carry the thing through," he wrote later, "was the utter helplessness of this forlorn little group of people, the coloured clergyman in his strange position, the brave blue-eyed, grey-haired wife, the young daughter, baited by brutal boys and having the police, who should have been their natural protectors, adopting from the beginning a harsh tone towards them and accusing them, beyond all sense and reason, of being the cause of their own troubles and persecuting and maligning themselves."

At Great Wyrley, Doyle made a point of not meeting George. Not until every available fact had been examined did the two men meet in Birmingham.

"He had come to my hotel by appointment," Doyle wrote, "but I had been delayed, and he was passing the time by reading the paper. I recognized him by his dark face, so I stood and observed him. He held the paper close to his eyes and rather sidewise, proving not only a high degree of myopia, but marked astigmatism. The idea of such a man scouring the fields at night and assaulting cattle while avoiding the watchful police was ludicrous to anyone who can imagine what the world looks like to eyes with myopia of eight dioptres."

In January 1907 a London newspaper published the first installment of Doyle's 18,000-word summation of the Edalji case. Since the story was not copyrighted, every paper in the country was soon proclaiming the wrongs done to George.

In dealing with the problem of the pony hairs, Doyle was able to show that, according to medical testimony, all of the hairs on George's clothing were similar to the hairs on the strip of hide cut by the police. Doyle concluded his summation by taking a somewhat Holmesian position regarding the police. He accused Captain the Honorable George Anson of prejudice, deceit, and incompetence. About the ignominious release of George after authorities could no longer justify his imprisonment, Doyle was even less polite.

The result was that, throughout England, men called for an explanation of the government's failure to pardon or compensate George. The government responded by appointing an impartial committee of three to examine the facts. Of these three, one turned out to be a second cousin to Captain George Anson.

Meanwhile, Doyle was enlarging the scope of his investigation of the Great Wyrley affair. The problem now became: Who was the real criminal? Doyle soon received the first of a new series of vicious letters. Because of peculiarities in them, he contacted the Walsall Grammar School and asked if they had ever had a student, during the 1890s, who "had held a peculiar grudge against the headmaster, was known to have a vicious nature, and had subsequently gone to sea." The answer was yes.

"Peter Hudson," as Doyle chose to call him, expelled for being beyond control, had afterward forged letters and ripped, with a knife, the upholstery in railway cars. He had eventually been apprenticed to a butcher and had then gone to sea, sometimes on cattle boats. The interval between the two series of anonymous letters (1895 to 1903) corresponded to the period when Peter Hudson was absent from Great Wyrley.

Doyle also discovered that some of the vicious letters had been mailed from the Liverpool area, and that Peter Hudson had shipped out of that port. More important, a woman who knew the Hudson family sent Doyle a horse lancet that, about the time of the 1903 slashings, had been given to her by Peter.

"He appears to have taken little pains to hide his proceedings," Doyle wrote of Hudson, "and how there could have been any difficulty in pointing him out as the criminal is to me an extraordinary thing."

The government's three-man impartial investigating committee ended its deliberations and sent its report to the Home Secretary, who soon announced his opinion. Yes, the jury had erred in convicting George of horse maiming; nevertheless, George had definitely written the vicious letters, and accordingly had "to some extent brought his troubles on himself." Therefore, George would receive a pardon, but nothing in the way of compensation—not a penny.

Doyle, enraged, fought on for three months longer. He obtained the testimony of the foremost handwriting authority in Europe, who declared that the handwriting of Peter Hudson was identical to the handwriting in the anonymous letters.

Regardless, the government refused to acknowledge that any case existed against Peter Hudson. The Home Secretary arose in the House of Commons and declared that nothing new had arisen to change the decision made earlier. Despite the fact that the threatening letters received by Doyle were in the same handwriting as the earlier letters, the government continued to take the position that the letters had been written by George.

Doyle's work did have some positive results. The Law Society permitted George to resume his practice. George was presented with a sum of money raised for him by a paper in London, and the abuse he had suffered contributed to the establishment of a Court of Criminal Appeal.

When Doyle married Jean Leckie, the wedding guests included one half-caste barrister from Birmingham.

————

Thoreau thought of Man as the animal that seeks to know, the beast who craves reality; an appropriate concept when the subject is Conan Doyle.

"There was an orientation towards the unknown," Pierre Nordon wrote. "In a sense, all of Conan Doyle's writings are dominated by a desire to investigate and explore."

Very definitely, Doyle was in step with what the psychiatrist Henri F. Ellenberger has described as the "unmasking trend . . . the systematic search for deception and self-deception and the uncovering of the underlying truth. . . . This trend seems to have started with the French moralists of the seventeenth century. La Rochefoucauld in his Maxims . . . Schopenhauer . . . Karl Marx . . . Nietzsche . . . Ibsen . . . Max Nordau . . . Pareto."[8]

As a seeker Doyle was a reverent man, exceptionally aware of what he described as "the wonderful poise of the Universe," that and his own presence in the universe.

On his father's side he was descended from an ancient Irish family that had suffered for its Catholicism and took pride in that identity. At medical school in Edinburgh, after immersing himself in Darwin, Spencer, and Huxley, he lost his faith. He rejected Christianity, he rejected Catholicism, but he was never an agnostic.

He "entirely admitted a great central intelligent cause," he wrote later, "without being able to distinguish what that cause was, or why it should work in so mysterious and terrible a way in bringing its designs to fulfillment."

Otherwise, he accepted the materialistic views he had absorbed in medical school. "I saw, as a medical man, how a spicule of bone or tumor pressing on the brain would cause what seemed an alteration in the soul. I saw also how drugs or alcohol could turn on fleeting phases of virtue or vice. The physical argument seemed an overpowering one."

This was his attitude when he created Sherlock Holmes, a character with whom, even then, he was not entirely happy; a character whose methods are so rational and materialistic that, as Ross Macdonald has suggested, he seems the dominant hero of our technological society: the one great symbol of that mechanistic, materialistic effort, that relentless spirit of rational inquiry, which man for over two centuries regarded as his salvation.

Yet even as Holmes was solving his first problems, Doyle was moving in the opposite direction. He had become interested in telepathy and psychic problems.

His mind slowly concentrated on the problem of death, then moved on to the question of survival and the need for a universal religion. After a series of mystic experiences, he solved these problems to his satisfaction and became a convert to spiritualism. Between his conversion and his death, he toured the world championing its cause. He spent over a million dollars of his own money and brought to spiritualism "a combative and aggressive spirit that it had lacked before."

For Conan Doyle the enemy now, the root of man's misfortunes, was materialism. A year or so before his death, he traveled to Amsterdam to lecture on spiritualism. He reacted with dismay and even anger when, as the evening began, he was invited to say a few preliminary words about Sherlock Holmes.

JULES MAIGRET
Georges Simenon

I'm only a man.
When I Was Old

I

THE AGE OF THE GREAT DETECTIVE began, not with the advent of an analytical gentleman with a radiant, all-powerful mind, but with the arrival of a reformed criminal who solved police problems because he knew criminals and their world.

François Vidocq solved problems because of his exact knowledge, and because of his brilliant use of disguise and propaganda. Eventually, he became so successful that the regular policemen of Paris demanded he be retired. Vidocq then opened his own business, The Information Office, he called it, and became the world's first private detective. As such, he acquired so much inside information about events in France that the government, thinking itself threatened, forced him to close. His memoirs created a sensation.

"It was he who first struck the European imagination as the detective," P. J. Stead wrote. "Long before Poe created Dupin, Vidocq had established the legend of the all-knowing, omni-present detective."

François Vidocq was a muscular man, five feet six inches tall, with a pale face, auburn hair, and a red mustache. His features were mobile, like an actor's; he had penetrating eyes, cop's eyes, and the affable manner of an egoist. Vain, proud, delighted by his fame, he was absolutely possessed by the hunter's instinct. Balzac called him "a person of appalling greatness." He was a kind of monster, outsize in everything but height.

Vidocq was born in Arras, in northern France, in 1776. His first criminal act was unexceptional, tapping the till in his father's shop. Things changed when, at age fourteen, he killed a fencing master in a duel. At twenty-two he was one of France's most famous criminals, famous not for his crimes, but for his escapes. No matter where the authorities imprisoned him, Vidocq slipped out.

Once, recaptured and on his way back to prison, he planted in the minds of his guards the idea that he could not swim. As the cart creaked across a long bridge, the guards relaxed. Vidocq dove into the water and swam away.*

Vidocq's most famous escape was from the dreaded galleys in Toulon where, chained to other prisoners, he did convict labor. The chains were made of soft iron; and Vidocq and other prisoners used bits of watch spring, which they kept hidden in tiny packages in their rectums, to saw through them.

His actual crimes seem minor; desertion from the army was his original offense. The problem was his escapes—each time he was recaptured, his sentence was doubled. Even his most serious crime seems small: the forging of a pardon that set a fellow prisoner free.

In 1799 he was arrested in Lyons, where the police had been tipped off by former convicts. Jean-Pierre Dubois, an ambitious police administrator who hoped to win an appointment to Paris by reducing crime in Lyons, studied Vidocq's record, identified him as a man who had been harshly treated for minor offenses, and

*Most of the material in this sketch is drawn from Vidocq's *Memoirs,* from *Vidocq: A Biography,* by P. J. Stead, and from *The Vidocq Dossier* by Samuel Edwards. It should be understood that nothing like Gerald Howson's careful account of Jonathan Wild has been done in the case of the equally extraordinary Vidocq. As Samuel Edwards emphasizes in a note that precedes the brief bibliography of *The Vidocq Dossier,* "the pickings are slim, and these works borrow freely from each other."

The incident cited above, from *Memoirs,* may or may not be factually true. It and others are presented because they contain the taste of the man, as found in his accomplishments.

offered him a deal: "no charges would be placed against him," Samuel Edwards wrote in *The Vidocq Dossier,* "and he would be given his freedom if he became a police informer."

Vidocq agreed and entered the Lyons underworld in the role of a pimp. As his information came in, the police made arrest after arrest, and the crime rate dropped dramatically. Then came a case in which it would be necessary for Vidocq to testify in open court, thus blowing his cover. Dubois gave Vidocq papers identifying him as a peddlar and sent him on his way.

For the next eight years Vidocq lived cautiously and stayed out of trouble. He was thirty-four, and in the dry goods business in Paris, when he was identified by ex-convicts who either informed police or attempted to blackmail him into joining their gang. At any rate, he was soon back in jail, spying for the police in the most putrid prison in Paris. After twelve months, during which he provided his masters with a large amount of information, the authorities recognized that he would be even more valuable outside.

His release was disguised as another escape. The police made a noisy display of searching for him, and the prisoners celebrated gleefully.

But in jail or out, Vidocq's fundamental problem did not change. Legally, he was a fugitive from justice. At any time the police could ship him back to the galleys in Toulon. If he was to win his freedom, he had to perform brilliantly.

At first he was restricted to problems the regular police had failed to solve. One involved a suspected fence. Vidocq stationed himself near the suspect's house, and when the man appeared, hailed him by a false name, which was immediately disclaimed. Vidocq then talked the man into going to the police station to prove his identity. There he was searched by the police, who found three watches plus twenty-five rare coins wrapped in a handkerchief.

Taking the handkerchief, Vidocq returned to the fence's home and, using the handkerchief as identification, warned the fence's wife that the police were on her husband's trail. She told

Vidocq to get her three carriages. He did so, then helped her load them with stolen property. Afterward, he ordered the drivers to go to the police station. The fence and his wife were sentenced to prison.

Vidocq's second problem was that in Paris the criminals were winning the war against crime. Napoleon's military needs had drained France's manpower and the police were understaffed and demoralized. Once a criminal left one district for another, the police in the first district lost all interest in him. Vidocq proposed the formation of a special crime squad dressed in civilian clothes. Such a squad, he specified, would operate throughout Paris and its suburbs, and would be at the disposal of the *préfet de police.* It would maintain surveillance over ex-prisoners, pursue escaped prisoners, arrest persons wanted by the authorities, and catch criminals in the act.

The uniformed police, *officiers de paix,* fought the idea, but the authorities were interested. In October of 1812, Vidocq was allowed to choose eight assistants. He took them from the criminal class; no one else had the necessary knowledge. They were not paid a salary but received a fee for each arrest and were reimbursed for whatever expenses Vidocq thought necessary. Officially, they were known as the Brigade de la Sûreté; unofficially, they were Vidocq's gang.

He led them to jails for organized viewing and memory training. The prisoners walked around in a circle while Vidocq and his men stood in the center and studied them. He insisted that full records be kept of every criminal involved in any case, and appears to have been the first police official to recognize that criminals often give themselves away by their method of operation. He hired the first woman detective and was one of the earliest proponents of the use of fingerprints. But such innovations seem small when compared with his ability, so to speak, to climb right into bed with the criminals.

At a time when clothing and manner identified a man's station in life, Vidocq was a zestful and imaginative role player. For years he maintained, daily, three separate identities.

He was himself, François Vidocq, originally the escape artist and fugitive, hiding in a small apartment on the left bank; and then, gradually, the famous detective, friend of celebrated writers who based certain characters on him. He was also Jules, thirty years old, a burglar and all-around tough guy with a beard and a limp. As Jules, Vidocq was often accompanied by his girl friend, Annette, who also loved playing a part. And finally, he was Jean-Louis, a sixty-year-old fence with a Breton accent, gray hair, a big mustache, and old-fashioned clothes. As a fence, he paid the highest prices for stolen goods.

Although he was a master of costume, Vidocq believed that changes in appearance were actually controlled from within. It was not an art, he said, but a science. You observed how an old man walked, a gallant raised his glass, and a peasant nibbled bread. "Observe what you would become," he told Balzac, "then act accordingly, and you will be transformed."

Much of it was great fun.

Although Vidocq was five feet six inches tall, he once convinced an English newspaper reporter that he was considerably taller and possessed the ability to make himself shrink. He accomplished this by hiding packs of playing cards in his shoes.

"He is a remarkably well built man," the reporter wrote, "of extraordinary muscular power, and exceedingly active. He stands, when perfectly erect, five feet ten inches in height, but by some strange process connected with his physical formation, he has the faculty of contracting his height several inches, and in this diminished state to walk around, jump, etc."

Vidocq organized his crime squad in 1812, at a time when he had the rank, salary, and prerogatives of a *commissaire*. In 1813 Napoleon, who was always interested in the unorthodox, awarded him a letter of commendation, a medal, and a purse containing one hundred gold francs. In 1814 Vidocq was raised to Deputy Prefect, a sort of assistant chief, authorized to call for the help of the uniformed police when necessary.

This he rarely did. The rivalry between the uniformed and plain-clothes branches of the Paris police was bitter. The *officiers de paix* enjoyed reminding Vidocq of both his fugitive status and their willingness to drag him back to the galleys, where he legally belonged.

In 1817, according to one report, Vidocq's gang made 811 arrests. This included 15 assassins, 341 thieves, 38 fences, 14 escaped prisoners, 43 parole breakers, and 46 con men.

Vidocq's gang was, and had been from the beginning, the granddaddy of criminal investigation departments throughout the world; the origin of the Sûreté nationale and also of the Sûreté of the prefecture, known today as the *police judiciaire.*

On May 2, 1817, Vidocq was notified, in a letter from the president of the appropriate court, that the forgery charge that had existed since his youth had been erased from the record. And so his most threatening personal problem was solved. His enemies could no longer get to him. At least not that way.

———

By the middle 1820s Vidocq was a household name in Paris.

No one really knew where he was at any particular moment. He could be parading the boulevards in his caped coat, square hat, elegant calf-high boots and riding crop. He could be wandering about disguised as a porter. He could be boozing with thieves in basement taverns.*

"The legend of Vidocq, combining in one person as he did order and disorder, police and crime, dirty work and high minded politics, was an important element in popular thinking," the scholar Louis Chevalier wrote. "The massive silhouette, now reassuring and now terrifying, not only loomed in the background of the major contemporary works, but also dominated the people's fears and beliefs."

Although Vidocq lived in a handsome house and dined in the finest restaurants, he was never able to completely shed the rougher side of his character.

In the Sûreté his chief assistant was a reformed swindler named Goury, who lived with a beautiful woman. One night, as

———

*Vidocq made money by lending it, which was legal. Some of his profits were used to buy taverns in the slum districts where, in one or another of his disguises, he drank regularly. Some of the bartenders were actually members of Vidocq's gang.

she was arriving at Vidocq's house to dine with Vidocq and Goury, a well-dressed man mistook her for a prostitute and made a proposal.

Inside the house she reported the incident. Vidocq and Goury reacted quickly. The gentleman was invited in and conducted to a dark bedroom where he was soon joined by a woman whom he gradually discovered to be not the lady he had admired but an elderly crone, one of Vidocq's servants. "He was locked in with her for the night," Samuel Edwards reports, "and not permitted to leave the next morning until he had paid a large fee, which Goury and Vidocq gave to the crone."

Having established himself during the era of Napoleon, Vidocq improved his position through the reigns of Louis XVIII, Charles X, and Louis Philippe. He had no interest in politics as such, and did not care who was on the throne. Catching thieves and the enlargement of his personal power base were his only concerns. His relations with the rich were excellent. He was the man they came to when threatened by scandal. Gradually, he learned where the important bodies were buried.

When Charles X came to the throne, his ultrareactionary advisors directed Vidocq to forget about criminals and concentrate on traitors. Vidocq was disturbed. When the same reactionaries criticized the off-duty habits of his men, their visits to brothels and public drinking, his unhappiness increased. On June 27, 1827, he resigned. On October 2, 1831, a new government now in power, Vidocq returned as head of the Brigade de la Sûreté. On November 15, 1832, he resigned for the final time.

He did so because, in a nation that prided itself on being rational, the most prominent magistrates and lawyers were coming to believe that la Sûreté, meaning security, should be in the hands of men of good character, rather than reformed criminals. And there were rational reasons for their thinking so. During Vidocq's four-year absence, his reformed criminals had begun to return to their old habits. Only Vidocq could control them, and he could not be on the job forever.

But Vidocq's resigning did not mean his retirement. He could never do that, since everything about him was so much larger than life. His vanity and his love of fame made it impossible for him to become a private person.

But there was more to it than that. "What Vidocq wanted, even more than money, was power," Stead wrote. "He had been hunting men for a quarter of a century and no smaller game would serve him now. The hunter could not retire like a civil servant at his age limit."

There was much for him to do. In money-mad, mercantile Paris, a great new age of capitalism was creating a new breed of criminal, the con man. Many of them were from good families, elegant young men who had squandered their inheritances but had no desire to remove themselves from the sweet pleasures of society. Their favorite deception was simple. They bought on credit and sold, at a heavy discount, for cash.

Vidocq's response was to organize the world's first private-detective agency. The Information Office opened on January 3, 1834. "I now have . . . the list," potential clients were advised by Vidocq, "of all who have been brought before the courts, accused of or condemned for swindling during the last thirty years."

The Information Office was not named frivolously. Vidocq's curiosity was gigantic, and he had numerous ways of learning the exact state of affairs in France. By 1837 he had 3,000 subscribers, each one, a potential source of information. He also lent money, especially to government employees.

The government became anxious about the amount of information such clients might be giving away in a conversation with the affable sleuth. On a pretext, the police raided the Information Office and carried away 3,000 dossiers. Half of them, it was found, related to actual police business. Vidocq was in touch with every branch of the government. It was aggravating to the police; and what made things worse was that he was so talented.

When the brother of the *préfet de police* was robbed, the police could not recover the stolen property. Using an assumed name, the victim took his problem to Vidocq. Vidocq not only recovered the stolen goods; he identified his client as the brother of the *préfet* and wrote to him at his proper address. The *préfet* was outraged. Were the police in control of the streets of Paris, or was Vidocq?

The police response was to slip a man into Vidocq's organization. Eventually, in a case involving the apprehension of a swindler, Vidocq was charged with illegal arrest, sequestration, and obtaining money under false pretenses. The police raided the Information Office and seized its proprietor and all his dossiers.

Back in prison Vidocq, sixty-seven years old, received no consideration of any sort. At his trial he was sentenced to five years and fined 3,000 francs. He appealed, however, and won a complete victory, being discharged without a stain on his character and portrayed as a public benefactor. He immediately returned to his private agency.

Nevertheless, the police had won. They had smashed the Information Office by arranging, at the first trial, for numerous dossiers to be read aloud. As Stead wrote, "A confidential agency cannot afford to have its records seized and read out in the courts."

In his old age his mania for knowing the truth continued. "He besieged the officers of the police," Stead reported, "impervious to snubs and excuses, even to blank refusals. When they did not employ him, he sent in reports just the same."*

Throughout his life Vidocq had enjoyed women. In old age, living cheerfully in a comfortable apartment, his fondness for them continued; but he learned that he was expected to pay for their attention. When a woman pointed out that it was a harsh world, that money eased everything, he responded by asking her permission to make her his heiress.

He died on May 11, 1857. Claimants to his estate immediately began to appear. They included ten ladies of the evening and one actress from a boulevard theater, each of them carrying a will.

---

*In *Maigret's Memoirs,* Jules Maigret observes, "I repeat, it's a game that's being played, a game that has no end. Once you've begun it, it's difficult, if not impossible, to give it up. The proof is that those of us who eventually retire, often against their will, always end up by setting up a private detective agency . . . I don't know one detective who . . . isn't ready to take up work again, even unpaid."

Students of the Paris police inevitably encounter the statement of the critic Yves Gyot, made in 1884, "The citizen is free to do what he likes, but under police supervision." It is an important view because today France is, and is not, a police state.

"All the essential architecture for a police state is here," Blake Ehrlich wrote in 1962. "Yet even taking account of the occasional act of tyranny, the police state does not exist."[1]

And in 1969 Sanche de Gramont wrote, "France is a police state, not in a tyrannical, harshly punitive, or arbitrary manner, but in the broad mandate given to the enforcers of public order."[2]

The French concept of police was inherited from the Roman magistrates who governed Gaul and regarded the police as a managing bureaucracy. When Louis XIV, in 1666, appointed a soldier-lawyer named La Reynie to the newly created post of Lieutenant of Police and ordered him to end the urban disorder that was the worst problem in Paris, he made La Reynie, in effect, mayor of the city.

La Reynie was responsible not only for criminal affairs, but for action against fires and floods, the inspection of markets and brothels, the verification of weights and measures, the supervision of printing and publishing, and the study of illicit assemblies and any sedition and discord that might arise.

Today the duties of the Paris police continue to go far beyond the pursuit of criminals. It is the cops who, among other things, decide the question of legal sanity, say which buildings will be condemned, and who will sell lottery tickets.

They are also responsible for keeping the government informed about the state of the capital. For this particular task their most important weapon is the informer. "Do you have informers?" a recent Paris police commissioner asked his men. "No? Then find another job, for you may succeed in it, but you will never succeed in the police."*

---

*This remains true today, internationally. In *New York Magazine* (March 24, 1975), Robert Daley wrote, "In the final analysis, no detective or FBI agent ever really 'breaks' a big case; an informant comes forward and sells the solution." Daley continued, "The FBI informant programs are the envy of everyone in law enforcement and have been since J. Edgar Hoover set them up—secretly—more than 40 years ago."

In *Pioneers in Policing*, edited by Stead, Frank Thomas Morn wrote, "Criminal detection historically meant criminal collaboration."

During the later part of *l'ancien regime,* which began with Louis XIV and ended with the revolution, the Black Cabinet, as it was called, opened and read thousands of letters each month. When Napoleon was in power, France did become a police state. Everyone was spied on, including the Emperor.

"Everything is sedulously recorded, down to the hours and minutes spent in brothels," a British student of the period wrote, so that "one can only conclude that the authorities had a perfect mania for knowing other people's business and that endless time and money were lavished on trifles."

The Black Cabinet still exists in effect, but the telephone has shifted attention to the spoken word. The government is especially concerned with anything that might lead to what is called "disaffection of troops."

Today the successor of La Reynie is the *préfet de police.* He heads an organization that, as the police of the central government, is completely distinct from and independent of any other French police force. The *préfet* himself, part mayor of Paris, part cop, is essentially an administrator. When he leaves his post, he usually moves up to an ambassadorship or is placed in charge of a nationalized industry. His badge number is 0001.

Under him, wearing badge number 0004, is that character whom American and English readers know as Inspector Maigret, but who, in his native land, is more accurately described as Chief Inspector Maigret, of the *police judiciaire,* the central detective force of the Paris police.

II

AMONG PROBLEM SOLVERS in criminal fiction, Jules Maigret seems the most original.

Man as species, Loren Eiseley has observed, "suffers from a nostalgia for which there is no remedy upon earth except as to be found in the enlightenment of the spirit—some ability to have a perceptive rather than an explosive relationship with his fellow creatures."[3]

Maigret is the enlightened man in criminal fiction. Representing authority, he perceives instead of exploding.

When a woman brings a problem to him, she says, "From what I have heard of you . . . I think you are a man of understanding." When an old acquaintance who has gotten into trouble tells Maigret, "I dare say you despise me for it," Maigret replies, "I've never despised anyone in my life."

As a problem solver, Maigret can be accepted as a rational man, a logical Frenchman, provided it is understood that his rationale is centered in compassion. It is this quality that enables him to see himself in the situation of others. As his creator, Georges Simenon, explains in *Maigret's Boyhood Friend,* "It was Maigret's way, when he was working on a case, to soak everything up like a sponge, absorbing into himself people and things, even of the most trivial sort, as well as impressions of which he was barely conscious."

Holmes reasons; Maigret intuits.

In *Maigret and the Bum,* Simenon cites Maigret's "attempts to understand, to immerse himself in the way of life of people unknown to him the previous day.

" 'What do you think about it, Maigret?' an examining magistrate would often ask him.

"His invariable reply was often quoted in the law courts, 'I never think, monsieur le juge.'" Instead, Maigret immerses himself, absorbs, broods, and finally becomes aware.

"In the act of hunting, a man becomes, however briefly, part of nature again," Erich Fromm has written. "He returns to his natural state again, becomes one with the animal."

Maigret's ability to identify himself, sympathetically and intuitively, with the victim, is responsible for many of his solutions.

———

In *Maigret and the Dead Girl,* the corpse of a young woman is found in the vicinity of the Moulin Rouge in Montmartre. The dead girl wears a tawdry blue evening dress and has lost one silver evening slipper. She has been struck several times and her skull is fractured. The autopsy shows that she was between nineteen and twenty-two years old, undernourished, but otherwise in good health. She was a virgin. Her purse and identification papers are gone.

For Maigret the first problem is, Who is she? This he solves as follows.

Her blue evening dress comes from a small shop, Mademoiselle Irene. The proprietress reports that she rented evening clothes to the girl twice, the first time about a month before. She remembers that the girl's first name was Louise and that her last name began with L. She also recalls that Louise was in desperate need of the dress and only had about 300 francs.

After a photograph of Louise has been published in the papers, a voice over the phone advises Maigret to see a Madame Crêmieux and provides her address. Maigret does so and learns that the girl had been Madame Crêmieux's lodger for two and one half months and that she was named Louise Laboine. Madame Crêmieux describes Louise as an extremely unsocial girl who, during her entire stay, spent only one hour visiting with her and, in that hour, opened her mouth just five times. Louise possessed one dress and one coat, was behind in her rent, spent most of her time in her room, and went out no more than two nights a week.

When Maigret inspects her room he finds nothing but an iron, wrapped in a rayon slip, a few cosmetics, some aspirin, sleeping pills, and writing material. A notecase contains a photograph, approximately fifteen years old, of a handsome, distinguished-looking man in his forties. He wears a light suit and stands beside a palm tree. There is no visible resemblance between this man and Louise.

Madame Crêmieux says that Louise received only one telephone call. It came about a month ago. After receiving it, Louise went out into the night.

And so the first part of the problem has been solved.

"With Louise Laboine it was like a photographic plate put into the developer," Simenon wrote. Forty-eight hours ago they had known nothing about her. Then she became "a blue shape against . . . wet pavement . . . a white body on a marble slab." Now they knew her name and "a picture was beginning to form."

———

Slowly, Maigret acquires additional facts about Louise. A taxi driver reports having seen her leave the Romeo night club about fifteen minutes after midnight on the evening of her death. Maigret learns that the Romeo, that evening, was the scene of a wedding reception for Jeanine Armenien, a lovely French model, and Marco Santoni, a wealthy Italian man-about-town. The bartender at the Romeo reports that at the reception Louise spoke privately with the bride.

In Nice a newspaper reader recognizes a photo of Louise and identifies her as having lived next door four or five years earlier. One day Louise and her mother had simply disappeared. It was found that they owed money everywhere. Maigret receives an impression of Louise as a young girl sent to get fish at a store where because her mother owed money, Louise was received coolly.

The Nice police locate Louise's mother in Monte Carlo where, by doubling their bets, she and a number of elderly women make enough money to support themselves. The mother is interested in the news of her daughter's death, but is preoccupied by the play at the casino. She identifies herself as a former dancer who worked as a bar girl in Turkey, Egypt, and Lebanon. Louise left home at the age of sixteen, the mother reports, and had not written her one word.

It develops that Louise came to Paris on the same train as the model, Jeanine Armenien, and that during the journey the two girls became acquainted. Louise only had money for two or three weeks. When it ran out, she got in touch with Jeanine, who was living with an aunt. Jeanine let Louise share her bedroom, but without her aunt's knowledge, and because Louise could get jobs but never hold them, this arrangement lasted several months. It ended when the aunt discovered Louise hiding under the bed. A few weeks later, Jeanine moved into an apartment of her own.

———

Now Maigret reviews a few of his impressions of Louise.

The landlady called her standoffish. The servant said she sat alone for hours on a park bench. When she went to the dress shop she was alone . . . she was alone when she went to the Romeo . . . alone at the end.

In Nice, meanwhile, the police have again talked to Louise's mother. They learn that at the age of thirty-eight she had married Julius Van Cram in Istanbul. Afterward they had come to Nice, where Louise was born. When Louise was two months old her father stepped out for cigarettes and never returned. Once in a while he sent his wife money, sometimes quite large sums.

With this information, the police identify the father as an international con man who, at twenty-four, disappeared with a good share of the funds of a bank in which his father was a director.

Maigret visits the concierge of the building where Jeanine Armenien lived before her marriage. He learns that Jeanine continued to help Louise and permitted her to share the apartment. Every two weeks, the concierge says, Jeanine got a letter from her father, but a letter for Louise was a rare event. When Jeanine moved in with her lover, Louise was in trouble because she was still unable to hold a job.

The concierge remembers that, one night about a month before Louise was killed, a gossip column reported that Jeanine ("beautiful model") and her lover had spent an evening at Maxim's. She also recalls that a few days before the girl's death, a foreigner, a man in his forties, asked to see Louise and left a message for her. Three days later the foreigner returned, learned to his distress that Louise had not picked up his message, then retrieved it and left a longer one. A few days later, Jeanine came by and told the concierge that she would soon be a news item in the papers. When she left she took Louise's letter with her because she knew that once the news about her got in the papers, Louise would come to see her.

Maigret locates Jeanine and her husband on their honeymoon in Italy. Over the phone Jeanine tells him that at the Romeo Louise had said she was broke and was thinking of suicide. Jeanine then gave her three or four thousand francs and, because she had read Louise's letter, told her what was in it. Louise was to go to Pickwick's Bar on the rue de l'Étoile and ask for Jimmy. If Jimmy was not there the barman would tell her how to find him. If Jimmy had to leave France he would leave a letter for her with the barman.

Maigret then goes to Pickwick's Bar, As soon as he enters, a change comes over him. He recognizes the barman as Albert Falconi, a Corsican criminal imprisoned twice for gambling and once for smuggling gold, who had also been arrested on suspicion of murder.

After Falconi acknowledges that Louise was in Pickwick's the night of her death, Maigret asks him to describe exactly what she did in the bar. Falconi says she sat on a stool near the door and ordered a martini. He adds that she picked up her message, then went off with an American she met at the bar.

When Falconi is finished Maigret arrests him and takes him to headquarters.

There Falconi finally says, "How did you guess?"

Maigret replies, "I didn't guess. I KNEW at once. You see, at the first glance your story is perfect . . . and I'd have swallowed it if I hadn't known the girl."

Falconi is astonished. "You knew her?"

"I came to know her quite well," Maigret says.

As Maigret spoke he could visualize her hiding under the bed, quarreling with Jeanine, sitting alone on a park bench. He could remember everything anyone had said about her.

" 'To begin with, it's very unlikely she'd have sat down at the bar.'

"Because she would have felt that she was a fish out of water."

He tells Falconi that he made a mistake when he considered Louise to be like the rest of the women that came to his bar. And Falconi said she drank a martini. The papers did not mention that the only alcohol found in Louise's stomach was rum.

As it turns out, Albert Falconi opened Jimmy's letter to Louise as soon as Jimmy left for New York. In the envelope was another letter, this one from Louise's con-man father. Reading it, Falconi learned that the father had left some money for Louise with a friend in Brooklyn.

Falconi and his friends decided to steal Louise's identity card and collect the money. When they attacked her, planning only to steal her handbag, she had the silver chain of the bag wrapped about her wrist.

"She fell to her knees," Simenon wrote. "When she opened her mouth to scream, he hit her in the face. Apparently she clung to him, trying to call for help. It was then that he took a cosh out of his pocket and clubbed her."

Near the end of the story, Simenon observes that "no training course teaches policemen how to put themselves in the place of a girl brought up in Nice by a half-crazy mother."

———

Maigret's success as a problem solver results from his ability to immerse himself in the situations of others, to sop himself in someone else's world, and to intuit sympathetically. The fact that he is a professional police officer, supported by some thirty years of experience, also contributes to his success. He and his assistants —Lucas, Janvier, Laponte—are very capable men.

In *Maigret's Memoirs** he observes, "When people talk about a detective's flair, or his methods, his intuition, I always want to retort:

" 'What about your cobbler's flair, or your pastrycook's?' "

Such men have had long apprenticeships, he points out, and have a thorough knowledge of their jobs.

"The same is true of the man from Police Headquarters."

Maigret became a cop almost by accident. He was in his second year at medical school when his father died. He had to drop out and find a job. In Paris he stayed in a small left-bank hotel where he met Jacquemain, a Detective-Inspector in the Paris police. Through him, Maigret joined the force.

For the first seven or eight months that he wore the uniform,

*For Maigret buffs, an exceptionally interesting, amusing book. Published in France in 1950, and in England in 1963, it is not available in the United States.

he rode around Paris delivering notes to the various police stations. Months passed before he stopped losing his way. This was in the days when very few cops had more than a primary education. The song writers made fun of them for their "hob-nailed shoes" and "big moustaches."

Because he was poor, Maigret himself wore hob-nailed shoes when he was on the Public Highway Squad. He often worked thirteen or fourteen hours a day, in every sort of weather.

Then he was sent to patrol the railroad stations and later was assigned to detective work in hotels and department stores. He also covered "crowded gatherings"—sporting events, patriotic demonstrations, military parades, and circuses. In fact, during his first four or five years on the force, he was frequently moved from one position to another and so obtained wide experience in many types of police work. The reason for this was that he had what New York cops call a "rabbi," meaning a friend in high places. His name was Xavier Guichard, Chief of the Sûreté, the national police of France. Guichard had been a friend of Maigret's father's.*

Eventually Maigret was assigned to the homicide squad. On his first case he was ordered to assist in the capture of a dangerous Czech, responsible for several murders. The police had been shadowing him for five days and knew where he slept. The man was armed, clever, and realized that the cops were right behind him. In the daytime he kept in the middle of crowds, and the police knew that he would try to kill as many people as possible before being brought down himself.

" 'The problem was to immobilize him before he had a chance to defend himself,' " Maigret explains in his *Memoirs.*

The decision is to arrest him when he is asleep. The inspector handling the case has a key to the Czech's hotel room. He and Maigret take a room on the same floor, then wait until dawn (a man's resistance is always lowest about that time). Finally, with

*Guichard was for real. His actual name was E. Xavier Guichard and he was director of the *police judiciaire*. He was a friend of Simenon's and was sometimes described as the "doyen of the official detective chiefs of Europe." By the age of sixty-four, he had spent forty-two years with the police.

great care, they creep up to the Czech's door. Then the inspector quietly inserts the key in the lock.

"As I was the tallest and heaviest," Maigret remembers, "it was my job to rush forward first, and I did so with one bound." Of the struggle he remembers "a set of huge dazzling teeth. A hand clutching my ear . . . trying to wrench it off." When the fight goes out of the criminal it is because Inspector Dufour has given the man's foot what seems to be a double twist. "The sound of handcuffs put an end for me to a fight which might have ended badly."

In his day-to-day police work, Maigret uses every means available to the police, including phone taps and informers. These rarely contribute to the solution of a problem, but they provide interesting clues along the way.

In his *Memoirs* Maigret says that "a detective is, above all, a professional. He is an *official.* He's not engaged in a guessing game, nor getting worked up over a relatively thrilling chase."

Maigret has been an official for most of his life, but being a police official is different from being an official of another sort, for a police official is balanced between two worlds. As Maigret says, "I belong to a social group, of course. . . . But I know the others too."

He concludes, "Utterly rotten individuals are rare. . . . As for the rest, I tried to prevent them from doing too much harm and to see to it that they paid for the harm they had already done."

———

Although he does not like it, Maigret accepts the fact that powerful people require special treatment. It is a lesson he absorbed in *Maigret's First Case.*

In this story a struggle for power is taking place within the Gendreau family, manufacturers of Balthazar coffee. Maigret, in his mid-twenties, has been on the force for four years or so, and is the secretary at the police station in the Saint-George district of Paris. When someone is shot to death at the Gendreau mansion, Maigret is the only policeman available at the station.

After several days of hard work, he demonstrates that the

Gendreaus' explanation that the butler did it is ridiculous, and that, more probably, the victim was murdered by Lise, the Gendreaus' daughter.

Maigret's superior at the Saint-George station is Monsieur Le Bret, a worldly man, well connected in society. Le Bret thinks the evidence against Lise is so weak that in any court she would be acquitted. Therefore, he wants to close the case immediately by accepting the butler's story.

"There are cases where scandal serves no useful purpose," he tells Maigret, "when the blunt facts would do more harm than good."

Le Bret's attitude disturbs Maigret. He goes to the office of his "rabbi," Xavier Guichard, and has a heart-to-heart talk with the big chief.

"The lesson he had learned that day, given in a fatherly tone, didn't figure in the official police manual," Simenon observes.

"Do you follow? Cause as little trouble as possible. What good would come of it?"

"Massive," "broadshouldered," and "redoubtable" are the words Simenon most often used to describe the early Maigret. But through the years, his pipe has been Maigret's most constant identification. He has a large collection and every one in it is important to him.*

He lives with his wife, Louise, on Boulevard Richard Lenoix in the Bastille district, the XII *arrondissement.* It is the poorest, most anonymous section of Paris, mostly warehouses, foundries, and small businesses.

They have lived there almost from the beginning of their marriage, despite friends' efforts to push them into a better address. Madame Maigret is a superb cook and Maigret regrets that,

---

*For Maigret buffs there are at least three, and some would say four, Maigrets. In *Simenon in Court* John Raymond wrote, "There is certainly Maigret the First—a false or rough-hewn and uncomplicated Maigret . . . just as there is, in one or two of the later volumes, something of an Old Pretender. In between—indeed, all through the series, as much in some of the earliest adventures as in his most recent—is the Maigret that we recognize and feel we know."

rather often when he is working a case, it is impossible for him to go home for his meal.

"Mme. Maigret is the most unliberated of females," the English critic Richard Cobb has noted; "her function is to cook meals that her husband will never eat, to wait for his return, to get up before him so that he may wake up to the smell of freshly ground coffee . . . the relationship is sexless."

And a French critic has observed, "He never sleeps with anybody, not even with Madame Maigret, whose bed he shares."

This is true. Sex plays virtually no part in the Maigret stories, no more than it does in Holmes. When duty takes Maigret into the bedroom of a nightclub entertainer or a prostitute, the women are sometimes rather casual about taking off their clothes. Maigret just turns his back and stares out the window.

He and his wife's great personal loss is that they have no children. Their only child died at birth.

When Maigret is not well he stays at home and reads the novels of Alexandre Dumas.

Once, after buying a new pipe for himself, he felt remorse, went into another shop, and sent his wife a handkerchief.

When he buys new shoes, he breaks them in during the evening stroll that he takes with Louise.

He does not drive. He did for a bit but would begin to think about the case he was working on, then find himself and his automobile in great difficulties.

For three years, very much against his will, he was vice president of the Police Benevolent Association.

He has never been able to kill an animal, not even a harmful one.

His honesty is legendary. Even if he is in an otherwise empty bar, he pays up when he takes a drink. "The list of drinks and prices was posted near the window to his right. He consulted it, took some loose change out of his pocket, and dropped the money for the Calvados into the till. . . ."

He needs the human contact he receives during his investigations. "He needed to escape from his office, to be out and about in all weathers, to discover a whole new world with each inquiry,"

Simenon wrote in *Maigret and Monsieur Charles.* "He needed those long hours spent waiting at the counter of some *bistro*, drinking calvados or beer, depending on the circumstances."

Some of Maigret's characteristics are taken from Chief Superintendent Massu, who was Chief of the Criminal Brigade at the time Simenon created Maigret. "I owe him—*inter alia*—what I called in several of my novels *'l'interrogatoire à la chansonette,'"* Simenon has said.

He was referring to the long interrogations that take place in Maigret's office on the Quai des Orfèvres—those intense affairs when the battle is joined between the criminal and the detectives; and of the breaks for quick feasts of sandwiches and beer sent over from the Brasserie Dauphine. Then the battle is joined once more, the criminal repeats his story over and over until a contradiction appears, a wedge is made, and—sooner or later—the beans are spilled and a full confession is obtained.

Because he is a cop, an official of a bureaucracy, that is, and also a distinguished problem solver, Maigret sometimes seems to be in opposition to the mythology of detective fiction, as established by Poe. But like quite a few other cops, Maigret is neither a bureaucrat nor an administrator, and knows it.

As *Maigret and Monsieur Charles* begins, he is called to the office of an important bureaucrat and informed that the head of the *police judiciaire* is retiring and that he, Jules Maigret, has been selected to succeed him.

The bureaucrat tells him, "It's an important promotion; there's no higher position in the *police judiciaire.*"

But Maigret does not want it.

He declares, "I'd prefer to remain at the head of the Criminal Division." He asks the official not to be offended by his decision. "I've had forty years of active police service. It would be hard for me to spend my days cooped up in an office, looking through files and occupying myself with administration. . . ."

When all is said and done, Maigret is blood brother to Dupin and Holmes. He has been described by Brigid Brophy as "a private detective who, needing to earn a living, happens to be employed by the police." As such, she points out, Maigret "sticks to the myth pattern in which both the aboriginal Dupin and the central Holmes are private detectives. . . . In fact, the competition between the detective hero and the police is indispensable to the myth, because it is the police with their propensity to err continually, who are the threat to the population in the story."

Maigret's most prominent rival is a magistrate named Coméliau, who functions as the true representative of the police bureaucracy.

In Paris every detective working on a case does so under the supervision of an Examining Magistrate. Although these men are sometimes presented as unsympathetic persons who hinder Maigret, they are generally content, Simenon says, "to leave matters in the hands of the police until they have completed their inquiries. Not so Coméliau. He always insisted on directing operations from the onset, owing, no doubt, to his exaggerated dread of 'complications.' "

Coméliau is exceptionally afraid of newspaper criticism. To forestall the impatience of the press, he tends to jail the first available suspect.

He is also the brother-in-law of an ambitious politician, and is fond of saying, "You must understand, owing to his position I am much more vulnerable than my fellow magistrates."

In *Maigret and the Headless Corpse,* one of the finest of the Maigret stories, both Coméliau and Maigret give typical performances.

———

As this adventure begins, a man's arm, severed from the shoulder, is found in the canal Saint Martin beside the Quai de Valmy in Paris.

Maigret arrives and soon requires a telephone. He enters a murky little bistro and buys a glass of wine and a *jeton* for the telephone. He notices that the thin, sullen-eyed woman who serves him is exceptionally listless, and wonders if she is anticipating a dread disease.

A professional diver searches the canal bed and finds other parts of a man's body. Meanwhile, Maigret is in and out of the bistro and has become more and more puzzled by the woman's disinterest in things about her.

The woman is Madame Calas. She has spent twenty-four years in the bistro, which is owned by her husband, Omer, who, she says, has gone to the country to buy wine. Maigret soon recognizes that she is an alcoholic who nips from a bottle in the kitchen.

The police find evidence of red sealing wax under the finger-nails of the dismembered arm. Since it is the kind of red wax that is used for sealing wine bottles, it seems possible that the dead man worked in a bistro.

Maigret questions Madame Calas. He is puzzled by her com-posure and her willingness to acknowledge that in the afternoons, when her husband is out playing billiards, she gives herself to other men, to anyone who wants her.

Judge Coméliau is appointed to handle the case. Maigret reports to him and, in the process, tells him about Madame Calas. The judge, who has been described as "very much a man of the Establishment, guided by inflexible principles and hallowed taboos," immediately decides that she is a sexually promiscuous, drink-sodden degenerate.

Maigret cannot agree. He has sensed something extraordi-nary about Madame Calas. Because he cannot identify it, the woman has become a problem to him.

He interviews her daughter, born when she was sixteen, and learns that Omer Calas beats his wife almost daily. He also learns that there is one man of whom Madame Calas is fond. He is a red-headed, mild-mannered and pockmarked person named Pape who works in a warehouse near the bistro. He and Madame Calas have known each other for years and years. When they sit beside the stove in the bistro, they look like an old married couple.

A suitcase belonging to Omer Calas is found in a Paris rail-road station. The fact that it contains dirty clothes indicates that Calas had left the country and was returning to Paris. The police also learn that the suitcase was deposited by a young man who is one of Madame Calas's lovers.

Maigret tells Madame Calas that she will have to come to

headquarters to be questioned by Judge Coméliau. She goes up-
stairs to change her clothes. When she returns she is becomingly
dressed, and there is a hint of self-respect in her bearing. Her
appearance is so much improved that a detective working with
Maigret breaks out in applause.

As she leaves the bistro, she asks Maigret to take care of her
cat. He agrees.

The police then examine everything in the building. They find
that, although no effort has been made to clean up the living
quarters, the kitchen of the bistro has been recently and exten-
sively scrubbed.

Sherlock Holmes is interested in "Who"; Maigret is interested in "Why." He feels certain that a crime has been committed
on the premises, but cannot understand what lies behind it. He
understands the relationship between Madame Calas and her red-
headed lover. He understands the role of the casual lovers. "What
he did not understand at all," Simenon writes, "was the relationship between Calas and his wife. How and why had those two ever
come together, subsequently married, and lived with one another
for so many years?"

As he leaves the bistro he deposits her cat with a neighbor.

While Judge Coméliau is examining Madame Calas and her
red-headed friend, Maigret investigates her background. Knowing
that she was born in Saint-André, he gets in touch with a lawyer
there and begins to learn her story.

Madame Calas's great-grandfather, Christophe Dupré, was a
peasant who, after making a fortune, purchased the Château de
Boissancourt. Her grandfather took the name of Dupré de Boissancourt and then dropped the Dupré. She is Aline de Boissancourt.

When she was young, some unknown incident caused her to
turn against her father.

"Aline had only one idea in her head," the lawyer tells Maigret, "to defy and wound her father."

As a young girl Aline was not permitted to go to school or
play with other children. Her father insisted that she remain at
home under the care of a governess.

"Was it that she blamed her father for the fact that her life was so different from other children's?" the lawyer asks Maigret. "Or was there . . . much more to it than that? I don't know. It's often said that girls worship their fathers, sometimes to an unnatural degree. . . . Be that as it may, she seemed prepared to go to any length to drive Boissancourt to distraction, and at the age of twelve she was caught setting fire to the château. She was always setting fire to things at that time."

At sixteen, she became pregnant by Omer Calas. They ran away to Paris. Her father made no attempt to find her, and she never communicated with him.

Years later, about a month before the dismembered arm was discovered in the canal, her father died of a heart attack. Since he left no will, Aline inherited everything.

Her father's lawyer traced her to the bistro, where he found her sitting beside the stove with her cat on her lap. She informed him that she desired to refuse the inheritance. As the lawyer left, he suggested that she might change her mind, and he handed her his card. She put it in her apron pocket.

Later, Omer Calas discovered the card, went to Saint-André to quiz the lawyer, and so learned of his wife's refusal.

This information is passed on to Maigret during an evening when he and the lawyer dine together in Paris and afterward tour the bars.

Maigret is extremely affected by Aline's situation.

He recognizes that "everything she had done, even as a kid at the Château de Boissancourt, had been a kind of protest . . . the fire setting, her sexual relations with Calas, and finally her flight with him in circumstances in which most other girls would have procured an abortion. This too, perhaps, had been an act of defiance? Or revulsion?"

By the time the evening on the town with the lawyer is over, Maigret is quite drunk. Back in his apartment, he babbles in a maudlin way to his wife about Aline Calas.

"You talked almost like a man in love," his wife tells him the next morning. "If I were a jealous woman. . . ."

Maigret depicts for his wife what must have happened at the

bistro: Omer returns and demands that his wife accept her inheritance. When she refuses, he knocks her about. At that moment—Omer in a rage, Aline laying on the floor—mild-mannered Pape arrives. He, either accidentally or deliberately, kills Omer by hitting him over the head with a heavy instrument. Afterward, he cuts up the corpse and throws the pieces in the canal.

Maigret imagines Judge Coméliau's acid voice saying to him, "What can you call that but cold-blooded? You can't imagine, surely, that it was a *crime passionnel?*"

Meanwhile, at Police Headquarters, Aline and Pape confess to Coméliau. At the end of the session, Aline asks Coméliau if Maigret has seen to her cat. Coméliau loftily replies that Maigret has better things to do, and the story ends:

"Maigret could never forgive Judge Coméliau for that."

Jules Maigret is as he is because of Simenon's notable pessimism. He believes that the human situation is extremely weak, that man exists in a poorly organized place where most of the inhabitants are out of position and where the most trivial events, in combination, can transform an upright citizen into a criminal.

"My first Maigrets were imbued with the sense, which has always been with me, of man's irresponsibility," Simenon wrote in *When I Was Old,* his first book of nonfiction. "That is never stated openly in my writings. But Maigret's attitude toward the criminal makes it quite clear."

Jules Maigret was born not far from Moulins in central France. He was the son of what are called "enlightened" peasant stock. His father was the steward of a 7,500-acre estate and was responsible for twenty-six farms.

Maigret's father had a friend, an alcoholic doctor named Gadelle, who lived in a neighboring village. He "drank so much that, in a warm room," Maigret remembered, "the atmosphere would be pervaded by a smell of alcohol which I always sniffed with disgust."

When the time came to deliver his own wife's first child, Dr. Gadelle became drunk during the prolonged stages of his wife's labor. She and their baby died.

Some people would not permit Dr. Gadelle to treat their families, but Maigret's father stretched out a helping hand. When Maigret's mother became pregnant for the last time, Mr. Maigret took her to specialists in nearby cities, but allowed Dr. Gadelle to make the delivery.

She died at "seven in the morning," Maigret remembered, ". . . and when I came downstairs the first thing I saw was the decanter on the dining room table. . . ." The doctor never appeared in the house again, but Maigret never heard his father speak against him.

Her death "seemed to me so stupid a drama, so unnecessary," Maigret wrote in his *Memoirs*. "And all the other dramas that I knew, all these failures plunged me into a sort of furious despair. . . . I felt dimly that too many people were not in their right places, that they were striving to play parts that were beyond their capacities, so that the game was lost for them before they started."

Conan Doyle created Holmes at a time when science was undermining Christian beliefs, such as the Creation and Divine Providence, and was offering as consolation the doctrine of inevitable progress.

Man, helped by science, would eventually solve all his problems.

This Simenon rejected. As he said in an interview in the *Paris Review*, "For a long time man was . . . observed from the point of view that there was a God and that man was the king of creation. We don't think any more that man is still the king of creation. We see man almost face to face. Some readers still would like to read very reassuring novels, novels which give them a comforting view of humanity. It can't be done."

Simenon's pessimism is exceptionally deep. In *When I Was Old* he wrote, "I love man. His history, above all his first stammerings move me much more than all his dramas about passion. I love to see him in search of himself, century after century, failing each time, forcing himself to go on."

But this is only a mild statement of his position. In a much more formidable estimate of man, taken from the same book, Simenon begins by observing, "Certain methods of agriculture have killed the soil for hundreds of years. By destroying certain insects with DDT we have diminished fertility." He continues:

"How curious is man's fate! He is determined to know, discovers fragments of truth, draws conclusions, acts on them only to see afterwards that he has transgressed some still unknown rule and unintentionally unleashed catastrophes.

"He struggles to readjust his knowledge, makes new discoveries which, in turn, on application prove to be just as dangerous.

"What admirable and moving perseverance!"

Compassion—sympathy for the victim within the microcosm of an individual case, such as Louise Laboine; and sympathy for the victim within the macrocosm of the world, man as species— are the qualities shared by Simenon and Maigret.

Of the weapons invented by man, Simenon is most impressed by psychiatry.

"Psychiatrists aspire to facts," Karl Menninger has written; "they spend their lives trying to more accurately describe and understand misbehavior of all kinds."

It is the *human* factor rather than the criminal that Maigret searches for. His investigations suggest the psychiatrist searching for the childhood secrets of a kleptomaniac.

Simenon's interest in psychiatry is an additional reason for Maigret's being the way he is. Simenon's belief that man is now in a position to see himself almost face to face has been noted. In *Maigret and the Headless Corpse*, psychiatry is referred to as the vocation "whose function is to bring man face to face with his true self." As such psychiatry offers an entry into a larger reality, and it is reality that Maigret seeks.

Like Conan Doyle, Simenon is in step with what Ellenberger called the "unmasking trend," the systematic search for deception and self-deception and the uncovering of the underlying truth. Maigret is Simenon's instrument for bringing the reader a little closer to viewing himself, and the rest of mankind, face to face.

In *Maigret and the Old Lady*, the Inspector is required to investigate a crime in Le Visinet, a pretty, picture-postcard sort of town that he had known years previously.

Once, soon after Maigret joined the police, towns such as Le Visinet had seemed to him the most beautiful places in the world. "The rich still had their country houses. . . . The valets used to wear striped yellow waistcoats. . . . It seemed that only happy and virtuous families . . .

"Now, sure enough, he knew. In a way he spent his life seeing behind the scenes, but he still had a child's regret for the world 'in the picture.' "

In this story Maigret has to question a simplistic-minded member of the Chamber of Deputies about his relations with his beautiful stepmother, Valentine, who has been murdered. "When you were young," Maigret asks, "were you ever in love with Valentine? She was barely ten years older than you."

The deputy is offended. "Never in my life," he replies.

Maigret then asks about his attitude toward Valentine's daughter, Arlette. "And afterwards," he says, "you weren't in love with Arlette?"

The deputy, indignant now, replies, "I've always looked on her as a sister."

To himself Maigret comments, "This man was still seeing the world and the human race as in a picture."

Maigret was created in 1930 when Simenon was living aboard a redesigned fishing cutter, the thirty-seven-foot yacht *Ostrogoth,* anchored off Delfzijl in the Ems estuary of the North Sea.* Simenon, then twenty-seven, had been a professional writer for seven years and had published, under sixteen pseudonyms, some two hundred pulp novels. These he produced at the rate of eighty pages a day.

Simenon's goal at the time was to leave the pulp world and move on to what he thought of as "semi-literature." His immediate requirement was a central character for a criminal series, and he wanted that character to be sympathetic.

*A statue of Maigret now stands in Delfzijl. At the unveiling ceremony, the actors who played Maigret on the English, Italian, German, and Dutch television networks were present. So was Simenon, who was photographed while applying a handkerchief to one eye.

"Hitherto, in France, the sympathetic character has always been the offender, while the police have been exposed to ridicule, if not worse," he explained in *Maigret's Memoirs.* *

Simenon had also decided that in his criminal series he would take very little interest in professional criminals. In his *Memoirs,* Maigret recalls that at their first meeting Simenon explained, "You see, Chief-Inspector, I'm not interested in professionals. Their psychology offers no problems. They are just men doing their own job, and that's all."

Maigret then asked Simenon what he was interested in and Simenon replied, "The others. Those who are made like you and me, and who end up one fine day by killing somebody without being prepared to do so."†

The first Maigret book was *Maigret and the Enigmatic Lett,* known in French as *Piètre-la-Letton.* It was published in 1931. For the first year, Simenon wrote one Maigret a month. Each was revised in one day. "I daren't look at them," he said in 1960.

They were also written on wine. "While writing the first Maigrets, I got the habit of working on wine," Simenon wrote in *When I Was Old.* "From six in the morning . . . there was a barrel in the fork of a tree next to the boat . . . [and] the habit was formed."

After producing some twenty Maigrets, all of which were short books, averaging around 135 pages, Simenon attempted to evade his sleuth by writing 150 short novels without what he called "the prop of police detection." Thirty-nine of these were

---

*A character who is a lecturer observes, in Roy Fuller's novel *Second Curtain,* that "the novelist's rebellion in the industrial age was first expressed by making the hero the criminal . . . like Cabel Williams. . . . And then, as industrial society shows its great strength, the criminal becomes too dangerous a figure for the novelist to sympathize with. He gets changed into the private detective. The private detective is on society's side but he still retains sufficient freedom of action to be posed not only against the anti-social elements the police cannot reach, but against the police themselves."

†Professional criminals, who have possibly inherited their abilities and trade, make large profits out of crime, and are seldom caught. When they are, they accept prison as an occupational hazard. The idea that crime does not pay has been disputed since 1877 when Richard Dugdale, an American student of prisons, decided that "we must dispossess ourselves of the idea that crime does not pay. In reality it does." In 1949 Harry Barnes and N. K. Teeters wrote, "It is primarily the moralist who still believes that crime does not pay." The best contemporary treatment of the subject is Thomas Plate's *Crime Pays.*

made into movies. Nevertheless, like a dog that refuses to get lost, Maigret kept imposing himself on Simenon.

"Finally he and I reached a sort of compromise," Simenon explained, about 1950. "He would allow me to write, each year, three or four novels in a different vein, but each year also I would devote one or two of my books to him.

"This has gone on for years. We are both quite content with the arrangement. It has become a joy and a relaxation for me to meet up again periodically with my good old inspector. . . ."

In 1963, when he was interviewed by Ian Fleming for *The Sunday Times,* Simenon said Maigret was of no particular age, that he had been about forty-five when invented, and that he was still no more than fifty-three.

Since then, the great French problem solver's position has changed. The laws of France require that its police retire at fifty-five. This applies even to Chief Supervisors of the *police judiciaire*. Today Maigret lives in retirement in Meung-sur-Loire, some twenty-five miles west of Orléans. Around him, at his little house that looks like a presbytery, he has his strawberry plants, his espaliered apples, his chickens in the manure pile, and his fishing pole. Such, at least, is his position in the world of fiction. In real life he exists in 102 volumes and should be around for some time to come.

IV

IN 1903 CONAN DOYLE inserted himself into a real-life criminal problem and emerged with honor. In 1934, four years after he had created Maigret, Georges Simenon did likewise, and came away with a reward that was timely, handsome, and unanticipated.

The swindler Serge Alexandre Stavisky purchased protection by bribing officials and informing for the Sûreté. In 1926, after swindling a broker out of over 7 million francs, Stavisky was charged with fraud. He procured four lawyers, each of whom was a member of the Chamber of Deputies, one being its vice president. The case was postponed nineteen times and was still pending at the time of Stavisky's death.

Meanwhile Stavisky had organized and was operating a much more formidable swindling scheme. Disaster arrived, disguised as an unexpected audit. On January 9, 1934, as the police were pounding on his door, Stavisky either committed suicide or was murdered. Then began one of the more enormous scandals of a great nation.

It was learned that although a warrant for his arrest had been issued on December 23, 1933, the prefecture had, on the same day, given Stavisky a passport under a false name. It was also learned that by January 1, 1934, detectives from the Sûreté Generale knew his exact whereabouts but made no move against him. Someone had obviously protected Stavisky, and because it was in their interest to do so.

The political Right soon charged that Stavisky was murdered by the police, to prevent disclosures harmful to the government.* Both the political Right and the Communists organized huge demonstrations and on January 27 the French government fell. When the new Prime Minister unwisely fired the popular *préfet de police,* riots began, the second government fell, and there was talk of revolution.

On February 21, 1934, the corpse of Albert Prince, a judge in the Paris court of appeals, was found beside some railroad tracks near Dijon. He had been doped and tied across the rails. It was then learned that, until three years before, Prince had been

---

*In *France in Ferment,* Alexander Werth stated his conviction that Stavisky committed suicide "by persuasion." "Suicide by persuasion is not a new thing," he wrote. "The classic instance is that of Jean Galmot, 'the uncrowned King of Guyna,' gold prospector and rum magnate . . . . He was locked up for months in the foulest of all the foul cells in the Santé prison. All of his belongings were taken away from him *with the exception of a razor.* Not a safety razor, but a real open razor. And every hour the warder would peep hopefully through the door. Galmot's only diversion consisted of sitting down and gazing meditatively at the razor each time he heard the warder's approaching footsteps."

In *Paris Was Yesterday,* Janet Flanner wrote, "Galmot . . . is now supposed to have been murdered . . . in 1928 on the orders of his pal Stavisky, whom . . . he had sold out to the police in 1926."

the head of the financial section of the Paris Parquet which, technically, was responsible for the nineteen adjournments of the fraud charge against Stavisky.

The excitement was intense. It was charged that Prince's missing briefcase contained documents about Stavisky and that the Sûreté was dragging its feet. Inspector Bony, the Sûreté detective who was directing the Stavisky investigation, claimed that he was being hindered by agents of the prefecture. Soon afterward, the inspector came up with an important item, the stubs of some checks written by Stavisky.

On March 20, 1934, the newspaper *Paris-Soir* announced the formation of a team to investigate the deaths of Stavisky and Prince. It consisted of three famous English detectives: Sir Basil Thompson, retired head of Scotland Yard, and two French mystery writers, A. G. Leroux and Georges Simenon.

In the investigation that followed, the burden was carried by Simenon.

———

As his series began on March 20, 1934, Simenon complained to the reader:

"Do you think it is funny for me to have created a personage such as Maigret? It is really the worst lack of prudence, for this personage, to whom I've given life without thinking too much about it, has grown, gotten bigger, and is going at such a pace that he is about to become more important than I am.

"The best proof of this is that this very Saturday, at 11:00 in the morning, the publisher of *Paris-Soir,* who was seated opposite me in his office on rue Royale, cynically stated to me,

" 'Actually, it is not Simenon whom I called, but rather Maigret.' "

Simenon then moved on to Stavisky, asking:

"Who were the people with whom he associated? They were men who were notoriously corrupt. Always surrounded by rough guys. Just like Al Capone. We used to see him everywhere, even in official circles, always protected by a bodyguard of rough guys.

"If I mention the name of Al Capone it is for good reason.

The methods of the two men are strangely similar.

"Crook, no: gangster, yes."

In his second article Simenon announced, "For the last two days I have plunged into the world of certain bars, certain clubs, certain resturants which are scattered from l'Étoile to the Place des Ternes, from Notre Dame de Lorette to the Madeleine, and also around Place Clichy and Boulevard Montmartre."

This is the place to begin, he feels certain. The people who were close to Stavisky "belonged to that comparatively closed world." The more he hears, the more certain he becomes that both the Stavisky and Prince murders "are gangster connected and there is a definite correlation between the two incidents."

Gradually Simenon begins to hear rumors about three men: Romagnino, who was Stavisky's number-one man; Jo-the-Terror, another member of Stavisky's gang; and a third criminal, Angelo, who now lives in London.

Someone informs Simenon that Jo-the-Terror has gone to London eight times since January 1. It is believed that Jo-the-Terror has entrusted Angelo with the Stavisky jewels.

Simenon then learns that Romagnino, Jo-the-Terror's boss, has also visited Angelo in London. It is believed that Romagnino has had every Stavisky document, including letters and check stubs, photographed and deposited with Angelo.

On March 14 *Paris-Soir* had broken the story that the check stubs Inspector Bony had come up with had been passed to him by Jo-the-Terror in a darkened London theater. Now, in the bars, Simenon hears that not all the check stubs were turned over to Bony.

"We saw Jo in a little bar on the Avenue des Ternes," Simenon writes. "Soon we realized that he had not delivered all the documents in his possession and that he continued to meet with certain persons known to have been compromised in the Stavisky affair."

Simenon wonders if "there will be enough in circulation to make life miserable for their benefactors?"

He then asks, "And did not certain personages receive during the last few days the visit of a man who, gun in hand, demanded a sum more or less important in exchange for a stub or for a photograph? Once more, one name has run from mouth to mouth."

The name, obviously, is Jo-the-Terror, but Simenon does not specifically say so. He merely adds that Jo had the reputation of being "constantly escorted by Smith and Wesson."

———

Simenon's next article was an interview with Jo-the-Terror, also known as Jo-the-Grey-Hair.

Jo is a sometime boxer and artist whose real name is Georges Hainaut. He lives in Room 53 of the Hôtel de Chartres 8, rue du Dôme, Paris, an address from which he was absent on February 20 and 21, the period when Prince was done in.

The interview itself takes place in Jo's room, which contains a brass bed and a wardrobe closet. Many books are piled about.

"Jo is a man in his forties, vigorous, carefree, very much at ease in a robe which opened on silk pajamas," Simenon writes. "His white hair is quite a contrast to his energetic manner and his youthful face. During the entire interview his hand was in the right pocket of his robe and there was in evidence a revolver of strong calibre."

When the subject of check stubs comes up, Jo replies, "Checks? What do you expect me to do with them? I have a scheme which brings me one hundred francs a day. A wise man is happy enough with that."

He is then asked about his relations with Romagnino.

"Oh, we've been friends for twenty years. As for Stavisky, I've never seen him. . . . If I had the checks I would have been picked up a long time ago."

Jo then denies that he knows Inspector Bony and begins to defend himself with great conviction.

"It's a shame to attack a man like me who has never done a thing wrong in his life. We are in the twentieth century and there is nothing wrong in going to the races and gambling. Women don't interest me."

On a table there is a stack of books on top of which lies a

revolver. Jo points and says, "There is only one thing that interests me, books."

He is asked if he is interested in politics. He replies, "Everyone knows I am of the extreme Left. I am a child of the streets and I don't deny my origins. I have made a few errors in my life. I have spent three or six months in jail, which does not prevent me from having my voting rights."

With great pride, he shows his voting card. At the same time, he catches sight of a photograph which shows him in the company of Mistinguett, a famous music-hall star. He then comes out with the first of two alibis.

"Leave me alone with your story of checks," he tells Simenon. "The best proof that I have nothing to do with those checks is this photo that you see was taken the day before yesterday in a *bôite* in Montmartre.

"That photo is worth money. And I will ask her to write underneath, 'To Jo for Life,' and it will be worth more."

When Jo is informed that a lawyer friend of his has been arrested, he seems taken aback, and says sadly, "Ah, my poor friend, I am used to those things. People are so mean. Almost every month there are anonymous letters written against me, and the police come over to interrogate me. But there is nothing that one can reproach me with. In fact, what do you mean by individual liberty?"

Jo then makes the statement that Simenon will use more than once in the remainder of his articles.

"If I should be arrested you can't imagine the fuss that would ensue. I swear to you that an hour after my arrest, the government would fall."

Simenon now asks Jo, "Do you realize that everyone is talking about you concerning the affair Prince?"

Jo comes up with his second alibi.

"It doesn't bother me, but you are right on the button. I have a mania for persecution. Because of that, I never take a walk without my firecracker.

"Because of this mania I have been in the habit, hour by hour, of noting down in a special notebook all my comings and goings. And this is not a joke. The notebook exists."

He flashes it, then continues, "You want the proof that I have nothing to reproach myself for, I'll give you the proof, and here is the proof. Within recent days I have neither broken any windows nor created a fuss on the street."

Simenon is puzzled.

Jo continues, "I have already been sent to an insane asylum twice. Suppose that I should be afraid of something. All I have to do is get into a crisis and get picked up to be put in the asylum again. You see, I am not a candidate for jail, but for the asylum."

He smiles broadly, then adds, "You understand that I have nothing to fear."

————

On the morning after the Jo-the-Terror interview appears in *Paris-Soir,* police inspectors station themselves outside Jo's hotel.

Meanwhile, Simenon has previously stated, "Jo has been meeting regularly with a man who lives at the Hôtel de l'Étoile." This man is also mixed up in the Stavisky case and has given Jo money.

Simenon has also begun to use the phrase, "The gangsters of the Étoile."

Now, outside Jo's hotel, the police are waiting but do not as yet possess a warrant for Jo's arrest.

Simenon writes, "While the police are waiting for the warrant, a man leaves the Hôtel de l'Étoile at seven o'clock in the morning. He is a tall man. He wears a long beige overcoat and a broad-brimmed soft hat."

At ten thirty one of the inspectors outside Jo's hotel gets nervous and telephones headquarters and receives word that Jo is not to be arrested.

By this time Simenon has joined the inspectors outside Jo's hotel. There he remains, stationing himself prudently.

Later he writes, "At eleven thirty a blue car stopped at a corner of the street. A tall man emerges wearing a broad-brimmed soft hat and a long beige overcoat. He goes to the Hôtel de Chartres and Jo is in his room. Apparently the conversation was brief. Soon Jo comes out carrying a little yellow suitcase in his hand and he walks to the corner of the street. The man who arrived in the blue car leaves almost immediately behind Jo, runs to his car, and drives off. We know that that's it. Jo has fled. It's only at five o'clock that the judge sends a warrant for his arrest, and by then the police have lost his trace."

The next day Jo gives himself up at police headquarters. As Janet Flanner wrote in her Paris letter in *The New Yorker*, Jo "surrendered to the embarrassed police, who didn't want him, since they knew where he was and that he knows too much." She called Simenon's articles "magnificent for writing, sense, and bravery."

Simenon himself now raises the question, "On the facts so far uncovered can we establish a case?"

The truth is, he cannot. He can only do some hinting.

"One of the questions which has arisen," he writes, "is, Why did the gangsters kill Prince?"

One hypothesis that has been suggested, he reports, is that the killer or killers wanted to obtain two letters which reveal the weakness of a high-placed magistrate. It has also been suggested, Simenon adds, that a dealer in jewels could have given Prince the receipts for the Stavisky jewels.

Simenon's personal opinion is that "there must be an intermediary world between Prince and the underground which ordered his execution. We must first establish the fact that Stavisky, as far back as we might go into his life, has always made sure to be in touch with and to obtain the good will of people involved in rendering justice as well as with the police."

He continues, "With Stavisky dead, we find ourselves in the presence of a man, Romagnino, who was the lieutenant of his boss, and who inherited the loot. What was the loot? We know it today.

"1. Jewels or receipts of deposit of jewels with a value of around 10 million francs.

"2. Checks and stubs of checks of which only a small part was enough to create a tremendous upheaval in the political life of France.

"Just imagine what would have happened if, at the beginning

of January, Stavisky had been able to go to a foreign country with all those documents. And imagine Romagnino returning to Paris with that terrible weapon, the check stubs."

On March 30, 1934, Simenon breaks his most important story. The headlines of *Paris-Soir* scream:

THE GANGSTERS DE L'ETOILE ARE ARRESTED

In the account that follows, Simenon reviews his involvement in the Stavisky case.

I'm going to try the method of Commissioner Maigret, I said to myself.

It is not a method of deduction, nor a method of showmanship. It is a simple method, more human.

Stavisky being a gangster, I have said to myself, I must look for those who after his death took charge of the jewels, the checks, and because of those circumstances, assassinated Prince.

Stavisky used to meet his lieutenants in . . . the restaurant "Cotty," 12 avenue de Wagram.

When I had lunch for the first time at that resturant, there was a man in front of me, at the first table to the left, a man who surely attracted my attention: his skin was rather brownish, he looked energetic, and he walked like a feline; in his eyes, in his attitude, there was a feeling that he was in complete command.

This is the man whom Simenon calls the Baron.

It didn't take me fifteen minutes to know the pedigree of the Baron, one of the most famous or infamous personages of l'Étoile: bookmaker, drug dealer, procurer, and under the suspicion of having set fire, three years ago, to the casino in Menton.

At the same time I learned in that same restaurant that Jo-the-Grey-Haired used to take his meals there in company with Romagnino . . . and other friends of Stavisky.

The very same evening, as I was returning to my apartment in the Carlton, I was quite surprised to find the Baron in the hall, awaiting a telephone communication with Menton. And of all things, the Baron lived exactly in the room above mine.

And perchance I overheard the telephone pertaining to a question of jewels.*

From there on all I had to do was to follow the track hour by hour without hope, of course, of immediate success. My Commissioner [Maigret], as you know, installs himself in a certain place, appears awkward, calm, smelling the atmosphere, keeping his ear tuned to every sound, making a mental note of the smallest detail.

I composed myself like him, and little by little, there came other personages around Jo-the-Grey-Hair, around the Baron, which pretty soon created a solid block.†

Simenon's account ends with his report of a most interesting development. The French government has requested *Paris-Soir*, he reveals, to cease its investigation immediately.

Simenon writes that "at this time we are not permitted to continue our search, for the Department of Justice is facing a situation which it has to elucidate. We cannot allow ourselves to

---

*Maigret frequently uses phone taps, but does so as a cop. It seems probable that Simenon, throughout his investigation, had the cooperation of the police; either the police of the prefecture or the police of the Sûreté Générale, but most probably the former.

In *Secrets of the Sûreté,* retired Sûreté executive Jean Belin wrote, "The rivalry that existed between our two principal police organizations was such that time and again their men handled the same case in direct competition, and frequently they would try to discredit each other."

The existence of this rivalry is referred to in several of the Maigret books. One reason for it is that, at least up to 1934, the detectives from the prefecture were paid twice as much as the detectives from the Sûreté générale.

In *France in Ferment* Werth comments that "since the Prince murder it has been a standing joke that the detectives of the Préfeture and those of the Sûreté Générale deliberately sabotage each other's work by denouncing the other's informers, and playing all sorts of tricks on each other. Inspector Bony, of the Sûreté Générale, attributed his failure to discover Prince's murderers to the sabotage of the Préfeture, who, he claimed, had done him endless damage by providing amateur detectives, who wrote all those thrillers in the press [obviously Simenon] with a list of his informers and by committing dozens of other indiscretions."

Regardless of the complications of the situation, Simenon did, somewhere along the line, strike a nerve. He also exposed himself to danger, was several times threatened, was physically attacked at least once during the investigation, and may have suffered later.

It was not until the author wrote to Simenon and inquired about his relations with the police during the investigation that Simenon learned that this book would include an account of his Stavisky reportage. Simenon then replied, "I have no desire to rouse this affair which brought me so much trouble at the time and which I have for the greatest part forgotten. I apologize for not helping you further."[4]

†In *France in Ferment* Werth wrote that the Baron was only charged with the theft of a ring, and that this charge was dropped and the Baron was released after one month.

risk a maneuver which might hamper the Department of Justice.

"So until further developments, *Paris-Soir* will await the results of the official investigation."

Then came another interesting development. The management of *Paris-Soir* handed Simenon a complete set of tickets and whisked him away on a slow trip around the world.

V

ON HIS SEVENTIETH BIRTHDAY, February 13, 1973, Georges Simenon announced his retirement as a novelist. The creation of characters, he explained, had become too exhausting.

He had written and published some 200 pulp novels, 116 straight novels, and 102 Maigrets. These had been translated into 47 languages and distributed in more than 300 million copies.

Since then he has, almost daily, tape-recorded from ten minutes to an hour. By October, 1975 he had dictated six slim volumes of nonfiction.

Georges Simenon is a vital, candid man who stands five feet eight inches tall and weighs about one hundred and fifty pounds. Like Maigret, his trademark is his pipe. In photographs it is almost always with him, either cupped in his hand or clenched between his teeth.

Simenon is Belgian by birth and comes from Liège. His father was employed by an insurance company, and because he did not get many raises, his wife accused him of being lazy. When he collapsed at his office desk and died, his family learned that his health had been bad for years, so bad that his employer had refused to issue him an insurance policy.

In *Simenon in Court,* John Raymond wrote of this tragedy, "In Simenon it aroused a hatred of all summary moral judgements passed on human beings that has remained a permanent feature of his attitude to human character ever since."

———

Alcohol—Scotch, gin, bourbon, beer, champagne—is a constant companion of problem solvers in criminal fiction.

Holmes is the only exception, and he knew cocaine.

Maigret seems especially fond of calvados, but in fact he drinks to a point where there is a basis for wondering how he can function properly with all that booze inside him. Yet, even with Maigret, we only know that he drinks and sometimes becomes intoxicated. As for Simenon himself the situation is different, for he has written candidly about himself and alcohol.

In 1960, when Simenon was fifty-seven years old, world famous, cheerfully married, the father of three children, and about to buy a new Rolls Royce, he began to feel old, and to doubt himself.

One result was that he started to keep a series of notebooks in which he recorded his activities, memories, and thoughts. In 1971 these notebooks, reduced to one volume, were published in America under the title *When I Was Old.*

In it Simenon is exceptionally frank, not wanting to present himself as a man on a "picture postcard," a person like the deputy in *Maigret and the Old Lady.*

He does not want his children to have an exalted father image of him. "I would like them to know the vulnerable man that I am," he writes; "as vulnerable as they and perhaps even more so." He is disturbed about "the legend," the series of myths that have been created about him over the years in newspapers and magazines. He wonders if his children and grandchildren would find themselves tempted to believe this legend too.

Simenon was raised in a home where the phrase "he drinks" was uttered in consternation. On his mother's side his grandfather had been ruined by drink; one uncle was a bum; and an aunt was such an alcoholic that she had to be committed. Of his father he wrote—"Drink spoiled my father's life too."

When his father died he had to quit school and find a job.

His mother wanted him to be a baker, but he had better ideas. For several years he had been intrigued by the pencils, erasers, and paper that he saw in the windows of stationery stores.

"A special kind of yellow paper, too hard to be used in school, seemed to me more elegant, more aristocratic, than anything I could find," he has written. The windows of candy stores and bakeries did not intrigue him.

He got a job in a bookstore but was fired for publicly correcting his employer on a point of literary history. Next, sixteen years old and wearing his first long pants, he went to the editor of the most important newspaper in Liège and asked for a job. He was given a trial and at the end of the first month was doing every sort of general reporting and also writing a special humor column.

Georges Simenon had taken his first drink when he was fourteen: wine out of the sideboard decanter. At the newspaper he sometimes joined the older reporters in cafés where he drank wine out of silver goblets, as was the custom in Belgium. And once a week, he got drunk with other young writers and artists, admirers of Villon, who had formed a club called the Keg.

But at sixteen he was more interested in women than in wine. In *When I Was Old* he not only wrote freely about himself and alcohol; he also provided an unusual amount of information about his sex life. This was in the French tradition.

"In French literature," Lionel Trilling wrote, "sincerity consists in telling the truth about oneself to oneself and to others; by truth is meant a recognition of such of one's traits or actions as are morally or socially discreditable and, in conventional course, concealed. English sincerity does not demand this confrontation of what is base or shameful in oneself."[5]

And so, of his life between sixteen and nineteen, Simenon wrote, "I had two women available to me each day, almost every day, at one moment or another, I would be like a dog in rut."

At nineteen he married Regina Renchon, a painter, completed his military service, and left Liège for Paris. There, working as a reporter, he drank only a small bottle of wine with his meals, and was hyperactive sexually.

"During my first days in Paris . . . I remember that I would leave the arms of one woman at eleven o'clock in the morning to go back to another one only a few minutes later, and be obliged to . . . begin all over twice the same afternoon."

Years later he observed, "The sexual need . . . I wonder if it is not part of a need that is more difficult to communicate, the need to penetrate humanity. . . . This finally is reduced to an act that appears ridiculous but which is none the less symbolic."

Although Simenon's candidness may make him seem eccentric to some, he is in fact a very shrewd man whose ability to plan ahead has been noticeable at several points in his life. As a young man in Paris, he wanted to be a serious writer but understood that he could not become one until he had first traveled, met many sorts of people, and learned a great deal about the world. He therefore bought every pulp magazine and novel available and started to write stories of all kinds for an extremely varied public.

By 1926 he had a small apartment on the second floor of a building on the Place des Vosges in Montparnasse, and his drinking had increased.

He spent much of his time making complicated cocktails and inviting his friends to sample them. But there was a reason behind his hospitality. He understood that men revealed more of themselves when they were having a good time, and so, officiating "with professional flourish," he "forced cocktails on my friends in order to produce more quickly the release that would permit me to see them naked."

Still interested in studying the behavior of his male guests, he sometimes arranged for the presence of naked women.

When this life paled, he bought a boat and sailed the rivers and canals of France. By 1930 he owned the *Ostrogoth*, aboard which he invented Maigret and got into the habit of writing on wine. Between then and 1945 he "was rarely drunk, but I needed . . . especially to write, a pick-me-up. I was persuaded in good faith that it was impossible to write otherwise. And, away from work, I drank anything."

After the Stavisky investigation, making his way around the

world, he searched for experience, including the sexual kind, in many countries. He spent hours roaming through the most disreputable districts of cities such as Cairo, Aswan, Panama City, and Guayaquil.

Returning to Paris, he moved into an apartment on the Boulevard Richard Wallace. The interiors were designed by a "decorator deluxe." By this time Georges Simenon was definitely living it up.

"I did not miss a chance to dress in tails and high hat. I was a member of the Yacht Club of France, the Escholiers, the Sporting Club. . . . I was even wearing a pearl in my necktie!"

During World War II he organized aid for refugees and served in the Resistance.

In 1945 he went to the United States. At the Brussels restaurant in New York he met his second wife—a Canadian, described by one reporter as "a tearing beauty." They began to drink American style, and enjoyed the great city tremendously.

"Alcoholism for two, accompanied by life, by passion, by exacerbrated sexuality, is not at all disagreeable, quite the contrary," he wrote in *When I Was Old*.

"All life is colored by it. New York, for example, seems made to be seen in this state, and then it is an extraordinary New York and, strange as it may seem, comradely.

"The crowds cease to be anonymous, the bars cease to be ordinary ill-lit places. . . . It is the same in all big American cities. . . . From one end of the country to the other there exists a freemasonry of alcoholics. . . . For two, I repeat, it's marvelous."

After three months or so of the wild life in America, "which I don't regret and which I often think of nostalgically," the pace began to catch up with him, and he "began to have painful awakenings, hangovers, attacks of gas pains."

He and his future wife moved to Canada and installed themselves beside a lake in a cabin with a huge fireplace. There, she proposed that he try to work on tea instead of liquor. He agreed to try, and she waited behind the door of his study and "cease-lessly" brought him hot tea.

"I left the door half open, stuck out my hand and grabbed the cup without a word. . . . She had reason to tremble, for if the experiment had failed . . . I would have been dead at this mo-ment."

Returning to the United States, they lived for a time in Arizona. "We continued to drink pretty seriously from time to time. Then we cut the liquor, allowing ourselves only beer. . . . One fine day in Arizona, we decided to put ourselves on the wagon."

From Arizona they went to California and spent the win-ter of 1949–1950 in Carmel. There he wrote, among other things, the novel *Maigret and the Old Lady* and the short story "Maigret's Christmas." Then they drove east and bought a five-acre farm in Lakesville, Connecticut. "Every two months, every three months, we got off the wagon for an eve-ning, or for two or three days."

In the meantime, many of the great names in modern litera-ture, Gide, Maugham, Hemingway, had praised his abilities as a writer. Gide was particularly fascinated by Simenon, corre-sponded with him for several years, and planned to write a book about him. "He makes one reflect," Gide said of Simenon, "and this is close to being the height of art."

In 1950, in California, Dashiell Hammett told a reporter from the Los Angeles *Times* that "the best mystery writer today is a Belgian who writes in French." When the reporter asked, "What makes him the best?" Hammett replied, "Well, he is more intelligent."

As Simenon grew older his drinking habits changed. He began to sip Coca-Cola. When he presided over the Cannes Film Festival in 1960, he succeeded in getting through a luncheon banquet and three or four cocktail parties each day "without touching a drop of alcoholic beverage."

———

In *French Crime in the Romantic Age* Rayner Heppenstall referred to crime as "something indissolubly there. . .an irreducible phenomenon. The forms it takes change with those of society, but no social reform yet ever diminished its incidence."*

Simenon, who has praised Heppenstall, would certainly agree with the above. In *When I Was Old* he observed, "I wonder if the essential character of crime isn't its illogic, which would explain why in the Middle Ages it was attributed to demons taking possession of a human being and why today the psychiatrist is more and more often called in. . . . Following a recent airplane crash, specialists in charge of the investigation . . . have been stressing that an airplane is a man-made machine, that airlines are managed by men, pilots are human beings, etc., concluding that for this reason a certain percentage of errors and failures is inevitable.

"Doesn't this apply to crime? And isn't a certain percentage of human beings almost inevitably destined to . . . etc.?"

Georges Simenon's interest in the criminal and his fate is exceptionally personal. "I am, by nature, a man who respects rules," he wrote in *When I Was Old.* "If I do not believe in them I pretend that they must be followed out of respect for others. And in forty years driving I have never had a single ticket, not even for parking my car illegally."

But he also knows there is another side to him. "In order not to feel a prisoner of society," he writes, "I need to pat a thigh, to make love without declaring it, without passion, to have sex on the spur of the moment as it is still done in the equatorial forests or in Tahiti."

He reveals that once when he was having an affair with a married woman, he took her "when her husband, busy in a neighboring room, was talking to us through the half open door."

For such needs and actions he excuses himself by saying, "I'm only a man."

---

*Crimes are what the law says is criminal, and the law is what legislators say it is. In *Politics* Aristotle wrote, "There are some crimes which are due to lack of necessities. . . . But want is not the only cause of crimes. Men also commit them simply for the pleasure it gives them, and just to get rid of an unsatisfied desire. . . . The greatest crimes are committed not for the sake of necessities, but for the sake of superfluities."

High-echelon commentators on law enforcement use phrases such as "socially tolerable limits," consider a certain measure of crime "unavoidable," and prefer "organized crime" to "anarchial violence."

From youth on Simenon has been exceptionally conscious of what he describes as "man's irresponsibility." In 1960, reading *Newsweek* magazine, he came across an article on Sir Sydney Smith, a professor at Edinburgh University and one of the pioneers of forensic medicine. One question asked of the professor was, "After a lifetime spent in the study of murder and murderers, does Sir Sydney have a theory about the kind of person who kills?" The physician replied, "In my recollection they have been devoid of the characteristics they are commonly credited with, and are quite ordinary individuals such as you and me."

Sir Sydney's reply delighted Simenon. In *When I Was Old* he underscores the last eight words of the physician's statement, then exclaims to himself—"For thirty years I have tried to make it understood that there are no criminals."*

Most of the Maigret books can be viewed as attempts to present the circumstances which lead to an individual's performing an action that society identifies as criminal.

In *Maigret and the Headless Corpse,* Aline Calas's redheaded lover had no intentions of killing Omer Calas. He simply walked in at the worst possible time, when Calas was beating his wife in an attempt to force her to accept her inheritance. In *Maigret and the Dead Girl,* the situation is not too different. Albert Falconi, bartender at Pickwick's, intended to steal from Louise, but he had no thought of killing her. He only planned to grab her handbag, but its chain was wrapped around her wrist.

A passage in *When I Was Old* shows Simenon's awareness of how easy it is for people to lose control of themselves.

"After luncheon, slight argument with my wife, Not even disagreement. Misunderstanding, for no reason. That was enough. A little afterwards, in town, vertigo, pain in my shoulder, etc. And if I let myself go it would have been total collapse. Everything takes on another color.

"The slightest touch is enough. The body follows."

---

*In the above statement, "there are no criminals," Simenon is excluding completely the person who approaches crime as a profession.

In the early Maigrets, Simenon's sympathy with his characters, and with man as a species, is present, but is not especially notable. It is this quality, as the series grows, that is so quietly impressive.

In *Maigret Loses His Temper* a lawyer is able to get high fees from his clients by lying to them that he has bribed Maigret. When Maigret learns of this, he is affronted. After an aggressive investigation he arrests the lawyer.

As the lawyer is about to be led away to a cell, he turns to Maigret and explains that he did what he did because his wife had become a bedridden invalid, and he, needing some way to amuse himself, "found gambling."

The explanation disturbs Maigret. He permits the lawyer to go to the cell without having his tie, belt, and shoelaces taken from him. That night in the cell the lawyer hangs himself.

Maigret, when he hears of this, is shaken.

—• SAM SPADE •—
Dashiell Hammett

Your Sam's a detective.
The Maltese Falcon

I

THE STATEMENT "Dashiell Hammett was a Pinkerton detective" becomes more meaningful when something is known about the Pinkertons.

———

Allan Pinkerton descends from Vidocq. The Frenchman's *Memoirs* were obtainable when Pinkerton was a young detective, and he studied them thoughtfully. Later, in a handbook for his employees, Pinkerton put down his own ideas.

"It has hitherto been held as a leading canon of detective practices that 'a thief only can catch a thief,' " he wrote, "and, to a very great extent, this has been acted upon, not only by the Police of America, but of all the world. Nearly the whole detective force of Paris are men who have themselves either been convicted of Crime, or who have committed it. . . . The same principle has also prevailed in the 'Stool Pigeon' system of England and America."[1]

It was a poor way, Pinkerton thought, to catch a thief. The informer profited more than the police. And it permitted the thieves to remain in control. They presented the detectives with "information in regard only to the smaller and less important

98

thieves, who would from time to time be arrested by the Detectives while the great criminals went free. . . ."

For Allan Pinkerton the fundamental problem was, Could an honest man catch a thief? He said yes. He was an honest man, and he had caught scores of thieves. "I am overwhelmed with business," he wrote a friend.

Secrecy, he believed, was the honest detective's most valuable weapon, "the chief strength which the detective possesses beyond the ordinary man."[2]

Secrecy was the word he used, but he could have called it deception. "It frequently becomes necessary for the Detective, when brought in contact with Criminals, to pretend to be a Criminal," he wrote in his handbook; "in other words, for the time being to assume the garb of crime . . . the detective has to act his part, and in order to do so, he has, at times, to depart from the strict line of truth, and to resort to deception, so as to carry his assumed character through."

Because the public associated the word detective with the idea of the palm extended to be "greased," he called his employees operatives. Few of them had law-enforcement backgrounds. They were "former clerks, ships' officers, farmers, merchants," James D. Horan reported in *The Pinkertons: The Detective Dynasty That Made History.* "Pinkerton taught them the art of 'shadowing,' disguise, and playing a role. From an early account the Chicago office at times resembled the backstage of a theatre, with Pinkerton . . . demonstrating to an operative ready to go out on assignment how to act like a 'greenhorn just off the boat,' a bartender, horsecar conductor, or gambler. Pinkerton kept a large closet in his private office filled with various disguises."

By the time his Pinkerton National Police Agency was five years old, Allan Pinkerton had refined Vidocq's methods to a point which can be described as "marking an important shift in the evolution of sleuthing and the imaginative temperament of the man hunter"—highfaluting talk which only means that on any list of historically important sleuths, his name has to be there or it is no list.

———

The Adams Express Company was the largest public carrier in America, operating in most of the East, all of the South, and in the frontier territories. In 1854, somewhere between Montgomery, Alabama, and Augusta, Georgia, $10,000 disappeared out of a locked Adams pouch.

E. S. Sanford, vice president of Adams, sent Pinkerton a letter outlining the problem and was advised that the money appeared to have been stolen by Nathan Maroney, manager of the Montgomery office. But Sanford did nothing, and a year later another Adams pouch, this one containing $40,000, vanished en route from the Montgomery office.

Maroney was now arrested. Since he and his wife were popular young members of Montgomery society, many of the city's leading citizens contributed to his bail fund.

At the hearing it became obvious that there was little evidence against Maroney, and Sanford asked Pinkerton to take charge of the case. Pinkerton agreed and went East to construct around the Maroneys what can be thought of as a "reality."

———

As Horan tells the story seven Pinkerton operatives played important roles in the deception of the Maroneys:

Costumed as an immigrant from Holland, the first operative shadowed Mrs. Maroney. When she put a letter in a hotel mailbox, he got a look at the envelope, then notified Pinkerton that it was addressed to a party in Jenkintown, near Philadelphia.

The second operative, a former watch repairer, went to Jenkintown and set up in his old profession. He soon advised Pinkerton that the Maroneys had relatives there.

The third operative, a woman, went to Jenkintown and posed as the wife of a wealthy forger. When Mrs. Maroney arrived she was cultivated by the "forger's wife."

The fourth operative copied down the address on a letter Maroney sent to New York. It turned out to be the address of a locksmith who was copying a key for Maroney. In New York Pinkerton operatives identified the key as the property of Adams Express. Because the case against Maroney was weak, and because Maroney was broke and could not put up bail, Allan Pinkerton decided to have him rearrested, this time on a conspiracy charge based on the key.

The fifth operative, an exceptionally handsome man, then arrived in Jenkintown. Pinkerton began to mail Maroney, now in jail in New York City, anonymous notes stating that Mrs. Maroney was seeing a handsome stranger.

The sixth Pinkerton operative, playing the role of a big-time forger, became Maroney's cellmate.

The seventh operative posed as the lawyer of the big-time forger and made frequent visits to Maroney's cell. During these visits he repeatedly sneered at the law and joked about how easily fixes were arranged. Such talk had its effect on Maroney, who was brooding about his wife, the handsome stranger, and the money. When the time was ripe, the lawyer swept into the cell with a release for the big-time forger. It was too much for Maroney. He begged for help. After the big-time forger had explained that considerable money would be required, Maroney sent his wife a note instructing her to turn the money over to the forger.

In Jenkintown Mrs. Maroney consulted her new friend, the forger's wife, asked if it was all right to give the money to a total stranger, and was assured that it was sensible. She then dug up the money pouch and gave it to the so-called forger. He passed it on to Pinkerton who found that out of the stolen $40,000, the Maroneys had spent only $400.

In September Maroney's trial began in Montgomery. Young bloods, anxious to be character witnesses, jammed the courtroom. On the second day the prosecution called its first witness. For Maroney it was a shocking moment. He looked on unbelievingly as the big-time forger walked toward the witness chair.

Maroney turned to his lawyer and said that he wanted to change his plea to guilty. He received ten years. His wife's sentence was suspended.

Complex cases, simple cases; all were attacked with the same weapon—deception.

———

Allan Pinkerton was a giant: Homo sapiens exaggerated. One report says that he arose before sunup and took a twelve-mile walk and a cold bath while his wife was preparing breakfast. The mileage may be suspect, but the taste of the man is there.

A Scotsman out of Glasgow, he was born in 1819, the son of a blacksmith. In his teens he joined the Chartists, who were demanding that things in Great Britain be more equal. They assigned him to a physical-force team, which meant that when it came to street fighting, he was to be out in front.

Just as the British were about to arrest him, he was warned and fled to America with his bride. They settled in the Scotch community of Dundee, northwest of Chicago, and he resumed his trade of barrel making.

One day in 1847, while cutting trees on an island in the Fox River, he found the remains of a cooking fire. The Indians had been driven away and picnics were still unknown; Pinkerton was suspicious. For several nights he returned and watched. Finally, seven men landed from a rowboat and built a fire. The next morning Pinkerton informed the sheriff. When the island was raided, the strangers turned out to be counterfeiters.

From then on, around Dundee, Pinkerton was called in whenever a problem involved detection. Once, posing as a barefoot yokel, he helped catch another counterfeiter. His reputation as a crime fighter spread, the sheriff of Cook County offered him a job as deputy, and the Pinkertons moved to Chicago.

There Pinkerton's effectiveness, including his ability with his fists, caused the mayor to appoint him Chicago's first police detective. After a year, disgusted by political interference, Pinkerton resigned, took a job as a post-office detective, and soon captured a mail thief whose successes had upset the business community.

One Chicago paper boasted, "As a detective . . . Mr. Pinkerton has no superior, and we doubt he has any equal in this country."

———

Exactly when he started his agency is unknown; the great Chicago fire of 1871 destroyed his records. Horan places the founding in the early 1850s.

In those days Americans loathed the thought of a standing army, and the idea of police—any sort of authority supported by guns—was just as bad. The 1820s and 1830s were quiet years. In the cities a night watch of constables was sufficient. Then the great flow of immigrants began. In some cities the population multiplied eleven times.

A method of providing order and protection during the day, as well as at night, was now a necessity.

The first cops were political appointees. They rarely wore uniforms and spent most of their day talking politics outside street-corner groceries. In New York the *Herald* called the police "as lazy a set of fellows as ever broke bread."

In every community the cry was Home Rule—local jurisdiction—and the police effort was as slapstick as it was parochial. The laws favored the criminal; pursuit ended at the city limits.

In the frontier territories things were no better. The marshals and sheriffs, political appointees, were rarely chosen because of their honesty and courage. Men like the Dalton brothers began as sheriffs and finished as bandits.

Everything was booming, most of all the railroads. In 1851 Illinois had 93 miles of track. By 1896 the figure was 2,086. Up and down the line, law-enforcement officials were not much interested in protecting the valuables aboard a train that was rolling out of their jurisdiction at a speed of forty-five miles an hour.

Management really had very little control over what went on along their roadbed. Men with or without grievances were derailing trains; station agents were pilfering from box cars in freight yards; and conductors were selling tickets and pocketing the cash. Allan Pinkerton had caught men doing each of these things. In 1855 six midwestern railroads put up $10,000 and asked him to establish a force of railroad police.

"That was to be the role of Pinkerton," Frank Thomas Morn wrote in *Pioneers in Policing,* "establishing control in a fast growing industry that could not rely upon the official city police."

The Pinkerton National Police Agency began as a private firm of bounty hunters employed to protect the railroads and express companies operating on the frontier. Not everything they did was undercover work requiring disguise. Pinkerton "and his men chased lawbreakers on horseback, in carriages, wagons, and stagecoaches," Horan wrote. "They were on the expanding frontier and in the big cities."

By 1866 Allan Pinkerton's agency was better organized than any official police. He provided crime-fighting services for the railroads; he had a body of uniformed night patrolmen, the Pinkerton Protective Patrol; and he specialized in detection.

Local law authorities were eager to cooperate. Holmes permitted the cops to take all the credit. Pinkerton was even more generous. He let them pocket the rewards.

For his trademark he chose the open, unblinking eye, "The eye that never sleeps"—and it entered the language as "private eye."

Thieves knew him as the Eye or Big Eye, and it was an established fact that he would follow you to the end of the earth. He and his operatives were known, hated, and praised from Capetown to the Orient.

Horan described Allan Pinkerton and his sons as "opinionated and sometimes unbearably touchy." They possessed "a venom and fury that numbed suspected assailants."

Truth was Pinkerton's religion. After learning that Philadelphia operatives were attending revivalist meetings, he notified his Philadelphia manager, "Page 11 of the 'General Principles' speaks broad and wide enough for anyone. It simply asks all employees to speak the truth; is that not sufficient, is that not religion enough without hypocrisy?"[3]

From the beginning he lived by the belief that the end justifies the means: "it is held by the agency that the ends being for the accomplishment of justice, they justify the means used," he wrote in his handbook. If it was impossible to secure justice except by kidnapping, he and his men would kidnap.

It was a situation that would cause him large problems. Some of his men were sharp characters, and "the problem of disciplining agents for wrongdoing was tremendously complicated by the fact that the agents frequently knew too much for Pinkerton to incur their hatred," Wayne G. Broehl, Jr., wrote in *The Molly Maguires.* "Lurking in the background in some of the cases was the possibility that the agent if fired would attempt to blackmail Pinkerton for some of the excesses the agency occasionally slipped into."[4]

By 1870 the agency, Horan stated, had "filled the role of a paid national police force that cooperated with the principal police departments in Europe." In London the Pinkertons were known as "the American equivalent of Scotland Yard."

——

Allan Pinkerton's greatest problem had no connection with the pursuit of criminals. It was the state of the economy. Security was still a new idea, the first service corporations abandoned when times were depressed. By November, 1872, Pinkerton could only pay his bills by borrowing from employees.

Relief came when turbulence arose in the coalfields of northeast Pennsylvania. Railroad cars were being derailed, coal tipples burned, mine inspectors beaten. The Reading Railroad hired the Pinkerton agency to protect its property, and to investigate the Molly Maguires, a secret society of Irish coal miners.

Pinkerton developed a team of undercover operatives, and after a year's investigation, the Molly Maguires were destroyed. *The Molly Maguires and the Detectives,* a book by Pinkerton, or at least signed by him, was published in 1877.*

Originally, Allan Pinkerton had refused to investigate union officials in connection with their lawful union activities. But he was not really interested in social problems—except as outlets for his aggression.

———

*Some years later Allan Pinkerton's son William met Conan Doyle aboard a transatlantic liner. "One night in the smoking lounge," Horan wrote, "he told the famous English author the story of McParlan's [James McParlan was the most important undercover man in the Molly Maguire case] adventures in the Pennsylvania mine fields."

When Doyle, in 1914, published *The Valley of Fear,* based partly on the McParlan story, William Pinkerton was furious. "W.A.P. raised the roof when he saw the book," Ralph Dudley, Pinkerton's general manager, told Horan. "At first he talked of bringing suit against Doyle but then dropped that. . . . What made him angry was the fact that even if Doyle was fictionalizing the story, he didn't have the courtesy to ask his permission to use a confidential discussion of his work. They had been good friends before but from that day on their relationship was strained."

"His was not a mind for analyzing social problems," Oliver Wendell Holmes, Jr., wrote of Pinkerton, "but rather a genius for detail, organization, and practical results."

The unstable economy and the chance to save his agency by attacking the problems of the Reading Railroad permanently changed his attitude toward labor. By 1892, when the Pinkertons broke an important steel strike in Homestead, Pennsylvania, the agency had participated in seventy major labor disputes. Perpetually on the side of management, the agency was to labor what the U. S. Cavalry was to the Indians.

Allan Pinkerton was succeeded by his sons, first William, then Robert, and by his grandson, Robert II. They were "just as intolerant, vindictive, fiercely opinionated, resentful of criticism," Horan wrote. But also, he added, "They always appeared in Paul Bunyan's class—outsize."

II

THE PINKERTONS DID NOT show their hand prematurely. When a new employee was required they used a classified ad, but they did not ask, "Want to be a detective?"

Their ads were ambiguously worded and might run as follows:

WANTED—a bright, experienced salesman to handle a good line. Salary and commission. Excellent opportunity for right man to connect with first class house. State age, experience, and references.

One day in Baltimore, late in 1916 or early in 1917, such an announcement was answered by Samuel Dashiell Hammett. He had dropped out of school when he was fourteen, had knocked about in a series of beginners' jobs, and was now twenty-two years old and bored.

"I was the unsatisfactory and unsatisfied employee of various railroads, stock brokers, machinery manufacturers, canners . . . ," he eventually testified. "Usually I was fired."

But from the Pinkerton point of view, his background was interesting. And there was something special about the applicant.

"I don't know what makes this quality in certain men," his friend Lillian Hellman wrote years later. Whatever it was, she testified, it "comes out as something more than dignity and shows in the face."

Exactly when Sam Hammett, as he was called throughout his Pinkerton years, realized that he was being considered for a job as a detective is unknown, but he was hired and soon found himself doing, for the first time, work that excited him.

"The FBI of Hammett's day was the Pinkerton Detective Agency," Joe Gores, a private eye turned writer of detective stories, said in 1976. Gores also provided an insider's view of the sort of work Sam Hammett now found himself enjoying: "the special, little understood joys of manhunting. The blood sport of beating the man who was trying to beat you," Gores wrote in an author's note at the end of his novel, *Hammett.* "Most special when the stakes were high, when what you were trying to take from him was something he valued deeply, often his liberty and sometimes his life."

Hammett won his first promotion by hunting down a man who had swiped a Ferris wheel.

Later, playing the role of an ardent member of the International Workers of the World, he spent three months in a hospital trying to coax evidence from the suspected radical in the next bed.

Some of his cases involved tough men and dangerous situations, and Hammett became a tough man who, on occasions, carried a gun and possibly used it.

Years later Lillian Hellman remembered "the bad cuts on his legs and the indentation on his head from being scrappy with criminals."*

When America entered World War I, Hammett joined the army. After making sergeant, he came down with the flu, which led to tuberculosis. At the end of eighteen months of service, he received a medical discharge.

By March 1920 he was back with the Pinkertons, this time in the Pacific Northwest. In October he collapsed and was taken to a veterans hospital in Tacoma. There, at twenty-six, he met Lt. Josephine Dolan, a beautiful army nurse from Anaconda, Montana.

Eventually he was shipped to a veterans hospital near San Diego. His health improved; he was released and returned to work in the Pacific Northwest. On July 7, 1921, Sam Hammett and Josephine Dolan were quietly married in San Francisco, where no one knew them. He began to work out of the Pinkerton San Francisco office, and their first child was born on October 15, 1921.†

Not much is known about what Hammett did as a Pinkerton operative, but a nonfiction piece that he published in 1923 reveals a bit.

In Seattle, the wife of a fugitive offered to sell him a photo of her husband for fifteen dollars. He did not buy it because he knew where he could get one for nothing.

In a southern city, the chief of police gave Hammett a thor-

*In 1975, when David Fechheimer, who is beyond all doubt the leading authority on Hammett in San Francisco, interviewed Mrs. Hammett and her eldest daughter, Mrs. Hammett said, "He was shadowing someone but what he didn't know was that he was not shadowing one, he was shadowing two and the second one came up behind him and dropped a brick on his head."

Hammett's daughter added, "You could feel it in later years. There was a dent in the back of his head like the corner of a brick. Mother said he sat in a chair for a perfect couple of days." The interview appeared in the magazine *City of San Francisco* (November 4, 1975, p. 38).

†These facts were excavated by David Fechheimer, who is himself a private detective, and were made public at the Dashiell Hammett conference in San Francisco on July 24, 1976.

ough description of a criminal, complete to the mole on his neck, but failed to add that the criminal had only one arm.

While Hammett was trying to peer into the upper story of a roadhouse, the porch roof crumpled and he fell and sprained his ankle. The owner "gave me water to bathe it in."

One night the car which held Hammett and his prisoner broke down. Hammett was warmly dressed but the prisoner, who "stoutly affirmed his innocence, was clothed only in overalls and shirt. After shivering all night in the front seat his morale was low, and I had no difficulty in getting a complete confession from him while walking to the nearest ranch the next morning."

In his pioneer casebook, *Dashiell Hammett*, William F. Nolan reported that Hammett "arrested a smooth talking forger in Pasco, Washington; he rejected an offer to enter the narcotics trade with a pusher from San Diego . . . he worked with a stool pigeon to obtain criminal data in Butte, Montana; he tracked down a fugitive swindler in Seattle."

He is known to have worked on at least two notorious cases, the Nicky Arnstein swindle in New York City, and the Fatty Arbuckle rape case in San Francisco.

"I was a pretty good sleuth," Hammett once said, "but possibly overrated because of the plausibility with which I could explain away my failures, proving them inevitable and no fault of mine."

His wife remembered that when he worked for the Pinkertons he was not politically aware. She was shocked to learn that before the war he had worked in Butte against the IWW. And a daughter recalled, "He told me he was not politically aware at that time. He didn't care if his clients were bums. He was strictly out to do his job."

Lillian Hellman has reported that while Hammett was in Montana he was offered $5,000 to kill a labor agitator. But murder was not part of his job, and the idea that someone might think it was gradually became important to him.

In February 1922 tuberculosis again attacked him, and he was forced to resign from the Pinkerton agency.

All in all, Fechheimer has reported, Hammett had been a

working detective for approximately thirty months, with his employment broken by his enlistment in the army and his illness. During much of his time with the agency, Fechheimer noted, he had worked a twelve- to sixteen-hour day.

As a detective, Hammett had moved in a world whose existence most people did not suspect.

In *The Maltese Falcon* Sam Spade tells Brigid O'Shaughnessy a story about a man named Flitcraft.

"Flitcraft had been a good citizen and a good husband and father," Spade says, "simply because he was a man who was most comfortable in step with his surroundings. He had been raised that way. The people he knew were like that. The life he knew was a clean orderly responsible affair."

One day Flitcraft was walking by the construction site for a skyscraper when a steel beam slipped and missed him by inches. For Flitcraft this event took the lid off life.

"What disturbed him," Spade continued, "was the discovery that in sensibly ordering his affairs he had gotten out of step, and not into step, with life."

Before Flitcraft had gone twenty feet he knew that he had to adjust himself to "this new glimpse of life." He abandoned his job, his wife, and his children, and drifted. Two years later, after no more beams had fallen, Flitcraft got back into the same business he had been in earlier, married a woman very much like his first wife, and readjusted completely to the idea that life is orderly, meaningful, and rational.

Like Flitcraft, most people live in stabilized situations. But not Hammett. Hammett was the man whose job had taken the lid off life, and he could not forget what he knew. He was also tubercular and may have believed that he did not have long to live. For these and other reasons, he wanted to express himself. His daughter Mary Jane remembers his reaction to one story in a pulp magazine.

"Oh, my God, I can do better than that."

When he resigned from the Pinkerton agency, he was so ill that the government granted him a full-disability pension. He rested, sometimes in the reading room of the San Francisco Public Library, then found a job as advertising manager of the Albert Samuels jewelry company in San Francisco. He would write for Samuels during the day and for himself at night.

"He'd write copy for me all day," Samuels recalled, "then go home to his apartment and drink during most of the night, sobering up enough to report in the next morning. Yet he was a man of honor, and he always did good work."

But it was costing Hammett a lot of sleep, and once again, his lungs gave way.

"You couldn't tell him to stop drinking or stop smoking," Mrs. Hammett remembered.

"When he was hemorrhaging," a daughter added, "he used to put chairs in a line across the room so that he could support himself over to the bathroom. He was very sick, and yet there was something indestructible about Papa."

His first published short story appeared in 1923. In the next six years he sold approximately sixty short stories. Most of them ran in the pulp magazine *Black Mask.**

Red Harvest, his first novel, was published in 1929. His second, *The Dain Curse,* came out later that same year.

Each sold well and was admired internationally. "I regard his *Red Harvest* as a remarkable achievement," André Gide wrote, "the last word in atrocity, cynicism, and horror." Robert Graves described the same book as "an acknowledged literary landmark."

―――

In his stories and novels Hammett provided an alternative to the genteel tradition in detective fiction.

At the time, particularly in England, the formal detective novel had become more and more of an abstraction: "the form was approaching the place where it would be almost totally cerebral," Aaron Mark Stein has observed, "with characters recognizable only as symbols moved about in a game of wits; bloodless people,

―――

*In his introduction to *The Hardboiled Dicks,* crime-buff Ron Goulart writes, "The pulps, which flourished in the years between world wars, were seven by ten in size with bright enameled covers and some 120 untrimmed wood-pulp pages."

carrying bloodless corpses through the maze of a formal garden."

The genteel detective novel was not only bloodless and an abstraction, it was, as George Grella has pointed out, a comforting social ritual.

Several people have gathered for a weekend in an isolated country home. The group is small, elite, homogeneous, a microcosm of posh society. There are a representative of hereditary wealth, a distinguished professional man, a husky Christian vicar, a retired colonial official, a sporting man, and a soldier who is most often a colonel or brigadier general—these and their bloodless ladies.

A terrible thing is suddenly discovered. One of this crew has been murdered. The police arrive and find sometimes fifty clues, sometimes none at all. Either way, the situation is baffling. To the rescue comes an eccentric but intelligent problem solver. This gentleman-amateur, blithest of dilettantes, sleuths around, puts together a sort of fabric of truth, and in the final scene—because of his special knowledge of matters such as rare South American poisons—fingers the villain.

Except in cases where he or she is a foreigner, the villain is usually the person the reader would least suspect. In fact, however, this individual has been hiding some dark, unpleasant secret, is not at all what he or she seems to be, and is, as Grella has demonstrated, an exploiter of society and its rituals.

With the villain in handcuffs and the case closed, the various members of the house party, including the reader, can relax back into a benevolent world where, perpetually, Silver Blaze is pounding to victory.

So much for crime.

Hammett said it wasn't so. He removed the crime story from the world of Poe and put it back into the world of Vidocq. "Hammett took murder out of the Venetian vase," Raymond Chandler said, "and dropped it into the alley."

At the time, in America, the reigning detective-story writer was Willard Huntington Wright, who used the pen name S. S. Van Dine to record the deeds of Philo Vance, suavest of problem solvers.

Eventually the *Saturday Review of Literature* asked Dashiell Hammett, as he was now known, to review Van Dine's latest, *The Benson Murder Case.*

"Alvin Benson is found sitting in a wicker chair in his living room," Hammett wrote, "his legs crossed, and his body comfortably relaxed in a lifelike position. He is dead. A bullet from an Army model Colt .45 automatic has passed completely through his head. That his position could be so slightly disturbed by the impact of such a bullet at such a range is preposterous. . . . This Philo Vance is in the Sherlock Holmes tradition and his conversational manner is that of a high-school girl who has been studying the foreign words and phrases in the back of her dictionary. . . . His exposition of the technique employed by a gentleman shooting another gentleman deserves a place in a How-to-be-a-detective-by-mail course."

In place of the pseudo, Hammett supplied authority. In a story titled "The Whosis Kid," he put his detective, the Continental Op (employed by the Continental Detective Agency), in a room with five other people, three of whom are aiming at each other with drawn guns. In this situation the Op knows exactly what to do.

"As for myself," he says, "I counted on coming through all in one piece. Few men *get* killed. Most of those who meet sudden ends *get themselves* killed. I've had twenty years of experience dodging that."

But Hammett was not just writing accurately about guns. He was writing accurately about the people who were holding them, and the world they lived in. Hammett's books, Raymond Chandler said, were written "for people with a sharp, aggressive attitude to life. . . . They were not afraid of the seamy side of things. . . . Violence did not disturb them."

As a Pinkerton Hammett had been involved with deception; as a writer his concern was reality. He was fictionalizing deception and presenting it as reality.

Steven Marcus has said of the Continental Op, "The Op interviews the person or persons immediately accessible. They may be innocent or guilty—it doesn't matter . . . they provide the

Op with an account of what they know, of what they assert really happened. The Op begins to investigate; he snoops about. . . . What he soon discovers is that the 'reality' that anyone involved will swear to is in fact itself a construction, a fabrication, a fiction, a faked and alternate reality—and that it has been gotten together before he ever arrived on the scene."[5]

III

BY 1930, some eight years after he had begun to learn his trade, Dashiell Hammett had published fifty-six short stories and two novels. In them he had moved the hard-boiled school of fiction "out of the back room of the pulps," as one critic phrased it, "and into the bright lights of the best bookstores." Yet his tales were still somewhat primitive, and he had created no memorable characters. Things changed dramatically on February 14, 1930, with the publication of *The Maltese Falcon.*

He had begun the book with at least three ideas in the back of his mind.

He was dissatisfied with the way he had handled two short stories. The first, "The Gutting of Couffignal," was a romantic tale in which the leading character, a Russian princess, was out to recoup the family fortune by looting an island resort. The second, "The Whosis Kid," featured Ines Almad, a woman who used dangerous men as "something to put between herself and trouble," and had a special talent for pleading her innocence. Hammett thought both stories were failures.

He had read somewhere of a peculiar arrangement between Charles V of Spain and that band of Crusaders known as the Order of the Hospital of St. John of Jerusalem, an agreement involving one falcon from Malta.

In a piece called "The Wings of Henry James," James Thurber recorded that, one night in a New York bar, he and others were startled by Hammett's announcement that in writing *The Maltese Falcon,* he had been influenced by Henry James's *The Wings of the Dove.*

"I was unable, in a recent investigation," Thurber reported, "to find many feathers of *The Dove* in the claws of *The Falcon,* but there are a few. . . . In both novels, a fabulous fortune—jewels in *The Falcon,* inherited millions in *The Dove*—shapes the destinies of the disenchanted central characters; James's designing woman, Kate Croy, like Hammett's . . . Brigid O'Shaughnessy, loses her lover."

Hammett also understood that the Continental Op would be out of place in the story as it was shaping up; a new problem solver was required. And so he created Sam Spade, who over the years has received what today seems an unreasonable amount of hate mail.

The fact is, when *The Maltese Falcon* was published, it was commonly believed that a man who slept with a woman was supposed to marry her. But Sam Spade slept with Brigid O'Shaughnessy and, instead of marrying her, sent her to jail. It was an act that led to his being condemned by two of the best:

Somerset Maugham: "A nasty bit of goods . . . an unscrupulous rogue and a heartless crook . . . there is little to choose between him and the criminals he is dealing with."

Ross Macdonald: "Spade— . . . his lover is guilty of murder; his narrow, bitter code forces Spade to turn her over to the police."

Today it seems possible that too little attention has been paid to Dashiell Hammett's women. When Gertrude Stein came to America in 1935, she was especially interested in meeting two people, one of whom was Hammett. A dinner was arranged in Beverly Hills. There, Lillian Hellman reported, "Miss Stein told Dash he was the only American writer who wrote well about women."

It is true that strong-willed women who are also handsome are standard features in the fiction of Dashiell Hammett. In many of his stories such adventuresses are the deus ex machina.

At the end of "This King Business," the Continental Op tells the female lead, "You're a cold blooded hussy." It is an exact description of most of Hammett's leading ladies.

Of Hammett's hussies, Brigid O'Shaughnessy is his finest Because the story told in *The Maltese Falcon* is presented dramati- cally, a great deal of Brigid's cold bloodedness is concealed. He1 viciousness is much more evident when the events are examined chronologically.*

———

In 1530 a group of Crusaders, the Order of the Hospital of St. John of Jerusalem, invite Emperor Charles V of Spain to give them Malta, Gozo, and Tripoli. He agrees, providing that annu- ally the Order sends him a falcon from Malta in acknowledgment that they are only renting, and that the territories remain Spanish property.

The knights of the order are grateful, and they are also rich; so rich that as payment for the first year's rent, they send the Emperor "not an insignificant live bird, but a glorious golden falcon encrusted from head to foot with the finest jewels in their coffers."†

On the way to Spain the foot-high statue is captured by pirates. During the next 300 years it is possessed by a series of Algerian, Sicilian, and Spanish nobles and eventually, during the Carlist troubles in Spain in 1848, arrives in Paris. There, "painted or enameled over to look like nothing more than a fairly interest- ing black statue," it passes from one dealer to another.

*Literary critics are often offended when events in a novel are put in chronological order rather than in the order devised by the author. This is understandable.

The present writer does as he does for three reasons.

He believes that the chronological approach sheds new light on the fundamental relationship between Brigid and Sam.

He believes it makes Sam's sending Brigid to jail, an act for which Spade has been condemned in the past, seem more reasonable.

He believes it permits a closer study of Spade's conception of himself as a detective.

†Representatives of the Grand Priory in the British Realm of the Most Venerable Order of the Hospital of St. John of Jerusalem report that none of the historians of the order mention such a gift being made.

In a letter dated September 8, 1976, Diane Moore, Assistant Curator of the Order, informed this writer, "A live Maltese falcon *was* presented each year . . . not, however, to the King of Spain, but to the Viceroy of Sicily (Sicily, at that time, was a Spanish territory). The presentation of this gift was one of the conditions attached to the grant of Malta and Tripoli made to the Order by Charles V in 1530."

Until 1911, no one is aware of its value. Then Charilaos, a Greek who has researched the bird's history and knows what he is looking for, spots it in a shop and buys it. But Charilaos does not hurry to convert his discovery into money. He knows its intrinsic value, but he also knows he can obtain a far higher sum after he has established the falcon's history. A year or so later he is murdered, and a number of his possessions are stolen. Among them is the falcon.

Meanwhile, an international criminal named Casper Gutman, learning of the falcon, has become fascinated by its story.*

After a seventeen-year search, Gutman traces the statue to the home of Kemidov, a Russian general who lives in Constantinople. Gutman then attempts to buy the falcon from the general, but overplays his hand. The general has the statue examined by experts and learns its true value. He has it copied, black porcelain over lead, then substitutes the fake bird for the real falcon.

Gutman, continuing to misread the situation, hires Brigid O'Shaughnessy and a Greek, Joel Cairo, to steal the falcon. They do, but keep it for themselves.

Brigid then allies herself with Floyd Thursby, an American

---

*Anyone who has speculated about what types such as Gutman do when they are not chasing the falcon might enjoy *The Playful Panther,* a biography of an English rogue, A. Maundy Gregory, written by Tom Cullen. It was published in America in 1975.

As an Oxford undergraduate, Maundy Gregory drifted into acting, then ran a detective bureau. By 1914 he was organizing "listening posts" for Sir Basil Zaharoff, "the mystery man of Europe." This brought him into politics and from 1916 to 1922, A. Maundy Gregory was a leading fund raiser for the Lloyd George Coalition governments. He was in charge of the sale of honors.

In *Peddler of Death,* a biography of Zaharoff, Donald McCormick reported that Maundy Gregory "wielded immense power behind the scenes in politics and was the keeper of innumerable shady secrets concerning the men of power in those days."

At the same time, Gregory owned one of London's smartest nightclubs. After World War I, according to Cullen, he became "Deputy Director of the £100,000 centenary appeal launched by the Most Venerable Order of the Hospital of St. John of Jerusalem, whose Grand Prior was a member of the royal family."

Gregory later converted to Catholicism. He was soon doing a good business selling papal honors. On the side, he financed literary efforts such as A. J. Symons' *The Quest for Corvo.* In 1932, at a time when Maundy Gregory was desperate for money, his friend Edith Rosse, with whom he shared a house, died under mysterious circumstances. Her modest fortune was inherited by Gregory.

The real prototype for Gutman, as Hammett has said, "was suspected—foolishly, as most people were—of being a German agent in Washington, D.C., in the early years of the war, and I never remember shadowing a man who bored me as much."

gunman. After framing Cairo, who is imprisoned over a bad check, Brigid and Thursby leave Constantinople with the bird. Brigid, afraid that Gutman may be on her trail, and scheming to become the falcon's sole owner, deposits it with an old friend, Captain Jacobi of the freighter *La Paloma*.

She and Thursby then sail for San Francisco on a faster ship. In San Francisco they check into separate hotels and Brigid, without telling Thursby, rents an apartment for herself.

Her relations with Spade begin when, moving to rid herself of Thursby, she goes to the firm of Spade & Archer, a partnership of private detectives, and hires them to shadow the gunman.

Neither Sam Spade nor Miles Archer is interested in the trumped-up tale she tells them. What does impress them, however, is the exorbitant sum of $200 which she offers, provided one of them handles her problem personally.

Archer begins the job that evening, shadowing Thursby and Brigid, who soon informs Thursby that they are being followed. She does so because she imagines that Thursby will become alarmed and go after Archer. If Archer shoots Thursby, the falcon is hers; if Thursby shoots Archer, the bird is still hers, because she can inform on Thursby. But the news that they are being tailed does not disturb Thursby.

Later that night, Brigid borrows Thursby's gun, contacts Miles Archer, then leads him down an alley and kills him. After midnight his corpse is discovered and the police notify Spade.

Spade does not grieve over his partner's death. He considers Archer a "son of a bitch," and has known it since the second week of the partnership. Also, he is having an affair with Miles's wife. Nevertheless, it is bad for business when a professional detective is murdered and the killer goes unpunished. It is particularly bad when that detective is your business partner.

British reporters once asked William Pinkerton about Sherlock Holmes. "Gumshoe detectives of fiction are usually just plain rot," Pinkerton replied. "Detective work is only using good common sense and nothing else."

Sam Spade is Pinkerton's sort of detective. At the scene of the crime, he learns from the police that Archer's gun was still on his hip and that his overcoat was still buttoned. Whoever got Archer that far down an alley, Spade reasons, could only have been someone Miles trusted.

It could not have been Thursby, Spade decides, because Archer was an experienced detective and would not be caught by the party he was shadowing. But it is not hard to imagine that Archer could be lured down an alley by a woman, so that from the start Spade figures that the killer is probably Brigid.

He has his hand on one piece of reality and wants more.

Meanwhile, Thursby is murdered, shot down while entering his hotel. Brigid realizes that Gutman and the young killer, Wilmer, have arrived in San Francisco. She also realizes that she has no protection. In the morning she calls Spade's office and leaves word that she has just rented an apartment and wants Spade to come out as soon as possible.

When Spade arrives they have a long conversation. He is able to extract $500 from Brigid but does not learn anything that will help him solve Archer's murder. During most of their discussion, Brigid and Spade tell each other nothing but lies. He lies because he suspects that she is a murderer. She lies because she is a congenital liar.*

Weeks earlier, in Constantinople, the Russian general who owns the real falcon had made a strategic move to further deceive Gutman. He hired Joel Cairo, just released from jail, and ordered him to steal the fake falcon.

Now, after Spade has left Brigid's apartment and returned to his office, Joel Cairo shows up. From him Spade learns several things: that Cairo is searching for "a statuette . . . the black figure of a bird" and that he is prepared to pay $5,000 for it.

---

*In John Huston's classic film version of *The Maltese Falcon*, Brigid was played by Mary Astor.

"I had a lovely pot to boil for Brigid," she wrote in *A Life on Film*. "First of all, she was a congenital liar ('I'm a liar. I've always been a liar!') and slightly psychopathic. And that kind of liar wears the face of truth, although they send out all sorts of signals that they are lying . . . . One of the tip-offs is that they can't help breathing rather rapidly. So, I hyperventilated before going into most of the scenes. It gave me a heady feeling, of thinking at cross purposes. For there wasn't a single scene in the picture where what I said was even close to what I was thinking."

Spade agrees to help and takes an advance of $200. That evening Spade returns to Brigid's apartment and tells her of Cairo's offer. She says she must see Cairo. They go to Spade's place and he calls Cairo, who agrees to come over.*

During the next few hours there is considerable action, but Spade picks up only one piece of information; both Brigid and Cairo are nervous about a man whose name begins with G. After Cairo departs Spade cross-examines Brigid and learns that she does not know why the black bird is so valuable.

They spend the night in his bed. Early in the morning he slips out, goes over to Brigid's apartment and searches it. He finds a week-old receipt for the rent. Because she has told him that she rented the place two days ago, the receipt supports his suspicions.

Back at his place, Brigid and Sam breakfast, then separate. She soon appears at his office. Someone has searched her apartment, she reports; she has got to have protection. He arranges for her to stay with his secretary's mother, then accompanies her partway in a cab. From the moment Spade leaves the cab, he does not see Brigid for thirty-six hours.

During this interval he is totally absorbed with solving the problem of the two murders. He picks up one clue when a friendly SFPD detective tells him that Archer was killed with Thursby's gun. He also arranges a situation that puts him in touch with Gutman and, at the price of being drugged by knockout drops, learns the full history of the Maltese falcon.

He even gets possession of the bird itself when Captain Jacobi of the *La Paloma* stumbles into the office with a package in his arms, then falls dead of bullet wounds. But he picks up very little information that will help him answer the questions—Who killed Archer? Who killed Thursby? Who killed Jacobi?

During this same thirty-six hours, Brigid's only interest is the falcon. Except for one treacherous phone call that lures Spade into a set-up, she ignores him. Eventually she forms a temporary alliance with Cairo and Gutman. After they have broken into Spade's

*Hammett-buff Joe Gores places Spade's apartment at 891 Post Street. Hammett was living at this address when he wrote the first draft of *The Maltese Falcon.*

apartment, she goes downstairs and waits for him outside. Sam arrives about midnight, finds Brigid on the steps, and follows her into the apartment where her allies are waiting with drawn guns.

In the scene that follows, the climax begins when Spade agrees to accept Gutman's offer of $10,000 for the bird. Spade then confronts them with their common predicament.

Three murders have occurred on the streets of San Francisco; and in various ways each of them, Gutman, Cairo, Brigid, and himself are connected to the carnage. "The police have got to have a victim," he explains, "somebody they can stick for those three murders."

Throughout the case Spade has used his talents as a role player. He has hinted that he is corruptible; he has also taken calculated risks and staged small dramas. "My way of learning is to heave a wild and unpredictable monkey wrench into the machinery," he has told Brigid.

Among his calculated risks is his repeated needling of Gutman's adolescent gunman, Wilmer. Now Spade begins to press for a fall guy—specifically, Wilmer. By this time, because of what has been revealed during the discussion, Spade is just about certain that Wilmer killed Thursby and Jacobi. A fall guy like Wilmer, Spade argues, will satisfy the district attorney.

"Bryan is like most district attorneys," Spade says. "He's more interested in how his record will look on paper than in anything else. He'd rather drop a doubtful case than try it and have it go against him . . . . To be sure of convicting one man he'll let half a dozen equally guilty accomplices go free—if trying to convict them all might confuse his case.

"That's the choice we'll give him and he'll gobble it up. He won't want to know about the falcon. He'll be tickled pink to persuade himself that anything the punk tells him about it is a lot of chewing gum, an attempt to muddle things up."

When it's just about all over, after Gutman and Cairo have jumped Wilmer, and after the falcon has turned out to be a fake, and Spade and Brigid are alone in the apartment, Spade calls the police. He identifies Wilmer as the murderer of Thursby and Jacobi, naming Gutman and Cairo as associates.

Then comes the climax of the story, the final scene between Brigid and Spade. As it begins Brigid has known Spade since Wednesday afternoon, and it is now Sunday, some ninety-four hours later.*

During this period Brigid has had three talks with Spade and has slept with him once. Afterward, from the time of learning that the *La Paloma* had arrived in San Francisco, she has not only disregarded him, she has worked against him.

Now, prodded by Spade, she acknowledges that she shot and killed Miles Archer.

"When you found," Spade tells her, "that Thursby didn't mean to tackle him you borrowed the gun and did it yourself. Right?"

"Yes—though not exactly," she answers.

She is willing to acknowledge this because she cannot imagine that Spade would turn her in to the cops. As she sees it, Spade is just one more man, the latest in a long string of masculine protectors whom she has manipulated.

But it is not so.

"You're taking the fall," he says. "One of us has to take it, after the talking those birds will do. They'll hang me sure . . . "

"You didn't care—care at all," she says. "You didn't, don't —l-love me?"

In this scene Sam is a shaken man. He is attracted to Brigid and does not like to do what he has to do, but he knows that the only truth they have shared is sex. He tells her she has "never played square with me for half an hour at a stretch since I've known you." He understands that if he does not turn this murderess in, she will have a subtle hold on him. He realizes that, as he says, "I couldn't be sure you wouldn't decide to shoot a hole in

*Sam and Brigid knew each other over a period of five days. In a close reading of the book, only two specific references to the day of the week could be found. The first is Spade's statement, on p. 144 (Vintage paperback edition), "Hello, Sid—Sam. I've got a date with the District Attorney at half-past two this afternoon. Will you give me a ring—here or there —around four, just to see that I'm not in trouble?. . . . Hell with your Saturday afternoon golf: your job's to keep me out of jail. . . . Right, Sid. 'Bye."

The second is the title of chapter 17, "Saturday Night." These references are the basis for saying that the acquaintance began on a Wednesday and ended on a Sunday.

me some day." As the scene ends he declares, "I won't play the sap for you."

Brigid responds with the only weapon that remains. "She put her mouth to his, slowly, her arms around him, and came into his arms."

Everything in *The Maltese Falcon* suggests that she sees Sam as just another man to be used. Nothing suggests that she has any special feeling for him, or that she is interested in anything but profiting from the black bird.

Brigid, truly, is a "cold blooded hussy."

———

Sam Spade's attitude toward the law-enforcement bureaucracy in San Francisco is like Holmes's attitude toward Scotland Yard. And for similar reason.

Lt. Dundy, chief Spade-hater in the SFPD, favors the idea that Spade killed Archer in order to marry Archer's wife. It is the sort of pedestrian stuff displayed by the inspectors from Scotland Yard. In Hammett, as in Doyle, the reality is far over the heads of the police.

On a higher bureaucratic level, Hammett's District Attorney Bryan, like Simenon's Examining Magistrate Coméliau, shows little interest in complication.

At a time when Spade knows about the falcon and its remarkable history, Bryan regards the killing of Thursby as a gangster slaying which, properly handled, can generate headlines for himself. When Bryan charges Spade with withholding information, Spade replies scornfully, "You wouldn't want the kind of information I could give you, Bryan. . . . It'd poop this gangsters-revenge scenario for you."

Nevertheless, the bureaucracy is a much more formidable problem to Spade than to Holmes or Maigret. Holmes is protected by his position in the class structure, and Maigret is a high official in the police. But in *The Maltese Falcon* the police are almost as much of a problem to the problem solver as the criminals are.

Spade's original goal was to identify and capture the murderer of his partner. Legally, it is a police affair, but Spade is not accustomed to having the police solve his problems. "I'll bury my own dead," he says.

Before the case is over, not one but three men have been killed on the streets of San Francisco, and Spade is connected to each. Because he has not cooperated with the police at any time during these events, squaring himself with authority itself becomes a difficulty. That he succeeds in solving both his problems is most admirable.

Ellery Queen called Dashiell Hammett a "romantic realist"; and *The Maltese Falcon* is Hammett at his realest and most romantic. The romance surrounding the falcon is as sensational as anything in the best Holmes adventures; but there is nothing romantic about the story's central theme, which is deception.

In the Adams Express case Allan Pinkerton constructed a false reality around Nathan Maroney. Kemidov, the Russian general who owns the real falcon, rigs another false reality around Gutman. Both cases contain the same sort of built-in illusion. Gutman is deceived, along with Brigid and Cairo. Each of them attempts to deceive Spade.

When Gutman raises his glass and proposes a toast to Spade, he says, "Well, sir, here's to plain speaking and clear understanding." He means, of course, the direct opposite.

It is just as André Gide said: "Dashiell Hammett's dialogue ... in which every character is trying to deceive all the others, and in which the truth slowly becomes visible through the haze of deception."

Except for its gorgeous details, the story told in *The Maltese Falcon* is the same story that Hammett told in earlier tales. The Continental Op regularly discovered that the situation which other characters accept as reality is actually, as Steven Marcus has pointed out, "a faked and alternate reality."

In *The World of the Thriller,* Ralph Harper wrote, "The heart of evil is deception, a power of lies. This is Dashiell Hammett's contribution, and it is absolutely fundamental."

For Harper, a Protestant minister, violence "is but the explosive result of the tension generated by deception." Spade and other

Hammett heroes "press the crossed wires tighter and tighter until the charge they carry is too burning for them to bear, and the subsequent flash melts them down. The hero himself is left limp and empty; there is no joy, not even satisfaction."

That "there is . . . not even satisfaction" is questionable. A detective is not an ordinary person. Unlike Flitcraft, the character Spade told Brigid about, a detective is aware of the violent nature of society, the extent of man's criminality. At the same time, he has a very strong sense of his own identity.

"I'm a detective and expecting me to run criminals down and then let them go free," Spade tells Brigid, "is like asking a dog to catch a rabbit and let it go," and "if I send you over, I'll be sorry as hell—I'll have some rotten nights—but that'll pass."

His emotional situation is more complicated than the Op's, but both men are detectives and both see things the same way.

In "The Gutting of Couffignal" the leading lady offers the Op her body in exchange for freedom.

"You think I'm a man and you're a woman," the Op replies. "That's wrong. I'm a manhunter and you're something that has been running in front of me. There's nothing human about it."

It all connects with Joe Gores's phrase in *Hammett*—"the special, little understood joys of manhunting."

Most detectives, it seems, like being detectives. In his last years Vidocq, with his mania for knowing, besieged the police with reports that they had never asked for. In his *Memoirs* Maigret declared, "I repeat, its a game that's being played, a game that has no end. Once you've begun it, its difficult . . . to give it up."

Sam Spade is a veteran detective. He has experience and he has courage. He can stage a scene, but he is not a show-off. He is a rational man who does not mind seeming irrational. He is a professional. Within his trade he does much the same thing that Allan Pinkerton did; he adds drama. He is an actor. He is not what he seems. Like everything else in *The Maltese Falcon,* he is deceptive.

Hammett called Spade "a dream man in the sense that he is what most of the private detectives I worked with would like to have been and what quite a few of them in their cockier moments thought they approached . . . your private detective . . . wants to be a very hard and shifty fellow, able to take care of himself in any situation, able to get the best of anybody he comes in contact with, whether criminal, innocent bystander, or client."

Hammett specifies "or client." In *The Maltese Falcon* all of Spade's clients ended up in jail. He came out of the affair with $800. Not bad for five days' work in the late 1920s.

IV

HAMMETT ONCE TOLD a reporter that politics in California were the world's most corrupt. The reporter did not press the matter, but the British historian Lord Bryce had made the same point in *The American Commonwealth,* published in 1888, and had lingered to explain why.

He began by generalizing about California: "A great population had gathered there before there was any regular government to keep it in order, much less any education or social culture to refine it. The wilderness of the time passed into the soul of the people, and left them more tolerant of violent deeds, more prone to interferences with, or suppressions of, regular law, than are the people in most parts of the Union."

His Lordship then got down to specifics. The overpowering reason for corruption in California, he declared, was the character of the citizens of San Francisco.

As to why this was so, he provided several explanations, the most intriguing being, "That scum which the western moving wave of emigration carried on its crest is here stopped, because it can go no further. It accumulates in San Francisco and forms a dangerous constituent of the population."

Throughout the years when Samuel Dashiell Hammett lived in San Francisco, political corruption hid behind the highly visible profile of Mayor James J. "Sunny Jim" Rolph, a short man who wore cowboy boots and a cutaway and specialized in dropping into the schools to join the students in giving the pledge of allegiance.

In Sunny Jim's city hall the philosophy was, "You make a buck, I make a buck." Graft and vice were accepted as necessary evils, and San Franciscans fondly regarded their town as "a robust-minded city."*

It was robust and it was wide open.

In New York the police identified themselves as being "on the force." In Los Angeles the phrase was "in the department." And in San Francisco, during the Rolph era, it was "in the business."

When San Francisco attorney J. W. Ehrlich wrote his autobiography, *A Life in My Hands,* he interpreted this phrase to mean "only and exclusively 'in the business' of being a San Francisco policeman with all of the commercial and other connotations that go with that phrase."†

But police graft was only a small part of the corruption in the San Francisco that Hammett knew. It was a city in which crime was organized to a degree that suggests the London of Jonathan Wild, with the role of Wild split between two brothers, Pete and Tom McDonough.

---

*"The thing I love about S.F. is its go to hell attitude," Raymond Chandler once wrote to his agent. "The narrow streets are lined with NO PARKING AT ANY TIME signs and also lined with parked automobiles which look as if they had been there all day. . . . The taxi drivers are wonderful too. They obey no laws but those of gravity and we even had one who passes street cars on the left, an offense for which you would probably get ninety days in Los Angeles."

†In an article in the San Francisco *Chronicle* (January 14, 1977) reporter Harry Jupiter quoted the Attorney General of California, Evelle Younger, as saying, "Compared to other police departments, San Francisco's was not a good police department. . . . For years, the attitude here has been, 'We're wide open. Come on out to San Francisco and have a ball.' . . . It's the most difficult city in the United States to police and the citizens, until recently, have not cared."

Despite such matters, the SFPD appears to have had its share of exceptionally capable officers. An article in the *Chronicle* (June 9, 1975) noted the retirement of Kenneth Manley as senior inspector of the SFPD homicide bureau.

During his twenty-five years on the force, the *Chronicle* stated, Manley took approximately 350 murder cases to court, and won them all. The newspaper quoted an associate of Manley's, "He worked a case like a bulldog, using intuition to get a focus, then holding on to every detail until he had enough evidence to overwhelm the district attorney."

The sign over their door said BAIL BONDING, but there was more to it than that.

"From their scrubby little office on Kearny," Ehrlich wrote, "close enough to the Hall of Justice for the chief to wince if Pete McDonough raised his voice in anger, these Argus-eyed squid-handed brothers supervised the many-splendored nightlife of San Francisco. They kept an eye on the nightly take of every hustling girl on Eddy Street, knew to the dollar how much Russian Mike or Bones Remmer or Eddie Sahati folded into their pockets after a night's play, and had the drawings of any burglary, con-game, or safeblowing that happened, *before* it happened—or it *didn't* happen.

"The McDonoughs had a scale of prices, in all categories," Ehrlich remembered. "They had their own lawyers. They created judges and uncreated them. They got city and county ordinances passed, defeated, amended, and shelved. . . . They 'laundered' soiled money. They cooled overnight beefs and saw the right people. Their office was a clearing house, an employment agency, a post office and a chancellery for the underworld. And . . . oh, yes, they wrote bail bonds."

It was an operation that the McDonough brothers established, by unrecorded means, sometime before 1918. They continued to direct it, unchallenged, until 1936 or thereabouts.

Based on the part of the story that is on the record, the troubles of Pete and Tom McDonough began one day at a service-club luncheon in San Rafael, a city north of San Francisco. The guest of honor was the Collector of Internal Revenue for Northern California. While making some off-the-cuff remarks, he mentioned that one San Francisco police captain with an annual salary of about $7,000 had recently paid taxes on an income of over $100,000.

As it happened, a reporter for the San Francisco *News* was present, and carried the story back to his editor. Before long a San Francisco County Grand Jury found itself hiring an outsider, a retired FBI agent from Los Angeles, to search for corruption in the SFPD. His investigation, for which he was paid $100,000, was not particularly aggressive, but his seventy-page report, and the newspaper publicity that followed, publicly revealed Pete and Tom's correct identity.

The McDonoughs weathered a series of trials, but were unable to resume their thieving. After their bail-bonding license was revoked, the former master criminals picked up their winnings and retired.

In his fiction Dashiell Hammett never referred to the McDonoughs, but his thinking, his view of life, may have been affected, at least in part, by his awareness of the real nature of their role in "The City That Knows How."

As a writer Dashiell Hammett had no answer. Conan Doyle championed the values of knighthood and chivalry. Simenon pities mankind; his Maigret is benevolent. But Hammett, until his last novel, offered nothing except the satisfaction of doing a job properly.

"Hammett's vision was of a society so corrupt," George P. Elliot wrote, "that it corrupts all individual relationships."

Most of the stories about the Continental Op included women who were not victims but aggressors. In *The Dain Curse,* however, after guiding the leading lady through a drug cure, the Op nearly declared his love for her.

The Maltese Falcon and Sam Spade were succeeded by *The Glass Key* and Ned Beaumont, a self-described gambler and politicians' hanger-on. He is actually a savvy but perplexing problem solver about whom the reader never learns much.

Although Janet Henry, the woman in the story, is attracted to Beaumont, the bleakness continues because Hammett permits no gestures of affection or sentiment. Since Ned Beaumont is a compulsive gambler—dice, horses, cards—and Janet Henry is young and has been sheltered, the reader is left with the feeling that they may not be able to make it together.

In 1930, after finishing *The Glass Key,* Hammett began the first draft of *The Thin Man.* At the time the name of the sleuth was John Guild; and when the female lead attempted to seduce him, he did not respond. After 18,000 words, Hammett put the manuscript aside.

A year later Hammett, then thirty-six, met Lillian Hellman, who was twenty-four. "Hammett and I had a good time together," she wrote, long afterward. "Most of it, not all of it. We were amused by each other."

For at least part of their long relationship, they were not particularly faithful to each other. Once, when things had reached the marriage-planning stage, Hammett, as she phrased it later, "disappeared with another lady."

He was not really a domestic man. Domesticity was something he had abandoned in 1927, when he sent his wife and his daughters to live in San Anselmo and remained in San Francisco to write.

When the final version of *The Thin Man* was published in 1934, the bleakness had vanished. Hero and heroine are married and delighted to be so; one of the happiest couples in literature.

He, Nick Charles, is a forty-one-year-old ex-private eye, retired for seven years, who keeps himself busy by managing his wife's timber holdings. She, Nora, is no "cold blooded hussy." Lillian Hellman, the model for Nora, was once described as "an intense, unsparing woman," and Nora, besides being a beauty, is independent and can be tough. She and Nick live in San Francisco but have come to New York for the Christmas season.

As the action begins Nick is reluctant to return to sleuthing. He is the first Hammett character to have an agreeable relationship with a woman, but the transition has been difficult, and in the mornings, at least on vacation, he prefers a martini to coffee.

The great link between Nora and Nick, it is implied, is sex. After Nick, working a case once again, has scuffled with an attractive woman named Mimi, Nora asks him, "Tell me the truth. When you were wrestling with Mimi did you have an erection?"

Nick replies, "Oh, a little bit."

It was sensational stuff in 1934. Hammett's delighted publisher, Alfred A. Knopf, advertised immediately, "We don't believe the question on page 192 of Dashiell Hammett's *The Thin Man* has the slightest influence on the sale of the book. It takes more than that to make a best seller these days. Twenty thousand people don't buy a book within three weeks just to read a five-word question."

Some critics found *The Thin Man* disappointing. "Instead of following his literary problem where it was leading him," David Bazelon wrote, "he preferred to follow his new-found Hollywoodism down whatever paths of pleasure it might take him. He postponed the attempt to resolve those problems which life had presented him."

Dashiell Hammett's literary problem can be divided into two parts. The first, concerning the relations between men and women, he was able to solve. It is the second that he has been accused of ignoring. This part of the problem is based on the fact that from the start, Hammett presented a reality different from what was found in previous criminal fiction.

"Hammett was the first American writer to use the detective story for the purposes of a major novelist," Ross Macdonald has said, "to present a vision, blazing of disenchantment, of our lives. Sam Spade was the product and reflection of a mind that was not at home in Zion or Zenith."

Judged by Christianity and its interpretation of reality, Hammett's world, and the characters in it, was corrupt. For his world to be identified otherwise required something very different from the concept of man as fallen angel.

Such an alternative Hammett could not provide. The size of his talent is suggested by the size of the problem for which he had no answer.

———

Dashiell Hammett was born May 27, 1894, on a farm in St. Marys County, Maryland. He died January 10, 1961, in New York, a victim of emphysema. For much of his life he played the dapper man-about-town, but inside he was as tough, and as extraordinary, as any of the characters in his stories.

One night when he and Lillian Hellman were drinking and she was striding around making angry noises, he ground the lighted end of a burning cigarette into his cheek. She, flabbergasted, asked what he was doing.

"Keeping myself from doing it to you," he replied.

A newspaper woman described him as "a fiction writer's version of a hard-boiled dream prince."

He had delicacy, was the opposite of a slob, but he was also tough, a roughneck with brilliance.

Lillian Hellman called him "a remarkably handsome man" with a "clear eyed, aristocratic face." She remembered the "proudness" of his bearing. His wife's first impressions of him included the fact that, "He always dressed beautifully and the area where he slept was very neat." Raymond Chandler, who met Hammett only once, remembered him as "very nice looking, tall, quiet . . . [with a] fearful capacity for Scotch, seemed quite unspoiled to me."

He was tall, over six feet, and thin, about one hundred and thirty-five pounds. His hair was prematurely white, his eyebrows black and thick, his mustache black and dapper. He was a dramatic figure, knew it, and posed for book-jacket photographs which emphasized that quality. Sartorially, he was not so much a dandy as a dude.

He was a sporting, gambling man who appreciated any sort of fun, including the most innocent kind of masculine clowning around. After the publication of *The Maltese Falcon*, he moved to New York and rented an apartment at 133 East Thirty-Eighth Street. One evening he was visited by *Black Mask* writer Fred Nebel. After a few drinks Nebel offered to make Hammett a bet: that even though the night was warm and dry, the sky cloudless and filled with stars, he and Hammett could walk along the streets under an umbrella without any New Yorker's taking notice.

Hammett accepted and provided the umbrella. Huddled beneath it, the two writers walked from Thirty-Eighth Street to Forty-Second, then entered the Oyster Bar at Grand Central Station, where they instructed the checkroom girl that the umbrella must be left open to dry. After dinner they retrieved the umbrella and, huddled beneath it, returned to Hammett's.

Nebel spent the night on the living-room couch. When he awoke in the morning he found, on the floor beside his shoes, a copy of *The Maltese Falcon*. It was inscribed, "To Fred Nebel, in memory of the night of the cloudburst when we were companions under the umbrella."[6]

As William F. Nolan has pointed out, Hammett never thought of himself as a Great Writer, a Man of Literature. He saw himself as a writer working in what was still a primitive field.

Partway through *The Maltese Falcon,* he told his editor he thought he had an opportunity to do something special. He succeeded. In doing so, he pushed hard-boiled criminal fiction up to the level of the superior novel. In the nearly half a century that has passed since then, his effort has rarely been approached and never beaten.

After *The Thin Man,* Hammett had done it all, everything he could possibly do as a novelist. Then, as Nolan has said, he "shifted gears" and for the rest of his professional career worked in films, radio, and syndicated newspaper comic strips. Since he could only create within a framework of violence, his situations and problems always dealt with crime.

Being a writer in Hollywood was a much better job than being a private detective.

Sometimes he had to work on a script for as long as thirty-six hours at a stretch, but otherwise the hours were a great improvement. Also, there was no physical danger. Then there was the pay.

The Pinkertons had paid him, part of the time, $105 a month. *Black Mask* paid $25 or so a story, and he had to support himself by daylighting at the jewelry store. At the studios there had been talk, in the beginning, of $300 a week, but he had demonstrated his value and things had improved. One report said Dashiell Hammett was making $1,500 a week. Another placed his annual earnings at $100,000.

Most of the time studio bosses would not allow him—this specialist in the bleak ending—to tell the whole story. He is credited with only one original screenplay and six original screen stories. No one will ever know how many movies he actually worked on. He was a problem solver, a patch man called in to improve a script, often when it was before the camera. He usually worked at night, and his name was seldom on the credits.

Better hours, no danger, and more money made up only a portion of the advantages of being a screenwriter. Hollywood was an amusing place. Some people thought the motion picture was a new art form, but in California the movies were controlled by a gang of junk dealers and glove salesmen from the East who had lucked into the nickelodeon, then carried their cameras west to the land of sunshine. The big idea was fun and money.

"Most of the important people got drunk after one o'clock, sobered up around three-thirty and got drunk again at nine," Ben Hecht wrote of Hollywood in the thirties. "Fist fights began about eleven. Seduction had no stated hours, and the skimpy offices shook with passion. The mingled sounds of plotting and sexual moans came through the transoms."

In this environment the lunatic proceedings of the early years were visible in the product. Gigantic egos were the norm, and few producers could resist the opportunity to improve a writer's script.

For $8,500, Warner Brothers had purchased all rights to *The Maltese Falcon*. The first version, retitled *Dangerous Female*, came out in 1931. Ricardo Cortez played Spade, Bebe Daniels was Brigid, and the director saw it as semicomedy. At the box office it fizzled.

In 1936 Warner Brothers tried it again. This time the production was even more mindless. *Satan Met a Lady* was the title, and the stars were Warren William and Bette Davis. Spade's name was changed to Ted Shayne, Gutman's role was played by a woman, Allison Skipworth, and the black bird was replaced by a jeweled french horn. It laid an egg.

In 1941, with John Huston batting for them, Warner Brothers knocked one over the fence. Except for the omission of a few scenes, Huston's classic version of *The Maltese Falcon* was a direct transcription of the book, and retained almost all of Hammett's great dialogue.

———

If you were lucky, or if you were talented, it was easy to make money in films, and even easier to spend it. Hammett was not only talented, he was a man who had been very ill; that he was alive at all was a miracle.

For these and other reasons, Hammett lived recklessly, behaving "as if he wasn't going to live past Thursday week," one friend said.

In a short story, "The Main Death," Hammett had written of a character, "He drank, he gambled, he loved, he spent—dear God how he spent. He was, in this drinking and gaming and living and spending a most promiscuous fellow."

He had been describing the life that he led himself, when he got a chance; the life that he would perfect once he got into the chips. "Hammett devoured money," William Nolan once said. "He ate it like lettuce."

For a time he had a suite at the Beverly-Wilshire. A Filipino butlered and Hammett lounged around in gorgeous dressing gowns. Later he and Lillian Hellman rented the Harold Lloyd mansion. It had forty-four rooms and had been built at a cost of $2,000,000. One night she, in a tantrum, destroyed the soda fountain.

At the racetracks Hammett was a regular. Another screenwriter reported, "Dash was a compulsive gambler who wasted a good deal of the money he earned from the studios."

A starlet named Elise de Viane charged that he had lured her to his apartment and attempted to seduce her. The jury awarded her $2,500.

"I think Hammett was the only person I ever met who really didn't care about money," Lillian Hellman once said.

In *An Unfinished Woman* she told a story about Hammett and a Hollywood street character of the thirties, an American Indian who made a living hawking postcards around Hollywood Boulevard and, on the nights of the great premieres, showed up in top hat and tails.

One night when she and Hammett were dining at the Brown Derby, the Indian slipped in and sat down beside Hammett. He said, Miss Hellman reported, " 'My grandfather was chief of the Sioux, my great-grandfather was killed by . . .'

" 'How much do you want?' Hammett asked.

" 'Nothing as a gift from you. You once told me you arrested an Indian for murder . . . '

"Hammett put his wallet on the table and said, 'Take it any way you want, but don't tell me what you think.'

"The Indian opened the wallet . . . and took out five twenty dollar bills. 'Be sure I do not take it as a gift. I take it as a loan. You are better than most, but you . . . '

"Hammett said wearily, 'Arrested an Indian for murder. That's right.'

"The Indian said, 'And thus it is impossible for me . . . '

" 'Sure, sure!' Hammett said. 'Mail it to me someday.'

"The Indian bowed . . . and was gone.

"I said, 'He's proud, isn't he?'

"Hammett said, 'No. He's a Negro pretending to be an Indian. He's a no good stinker.'

"I said, 'Then why did you give him the money?'

" 'Because no good stinkers get hungry too.' "

———

And it was this man, working in this place, who was gradually becoming involved politically. As a writer he had offered no solution; but as a man, eventually, he did.

For Hammett the problem, it seems, was corruption. How was society to become less corrupt?

"I am fairly sure that Hammett joined the Communist Party in 1937 or 1938," Lillian Hellman wrote in *Scoundrel Time.*

Except that the process occurred during an enormous worldwide depression, while he was employed in a dream factory that manufactured fancies for fugitives from reality, very little is known about the circumstances of Hammett's becoming politically radical.

Lillian Hellman believes the seed was planted years earlier, when Hammett was still a Pinkerton operative and an executive of the Anaconda Copper Company offered him $5,000 to kill a labor-union organizer named Frank Little.*

*Frank Little was known as the "hobo agitator." He was part Indian and had lost one eye. He came to Butte, Montana, late in July, 1917, and began making antiwar speeches to the miners. In the middle of the night he was seized by vigilantes and hanged from a railroad trestle outside Butte.

Hammett did not talk much about the past, Lillian Hellman has testified, but he often referred to the bribe offer, so often, in fact, that she regards it as a key to his life. "I think I can date Hammett's belief that he was living in a corrupt society from Little's murder," she wrote in *Scoundrel Time.*

In 1947 his affiliation began to catch up with him. In New York an organization known as the Civil Rights Congress had been developed as a more aggressive version of the American Civil Liberties Union. Hammett allowed its founders to list his name on its letterhead. He also became one of the three trustees of its bail-bond fund.

In 1951 the Attorney General designated the Civil Rights Congress a Communist front. Four of its officers jumped bail and vanished. In July, in New York, Hammett was asked to identify the people who had contributed to the bail fund. He refused.

The fact was, apparently, that Hammett did not know who the contributors were; but this was not the point.

On the evening before he was to testify, Lillian Hellman begged him to say, in court, that he did not have any names to give.

"I hate this damn kind of talk," he replied, then advised her that he would give his life "for what I think democracy is, and I don't let cops or judges tell me what democracy is."

He was sentenced to six months, allowed no bail, then handcuffed and taken to the West Street prison.

Sometime during the next few days, while he was waiting to be passed on to a federal penitentiary, a brief but interesting incident occurred, in which Hammett appears as a man of action facing the dangers that he had fictionalized earlier. He told Lillian Hellman about it later and she reported it in *Scoundrel Time.*

The scene of the drama was the area around the ping-pong table on the roof of the West Street jail. The characters were two sets of doubles partners, the first being Hammett and V. J. Jerome, the leading theoretician of the American Communist Party; and the second, two hardened criminals, a bank robber and a man accused of murder.

The trouble began when Jerome protested that his shot, called bad by the murderer, was really good. Hammett said it was foolish to expect criminals to be honest, and the socialist theorist replied that he believed in the potential reform of all men.

After the game had begun again, things went well for a few rallies, but then Jerome again protested that the murderer was cheating. The murderer threw down his paddle, pulled out a knife, and started toward Jerome.

"Hammett said, 'Mr. Jerome wishes to apologize,' " Lillian Hellman wrote.

"Jerome said, 'I do not wish to apologize. You should be ashamed of yourself for cheating a jailed comrade. You must learn—' "

As the murderer threw the knife, Hammett pushed Jerome out of the way "and held on to the murderer with repeated apologies that hinted Jerome wasn't all there in the head. Peace was restored when Hammett made Jerome buy the knifethrower two packs of cigarettes and take an oath not to play ping-pong again."

———

He did his time in the Federal Penitentiary in West Virginia and the Federal Correctional Institute near Ashland, Kentucky. He was released December 11, 1951.

Waiting for the plane for New York, he met a moonshiner who had also done time. The man was out of a job and broke. Hammett gave him all he had, which left him unable to eat on the plane.

In April 1952 he was called before Senator Joseph McCarthy, then investigating Communists. When asked if he was then or had ever been a member of the Communist party, Hammett took the Fifth Amendment.

"Mr. Hammett," Senator McCarthy asked later, "if you were spending as we are, over a hundred million dollars a year on an information program allegedly for the purpose of fighting communism, would you allow your shelves to bear the work of some seventy-five communist authors, in effect placing our official stamp of approval upon these books?"

"Well, I think—if I were you, Senator—I would not allow any libraries," Hammett replied.

This interrogation was televised and Hammett used part of

his screen time to communicate with Lillian Hellman.

"Dash had an . . . irritating habit of shrugging," she told an interviewer. "For years I would say, 'Please don't shrug.' " Before the McCarthy committee Hammett was "shrugging his shoulders like mad." When he phoned her later, he said, "Hey, how did you like it? I was shrugging my shoulders just for you."

————

Dashiell Hammett's formal education ended when he dropped out at the end of his first year of high school and became a messenger boy. From then on his effort to educate himself gradually led him to read widely about offbeat subjects.

In *Tulip*, his final, uncompleted manuscript, he described a character as having "a lot of what seemed to be accurate information and original ideas on any subject that happened to come up, as long as it was a little out of the ordinary." That was Hammett on Hammett.

By nature Dashiell Hammett was a democrat. He sympathized with the common man. In two wars he was not an officer but an enlisted man. Sergeant Hammett in World War I, Corporal Hammett in World War II. He seems to have enjoyed his associations as an enlisted man.

Like most Southerners, he was easy in the woods and a good shot, but his favorite sport was baseball, America's most democratic game.

In his later years, after he had given up alcohol, when he wasn't listening to baseball, or hunting, or working on the manuscript of *Tulip*, he read.

"Dash read like most people eat," a friend remarked. "He chewed up all kinds of books."

Lillian Hellman has reported that Hammett was an addict of books with titles like *Bees: Their Vision and Language* or *German Gunmakers of the Eighteenth Century*. He spent a year studying the retina of the eye. He became an expert on matters like how to play chess in your head, and the history of the snapping turtle. The Icelandic sagas absorbed his attention for a considerable period, as did plasma physics, the cross-pollination of corn, and tying knots.

Hammett once said that the private detectives he knew were very different from Sherlock Holmes, but he himself, it appears, had much in common with the great Englishman. Both sleuths were exceptionally curious, and both feared boredom.

The reading expeditions of his later years can easily be regarded as Holmesian episodes: "The Adventure of the Snapping Turtle," "The Adventure of the Icelandic Sagas," "The Adventure of the Eye's Retina." They removed Hammett from the commonplaces of existence and pulled him toward what Holmes once called "something transcendentally stimulating and clarifying."

In these intellectual investigations, made in the last years of his life, Hammett dropped all political affiliation, surmounted ill health, and returned to his role of the generous but street-wise ex-shamus who was not deceived by dark-skinned Hollywood characters who claimed descent from Indian chiefs.

During these years his greatest intellectual love was mathematics.

In *Tulip* he wrote, "I got to thinking about the notion of an expanding universe being only an attempt to bootleg infinity again, and of what rearrangements would be necessary in mathematics if one, the unit, the single item, were not considered a number at all, except perhaps as a convenience in calculating. And presently I was pretty sleepy and put out the light and went to sleep."

— A Note on — PAT GARRETT

COPS AS PROBLEM SOLVERS are rare in American fiction. Yet many exceptional men have worn the badge. In tribute to them, a sketch of an American lawman seems desirable.

Pat Garrett is an easy choice. Literary critics have noted a connection between frontier characters such as Natty Bumppo and urban sleuths like Sam Spade. In the flesh, Pat is blood brother to each. In addition, he provides a change of scene.

"The P.I. is invariably an urban character," George V. Higgins wrote; "the only time you find him in the woods is when he goes out from the City, into the Woods, to chase somebody else who has escaped from the City."

With Pat this ritual changes.

———

From 1901 through most of 1905 the United States Collector of Customs in El Paso, Texas, was a sporting, gambling man named Pat Garrett, "an important figure in barroom circles," one historian wrote. "There was no getting around the fact that Pat was more at home among the sporting element."

Pat drank, played poker, bet on the horses, and did not object to shady characters. When just about every man wore a coat of the plainest broadcloth, Pat "wore striped suits."

He was born in 1850 and died in 1908. In those fifty-eight years, the only way he was able to successfully fit himself into ordered society was as a hunter of criminals.

He was a gambler, but an unlucky one.

He was a rancher, but a disinterested one.

He was a husband and father, but imperfect.

He was an administrator, but inefficient.

Only as a man hunter was Pat in his element. "A one man striking force, a fearless individual," he has been called.

He was twenty-seven years old and in Fort Sumner, New Mexico, when the news arrived that Comanches had raided a horse ranch near Roswell. Pat joined the posse that went in pursuit. Many riders, low on food and water, eventually turned back. Pat became the leader of those who remained, and one week later, after he and his men returned to Fort Sumner, the Comanches were dead and the horses recovered.

Pat's courage and perseverance on the trail became a major subject in the Fort Sumner bars, and before long a representative of the largest landowner in New Mexico arrived to talk to him. Pat soon showed up in Roswell, seat of Lincoln County, where a weak sheriff could not handle the problem of rustling.

The situation was so bad that, in the remoter sections of the county, people no longer traveled far except in groups of six or more. Rustlers and outlaws prowled the roads, robbing and killing. Even U. S. Secret Service agents, looking for counterfeiters, demanded armed escorts.

Of the rustlers the most active was Billy the Kid. He was twenty-two, liked to dance and wear a flower in his lapel, and had already killed several men. A reward of $500 was posted for his capture.

Many months earlier, in the saloons and gambling tables at Fort Sumner, Pat Garrett, at six foot five inches, had been known as Big Casino, while his five-foot-seven-inch friend, Billy the Kid, was Little Casino. If either's luck with the cards was bad, the other would stake him. Now, supported by the power structure, Pat became sheriff of Lincoln County. In the bitterest part of the winter, even before his term as sheriff had legally begun, Pat and his posse cornered Billy the Kid at Stinking Springs.

After a shoot-out, Billy surrendered. He was tried for murder and sentenced to be hanged. "Well, Pat's right now a . . . head," he told a reporter. "We used to be friends, as you probably know. He's got senile. He's getting a lot of money for cleaning this area up—of us supposedly. I don't think much of him now."

One morning Billy killed his guards and escaped. A few weeks later Pat learned that Billy was hiding in Fort Sumner. Pat left immediately, found Billy at night, and shot and killed him.*

Pat Garrett had "mild blue eyes and a low pleasant voice, and gives the impression of being too modest and backward to fight even if imposed upon," as one reporter wrote. And a woman recalled, "Despite his crooked mouth and crooked smile which made his whole face seem crooked, he was a remarkably handsome man."

At the end of his term as sheriff, Pat ran for the territorial council, but lost by a few votes. He remained in Lincoln County and bought a ranch, but was never much interested in it. Eventually some ranchers from the Texas panhandle made him a proposition. Rustlers were driving their cattle into New Mexico and selling them with fake bills of sale. It had to be stopped. The Panhandle ranchers offered $5,000 a year and fringe benefits that would let Pat earn close to $10,000 a year. After the ranchers had agreed to support him with a legitimate legal apparatus, he accepted. He insisted on due process of law.

The giant LM ranch then loaned Oldham County, Texas, $25,000 to build a courthouse. After the county's first grand jury had been formed, 159 bills were issued, mostly for stock theft.

For various reasons, as Pat and his men were riding the bleak trails, he gradually began to believe that he had been hired as a mercenary; that he was expected to kill men instead of bringing them to trial. At the end of a year he quit and moved to Uvalde, Texas, to raise racehorses.

"He had taken up with the big men of property and ambition," Frazier Hunt wrote, "but he also wanted to play poker and drink good bourbon and loaf around bar rooms. . . . He was not quite hard enough and self-centered enough for this demanding thing called success . . . handicapped by some futile sense of the easy going and romantic."

*Billy the Kid was never famous in his lifetime. He did not become a legendary figure until 1926 when Walter Noble Burns wrote *The Saga of Billy the Kid,* which was based not on the facts but on the dramatic possibilities of the situation.

Meanwhile, in New Mexico, a situation was developing that would require Pat's talents.

Albert B. Fall and Colonel Albert J. Fountain were the two most prominent lawyers in the New Mexico territory.

Fall was a Southerner, the son of a Confederate officer, and a Democrat.* Fountain was a Northerner, the son of a Union officer, and a Republican. His wife was Mexican, and he was interested in the problems of Mexican-Americans.

By the time Fall arrived in New Mexico, Fountain was well established. Fall's situation did not begin to improve until he allied himself with Oliver M. Lee, a rancher and reputed gunman who took what he wanted and employed men like himself.

In the first two days of the three-day election of 1892, Fall and his Democrats did well. The Republicans responded by calling out the militia to guard the polls. These troops, mostly Mexicans, were known as "Fountain's greasers." Fall then sent for Lee and his fighting men.

"Lee's riders filtered into town all night long," Leon C. Metz wrote in *Pat Garrett,* the definitive biography, "and by morning had taken up positions on the Las Cruces rooftops. When the militia men marched up the street . . . Fall stepped into the road . . . and yelled to its leader, 'Get the hell out of here with that damned militia or I will have you all killed!' "†

The Democrats won the election.

———

Oliver Lee had begun by struggling against the New Mexican cattle barons. There were rumors that he was a rustler.‡ Rustlers did not move in on him until 1893. Lee killed two and pleaded self-defense.

In 1894 twenty-one New Mexico cattle barons, among them

———

*Albert B. Fall eventually became Secretary of the Interior in President Harding's cabinet. He was a leading figure, and chief victim, in the Teapot Dome scandal.

†This quotation and the one on page 147 are from *Pat Garrett: The Story of a Western Lawman,* by Leon C. Metz. Copyright 1974 by the University of Oklahoma Press.

‡"The average cattleman was honest, according to his ethical standards," Southwestern historian C. L. Sonnichsen quoted an oldtimer as saying in *Tularosa.* "He wouldn't . . . take from a little cattleman . . . but the big herds were legitimate prey. . . . The men were sometimes pretty hard customers, and you had to do pretty much as they did or you found yourself an outsider."

Oliver Lee, formed an association to stop rustling. The association's lawyer, in full charge, was Colonel Fountain. Concentrating on Lee, he slowly developed evidence that established one bona fide case of cattle theft. Then he wrote to the associations' members and accused Lee and his men of rustling hundreds of head of cattle.

Lee and Fall were not passive men. They were tough, courageous, and mean. In January, 1896, Fountain left his ranch and journeyed to court to secure the needed indictments. After he had presented his evidence and testimony, the court handed down thirty-two indictments, one of which charged Lee and an employee with rustling.

On January 30, Colonel Fountain and his nine-year-old son departed for the ranch. They never arrived. The press was upset. The fate of the Fountains, it was argued, was evidence of the lack of law and order in the territory. Unless the Fountain mystery was cleared up, statehood might be postponed. Rewards totaling $12,-000 were offered.

In February the governor went to El Paso to confer with Pat and was soon joined by a committee of prominent New Mexicans who offered Pat an "opportunity to make money, and a chance to get the sheriff's office of Dona Ana County," Pat wrote his wife; "they would pay my expenses of $150 a month and $8,000 in case I succeed in arresting and convicting the murderers."

Pat accepted and moved to Las Cruces, the county seat of Dona Ana County. At the same time the governor, knowing that Pat was not a professional sleuth, wired James McParlan (of Molly Maguire fame), manager of the Pinkerton office in Denver, to assign several operatives to help Pat.

The Pinkerton men—team players—wanted to have indictments sworn out for the arrest of Lee and three of his men. They considered arresting Fall as an accomplice. Pat—a loner, and on occasions a grouchy and sarcastic man, disagreed. He argued that they did not have enough evidence for a conviction.

In May the Pinkertons withdrew. As they did so, they acknowledged that Pat was the only man around with the guts to swear out warrants against Lee's gang, the only man courageous enough to go to Lee's ranch and make arrests. But there was no solid evidence against Lee and his men, and for the rest of 1896, all of 1897, and into the following year, there was not much that Pat could do except, as one commentator put it, "remain taciturn and moody."

In 1898 a new governor prodded him to act. There were rumors that he was going to seek indictments. One day, when Pat was riding the rounds, notifying prospective jurors about the new grand jury, he walked through the back door of a saloon and found Lee, Fall, and others playing poker. Pat took a hand and the game, which had been a modest one, turned into "a contest of grit, nerve, and endurance between two pistol-packing gladiators," as one historian put it. Seventy hours later one player brought up the subject of the grand jury. He said he guessed that someone at the table might need a lawyer before long, and that the lawyer he would hire was also at the table.

Lee took it from there. "Mr. Sheriff, if you wish to serve any papers on me, I will be here or at the ranch."

Pat replied, "All right, Mr. Lee. If any papers are to be served on you, I will mail them to you."

The game soon broke up peacefully.

On April 1 the grand jury met and adjourned. Since there was no mention of Lee or the Fountains, Lee left for El Paso. The next day, with everyone relaxed, Pat went before the judge and requested bench warrants for the arrest of Lee and four of his cowboys. His deposition promised to prove that these were the men who "murdered Colonel Albert J. Fountain and his son."

On the following day he went out to Lee's ranch and arrested and brought in two cowboys. When Lee returned Pat made no attempt to arrest him. Pat was gambling that one of the cowboys might talk in exchange for his freedom.

Meanwhile, the Spanish-American War was being fought, and Fall was in an army camp in New Jersey. When he returned he was confronted by an imposing problem. His most important ally, Oliver Lee, had vanished and was now a fugitive. Fall's solution was brilliant. Aided by the governor, Otero, and another politician who wanted to establish a new county elsewhere in New Mexico, he succeeded in splitting Dona Ana County in two, and creating an entirely new county, Otero County, in which Pat had no authority. The new county became a Lee stronghold.

On May 25, 1899, in Shasta County, Lee and his men were tried for murder. Their heavily armed friends escorted them to and from the courtroom, a number of prosecution witnesses forgot to show up, and the jury needed only eight minutes to reach its decision—Not Guilty.

Pat continued as sheriff of Dona Ana County until he was almost fifty years old. In 1902, tired of riding the back trails, he did not seek reelection.

President Theodore Roosevelt then appointed him Collector of Customs in El Paso. Three years later, when Roosevelt came to Texas, Pat's amiability got the best of him. He went to San Antonio to see Roosevelt and brought along a friend, a professional gambler, whom he introduced to the president as a cattleman. A group photograph then appeared in southwestern newspapers. In it the gambler was identified correctly. The embarrassed Roosevelt did not reappoint Pat to the customs job.

From then on Pat was in trouble. Things became so bad that a grocer refused him credit and entered him in the dead-beat book over a matter of ten dollars. Pat's drinking increased and he became quarrelsome. He returned to El Paso, sold real estate, and lived with a woman most people regarded as a whore.

Meanwhile, his son had leased part of Pat's ranch to Wayne Brazel and A. P. "Print" Rhode. It was then learned that they intended to use the land to raise goats on.

Like most ranchers, Pat scorned goats. When he heard what had happened he rushed back from El Paso and swore out a complaint. The trial took place in a butcher shop where Print Rhode repeatedly challenged Pat to a fistfight. After one day it was recessed.

On February 29, 1908, Pat and another man left for Las Cruces in a buggy. On the way they paused to urinate. Pat stepped down, walked around to the rear of the buggy, and, as Leon C. Metz wrote, "removed his left glove, and unbuttoned his trousers. That was the old former manhunter's position when a bullet slammed into the back of his head."

— ERIC AMBLER —

Isn't all research private-eye work, Doctor? Isn't an
inquiry into the possible relationship between virus
infections and cancer a detective process? . . . Isn't
every judgement made on a basis of information
received in its essence a form of assessment?
                                                    Dr. Frigo

I

ERIC AMBLER APPEARS to be a very private man, and to enjoy
being so.

He has published more than a million words, yet it is doubtful
that, reviews excepted, twenty thousand words have been written
about him. And although he was for many years a highly paid
screenwriter in London and California, his name is rarely mentioned in the memoirs of film luminaries.

Yet among friends he seems to be sociable, even gregarious.
Oscar Levant wrote, "Every time I see Eric, I am given a full
treatise on his opinions."

A lady in California remembered him as "very handsome and
very polite."

In *The Dangerous Edge* Gavin Lambert wrote of him, "The
neat, alert young man in the shabby Paris bar . . . has become a
scholarly figure. . . . Wary and spectacled, his eyes suggest that
the longer you study appearances the more deeply you distrust
them."

In 1975 he was interviewed by an American scholar, Joel Hopkins, who called at his home in Switzerland. The result, published in the *Journal of Popular Culture,* contains the only detailed account available of the Old Master in residence.

"Spacious . . . comfortably and tastefully furnished," Hopkins said of Ambler's apartment. "The walls are decorated with 19th century lithographs and oils by a contemporary Japanese action painter. Bookcases there are, but they do not dominate. The impression given is of a man with many interests and impeccable tastes."

And of Ambler himself Hopkins wrote that "one is impressed by his gracious and civilized manner. . . . His suit is well tailored, the knot in his tie is slightly askew, and his 'footwear' has that look of quality which comes from good care and buying at the right London shops . . . his overall appearance is somewhere between an Oxford don and a successful banker—not too tweedy and not too stuffy."[1]

He has no series hero, and no sleuth. There is, moreover, nothing exceptional about his interest in the character of the people he creates. It is the character of the world these people live in that preoccupies Ambler. It is an involvement that began when he was twelve years old and a student of Sherlock Holmes. Fifty-three years later, in his introduction to a special edition of *The Adventures of Sherlock Holmes,* he defined the great sleuth's role in his education.

"Holmes is not only a great detective, but also an aphorism dropper," Ambler wrote, who "turns usually for the apt comment, the summing up, to French or German writers."

Because the sources of most of Holmes's French aphorisms were not identified, young Ambler, whose great desire was to be an educated man, went to the public library to find them.

"It was valuable exercise," he recalled. It "taught me a lot about using certain books of reference."

But Holmes also influenced Ambler in larger ways. When the great sleuth advised Watson to read Winwood Reade's *The Martyrdom of Man,* Watson declined but Ambler was eager, although certain doors had to be unlocked before he could do so.

The Martyrdom of Man turned out to be among the books kept in a locked case in the librarian's office. Days passed before Ambler was permitted to read it.

An anti-Christian manifesto, it delighted Ambler. He had been taken to church since before he could toddle, and the entire proceeding bored him.

Now, "here at last, was a book by an articulate . . . educated writer, which proclaimed, with a wealth of . . . evidence and . . . argument . . . that the whole thing was, and always had been, an elaborate hoax. . . . After the first excitement of recognizing . . . a kindred spirit had worn off . . . I became more interested in the paths by which he had arrived at them than in the speculations themselves. Before long I had begun an exploration of social history which still continues.

"I remain grateful to Holmes."

Eric Ambler was born June 28, 1909, in Salford, a grimy, smelly manufacturing city next to Manchester. His parents were music-hall performers.

In his adolescence he was precocious in more than one way. "Burglary has always been an alternative profession," Holmes said, and Ambler picked up on that one too. "I was a juvenile delinquent," he has acknowledged. "We used to steal cars and such."

Formally, his education began in London at Colfe's Grammar School, which was not Eton or Winchester, and it continued at Northampton Polytechnic, a branch of London University, which was not Oxford or Cambridge. When he dropped out of the polytechnic at the end of his second year, his commitment to the status quo was nil.

Twelve years earlier, in the Somme offensive of World War I, the Allied armies had required three months to advance three miles. During that advance, England alone had lost 500,000 men. "The effect of the Somme," Martin Green has noted, "was something too profound to be satisfied by a substitution of one man for another as prime minister." London seethed with new social solutions, and Eric Ambler was engaged.

"I was ready for the barricades," he said years later. "Anything anti-Fascist, I was on its side. I was a *very* far left wing socialist. I thought this was the light and if only I could get clued-up on dialectical materialism I could go far."

A radical at night, he served capitalism by day, being, in his mid-twenties, vice president and general manager of an advertising agency. He had failed, meanwhile, as an apprentice engineer, as a song writer, and as a playwright; and he was still hunting for a field that he could improve by changing.

Finally he decided to try writing thrillers. "The detective story genre had been worked over and worked over," he has since explained, "but no one had looked at the thriller. It was still a dirty word."

In those days the thriller, the adventurous spy tale, the novel of intrigue, was still infected by the right-wing point of view imposed by "the war to end war." One Englishman equaled a dozen foreigners, and Good perpetually defeated Evil. Good was an English public-school type who killed cads and diced with death. Evil was foreign, a dirty dago, a dreadful wog.

"I set out to change the genre," Ambler explained in 1974. "I remember reading the accepted masters . . . Sapper and the rest —and deciding they wouldn't do. There was a Bulldog Drummond story, 'The Black Gang,' in which the heroes dressed in black shirts and went around beating up Bolsheviks and Jews, all with the general approval of the author. I decided to turn things around."

Innovation number one was "nice" Communist spies. They turned up regularly in his first three books, guiding, enlightening, and rescuing the hero.

Ambler also borrowed and modified certain concepts developed by John Buchan, an Establishment figure—he would eventually become Governor-General of Canada—who was a famous writer of thrillers.

The first thing he borrowed was the idea, maintained by some of Buchan's heroes, that the world was manipulated by a huge conspiracy. "Away behind all the Governments and the armies,"

Buchan wrote in *The Thirty-Nine Steps,* "was a big subterranean movement going on, engineered by very dangerous people." And in *The Power House* Buchan declared, "Civilization is a conspiracy" and "modern life is the silent compact of the comfortable to keep up pretenses."

Accepting such opinions, Ambler moved on. As a far-out leftist, he had a natural target—Big Business. Eric Ambler was the first thriller writer to attack capitalism.

"It was the power of Business, not the deliberations of statesmen, that shaped the destinies of nations," Ambler wrote in his second book, *Background to Danger.* "Rome might declare herself sympathetic to a Hapsburg restoration; France might oppose it. A few months later the situation might be completely reversed. For those few members of the public who had long memories and were not sick to death of the whole incomprehensible farce there were always explanations of the *volte face,* many explanations—but not the correct one. For that one might have to inquire into banking transactions in London, Paris, and New York. . . . One would have to grope through the fog of technical mumbo-jumbo with which international business surrounds its operations and examine them in all their essential and ghastly simplicity. . . . The Big Business man was only one player in the game of international politics, but he was the player who made all the rules."

Graham Greene has pointed out that John Buchan was "the first to realize the enormous dramatic value of adventure in familiar surroundings happening to unadventurous men." The Buchan hero was an innocent, an "honest soul" involved in desperate matters through no fault of his own. He was unadventurous and unaware, a well-connected outdoor type with no political sophistication.

This sort of unheroic figure Ambler appropriated and inserted into the world of commerce. One result is that in Ambler's books, the subject is always the same: the plight of the citizen swept into large events at a time when others are solving problems.

The major difference between the world of Ambler and the

worlds of Doyle, Simenon, and Hammett is major indeed. In most of Ambler's books the problem solvers are the bad guys.

In 1937 the success of his first two thrillers allowed Ambler to set up as a professional novelist. He moved to Paris, lived on fifteen dollars a week, read Nietzsche, and as he has since observed, started to become "less of an innocent."

Gavin Lambert wrote of Ambler then, "The young Englishman often seen at some shabby Paris bar in the early hours of the morning looks neat and quiet, almost dapper. People comment on his resemblance to the Duke of Windsor."

In 1939 Ambler published the novel which many consider his masterpiece. Its title in England was *The Mask of Dimitrios;* in America, *A Coffin for Dimitrios.* Its central character, Dimitrios Makropoulos, is the first, and most primitive, of that remarkable series of problem-solving criminals that Ambler has imagined and brought alive.

An acquaintance of Dimitrios once observed that "most of us go through life without knowing what we want out of it. But Dimitrios, you know, was not like that. Dimitrios knew exactly what he wanted. He wanted money and he wanted power. Just those two things, as much of them as he could get."

But this was not always so. As Dimitrios's story begins he is approximately thirty-two years old, a Greek who works as a fig packer in Smyrna, a seaport, now known as Izmir, in western Turkey. He is a quiet man, not especially strong, whom some men fear. "He was hated by many for his violence," Ambler wrote.

At the time Christian Greece and Moslem Turkey are at war. The drama of Dimitrios begins when Turkish troops capture Smyrna and massacre its Armenian residents. The next day the Turks attack everyone who is not Moslem. By September 15, 1922, over 120,000 people have been murdered, and Dimitrios has taken refuge in the house of a Moslem named Dhris Mohammed.

Disguising himself as a Turk, Dimitrios prowls through the city. He learns that Greek ships are lying off the coast.

Their captains will take aboard anyone who can pay.*

Dimitrios knows of a moneylender, a Jew turned Moslem, who keeps money under his floor. He invites Dhris Mohammed to join him in robbing the moneylender. Two men are required, Dimitrios says—one to hold the victim, one to search for the money.

A few days later, the moneylender is found dead; his throat has been slit. His relatives soon call the authorities' attention to Dhris Mohammed, who, spending easily in cafés, is boasting that the moneylender, Sholem, gave him a loan without interest.

Dhris is arrested and charged with murder. At his trial he says Dimitrios killed the moneylender. "I could see that he had meant from the first to kill Sholem. Why then had he brought me? He could have found the money for himself after he killed the Jew. But we divided equally and he smiled and did not try to kill me. . . . He knew that when my purse becomes full my head becomes empty."

The authorities do not believe Dhris and he is executed.

———

In Greece Dimitrios pulls off another robbery, is charged with attempted murder, and escapes to Bulgaria. In Sofia he takes a room in a cheap hotel and soon falls behind in the rent.

A prostitute named Irana lives in the next room. He tracks some of her clients to their offices, identifies them, then propositions Irana. He can get her more money than she is accustomed to, he tells her. To prove his point, he says he can get her 5,000 leva and will give her half.

"He told me to write a note that he would dictate," Irana explained years later. "It was addressed to a man whose name I had never heard of and it simply asked for 5,000 leva. I thought he must be mad and to get rid of him I wrote the note and signed it."

The next day Dimitrios hands her 2,500 leva and she, reluctantly, accepts him as her pimp. Dimitrios, now expensively

*In real life this included Aristotle Onassis, then fifteen years old. With the help of the American vice consul, he escaped in the uniform of an ordinary American sailor.

dressed, begins to frequent Sofia's political cafés. Cold-blooded and resourceful, he has solved the fundamental problem of staying alive. But he has not been able to put his abilities at the service of anything larger than himself, anything that might offer respectability.

This situation changes when he comes to the attention of A. Vazoff, a Sofia lawyer who is a director of the Eurasian Credit Trust. One result is that Dimitrios is frequently absent from Sofia.

"One morning he came to me in great agitation," Irana recalled. "I had never seen him so nervous. He took me by the wrists and said that if anyone asked me I must say that he had been with me for the last three days. I had not seen him for over a week but I had to agree."

That afternoon Irana reads a news story about an attempt to assassinate the premier of Bulgaria. Dimitrios soon disappears from Sofia, but his association with the Eurasian Credit Trust continues. In 1924 he plots to assassinate the premier of Turkey. When the scheme is discovered before the attempt is made, Dimitrios vanishes.

By 1928 he is in France, an important figure in white slavery. He uses his own money and funds supplied by others. "He represented certain very rich men," an associate said.

A year later Dimitrios abandons white slavery and gets into heroin. His contact with the suppliers is Vazoff, the Sofia lawyer, and he finances his purchases with drafts on the Eurasian Credit Trust.

To push the heroin, he hires six men and one woman. Years later one of the men in the gang, Petersen, reminisces about Dimitrios as leader. "Dimitrios dominated us because he knew precisely what he wanted and precisely how to get it with the least possible trouble and at the lowest possible price. He knew how to find people to work for him, too, and when he found them, how to handle them."

As a meeting place for the gang, Dimitrios purchases, in Petersen's name, three long-unoccupied and windowless buildings clustered at the end of an impasse near the rue de Rennes. The floors of the meeting rooms are covered with cheap Moroccan rugs.

Through all of 1929 and 1930 Dimitrios continues in the heroin business. His control over his gang is so tight that only one member, a Dutchman named Visser, knows anything about Dimitrios's personal life, and all Visser knows is that Dimitrios is now wealthy, calls himself Rougemont, and has a chic countess for a friend.

In 1931 Dimitrios gets out of heroin. Among other things, he has acquired the habit himself. He liquidates his assets, mails to the police a dossier on each member of the gang, then enters a private clinic. The gang is arrested, but the sentences are short. Visser, the only one who can finger Dimitrios, does not.

After taking the cure Dimitrios goes to Rome, purchases citizenship in a South American republic, and legally becomes Señor C. K.

———

By 1937 the one-time fig packer, Señor C. K.—murderer, pimp, possible assassin, spy, white slaver, drug dealer—is on the board of directors of the Eurasian Credit Trust. Because the trust is registered in Monaco, it is not required to open its details of registration to the public.

That same year Visser locates and begins to blackmail Dimitrios. Dimitrios recognizes that he must be killed. He decides to take care of two problems at once by using Visser's corpse to wipe away any possible consequences of his murder of the money-lender in Smyrna fifteen years earlier.

He first obtains a false French *carte d'identité* in the name of Dimitrios Makropoulos. He then charters a yacht, lulls Visser into a false sense of security, and invites him to join the cruise.

When the yacht reaches Istanbul, Dimitrios arranges for Visser's murder. The corpse, he specifies, is to be dumped into the Bosphorus at a point where the current will take it ashore. He supplies the *carte d'identité,* which is to be sewn into Visser's clothing.

Having arranged a situation, a faked reality that is not too different from the one created by the Russian general in *The Maltese Falcon,* Dimitrios departs by train for Paris.

His downfall now begins.*

Chance is Dimitrios's nemesis, and chance functions through Charles Latimer, a political innocent who is more or less Dimitrios's complete opposite.

Latimer is an English writer who makes a comfortable living turning out mysteries of the murder-at-the-vicarage variety. The world as he knows it is the same sort of world that he reflects in his books. It is a tidy, uncomplicated, genteel place, a "monochrome world," Ambler would call it, of innocence and guilt, right and wrong, good and evil.

At first Latimer has no idea that people like Dimitrios exist. He becomes aware of Dimitrios himself after the discovery of Visser's corpse.

The Turkish police take the *carte d'identité* bearing the name Dimitrios Makropoulos to the French consulate, where it is identified as genuine. The matter is then brought to the attention of the chief of the Turkish secret police, Colonel Haki.

In 1922 Haki had presided at the court that sentenced Dhris Mohammed for the murder of the moneylender. Over the years Haki has remembered that Dhris accused Dimitrios of the murder, and he has acquired considerable knowledge of Dimitrios's activities. But he does not know enough to identify Dimitrios as Rougemont or Señor C. K.

At a party in Istanbul Colonel Haki is pleased to meet Charles Latimer, whose books he enjoys because they have no connection to the sordid reality that he himself encounters regu-

*In *Who's Who in Spy Fiction* Donald McCormick noted that while researching *Peddler of Death,* his biography of Sir Basil Zaharoff, he "was convinced that Eric Ambler must have based some of *The Mask of Dimitrios* on first hand knowledge of Zaharoff's early career. . . . But a letter from Ambler revealed that the story of Dimitrios was thought up on a journey by train across Europe shortly before the war and that there was no connection with the Zaharoff saga."

When another writer, in the throes of becoming a Zaharoff buff, read pp. 39–43 of *Peddler of Death,* his reaction was similar to McCormick's. Ambler was queried, and he replied that Dimitrios was invented from top to toe and in no way linked to Zaharoff, whom he identified as "a rather second rate bogeyman."

The world being as it is, corpses carrying false passports may not be a rarity.

larly. The next day Haki tells Latimer about Dimitrios.

"His kind never risk their skins," Haki says. "They stay on the fringes of the plot. They are the professionals . . . the links between the businessmen, the politicians who desire the end but are afraid of the means, and the fanatics, the idealists who are prepared to die for their convictions. The important thing to know about assassinations . . . is not who fired the shot, but who paid for the bullet."

Latimer, intrigued, asks to see the corpse that has been dragged out of the Bosphorus. Afterward, he decides to investigate Dimitrios and his past.

"My curiosity about Dimitrios was that of a biographer," Latimer wrote. "I saw him . . . as a unit in a disintegrating social system."

Working with information supplied by Haki, Latimer goes to Sofia and interviews people who knew Dimitrios earlier. Then he goes on to Belgrade, where he meets Petersen, one of the members of Dimitrios's heroin gang.

Petersen, who now calls himself Peters, has managed to put aside much of his share of the drug profits. He is now moving about in the world and is also curious about Dimitrios.

Months earlier, Petersen had bumped into Visser, and after a few drinks Visser let slip his information about Dimitrios as Rougemont and Señor C. K. Recently, Petersen had read a news item about the death of Dimitrios. He then checked about in Paris and learned that the real Dimitrios was still alive.

Now he shows Latimer a photograph of Visser, and Latimer identifies him as Dimitrios.

Petersen explains the situation to Latimer, but omits two facts, the present name and address of Dimitrios. He informs Latimer that he intends to blackmail Dimitrios for one million francs and that because Latimer saw Visser's corpse, his cooperation will be essential.

Latimer agrees to help but wants no part of the blackmail money. His income from his writing is satisfactory, and he does not covet other people's money.

Petersen contacts Dimitrios and the three meet in Paris in a seedy hotel room.

Dimitrios agrees to pay the million francs and does so. Petersen and Latimer pick up the money, then retire to the old meeting rooms at the Impasse, which Petersen has purchased under a false name.

Entering the main apartment there, they find Dimitrios waiting behind a gun.

"Poor Dimitrios has no intelligence," Dimitrios says, mockingly. "Even if he finds out from the records that within a month of my coming out of prison, I had succeeded in selling three unsaleable houses. . . . Did you not know, Petersen, that before I bought those houses in your name they had been empty for ten years? You are such a fool."

Dimitrios then shoots and mortally wounds Petersen. As Dimitrios turns to shoot Latimer, Latimer jumps, stumbles on a rug, and Dimitrios's bullet misses him. They struggle, Dimitrios drops his gun, and Latimer recovers it.

The dying Petersen draws his own gun, covers Dimitrios, and tells Latimer to go for the police.

Dimitrios, certain that Petersen will kill him after Latimer goes, offers Latimer two million francs to stay. Latimer refuses and moves toward the door.

"In the end one is always defeated by stupidity," Dimitrios says. "If it is not one's own it is the stupidity of others." He then ups his offer. "Five million, monsieur. Is that not enough or do you want this carrion to kill me?"

As Latimer closes the door and moves down the steps, Petersen fires and Dimitrios dies.

———

The death of Dimitrios does not end the book. The end comes a few days later when Charles Latimer, specifically referred to by Ambler as a producer of pabulum for adolescent minds, and who is hard up for money, begins another of his mystery books. "The garden parties at the vicarage, the clink of tea-cups . . . the sweet smell of grass," Ambler wrote. "That was the sort of thing people liked to hear about. It was the sort of thing that he himself would like to hear about."

Thirty years later Ambler will pick him up again, with interesting results.

———

The difference between the attitudes expressed in *Dimitrios* and those found in earlier thrillers, such as Edgar Wallace's *The Black Gang,* is impressive.

Ambler does not present a world of Good and Evil; Dimitrios is not a villain. He is a criminal, but he is also a victim of circumstances. As a minor character observes at the close of the book, "Special sorts of conditions must exist for the creation of the special sort of criminal he typified. All I know is that while might is right, while chaos and anarchy masquerade as order and enlightenment, those conditions will obtain."

Colonel Haki judges Dimitrios harshly. "A dirty type," he says, "common, cowardly, scum. Murder, espionage, drugs—that is the history."

Petersen feels about the same. "I do not like Dimitrios," he tells Latimer. "Do not misunderstand me, please. I have no moral rectitude. But Dimitrios is a savage beast."

But Ambler himself, neither cop nor criminal, avoids the traditional point of view. Instead, he observes that "it was useless to try to explain him [Dimitrios] in terms of Good and Evil. They were no more than baroque abstractions. Good Business and Bad Business were the elements in the new theology. Dimitrios was not evil. He was logical and consistent; as logical and consistent in the European jungle as the poison gas called Lewisite and the shattered bodies of children killed in the bombardment of an open town."

With Eric Ambler and *Dimitrios,* the thriller, the novel of intrigue, grew up.

———

Dimitrios was immediately identified as the superb novel that it is, a classic of criminal fiction.

In Ambler's earlier books, which he has since described as "cartoons for later books," he cluttered the scene with characters, it was difficult to remember the plot, and his "nice" Communist spies interfered with the action by pausing to deliver long smarten-up lectures to the innocent hero.

But in *Dimitrios* Ambler is in complete control and presents his tale with great style, tossing off aphorisms that would have pleased Holmes. The opening sentence reads, "A Frenchman named Chamfort, who should have known better, once said that chance was a nickname for Providence."

II

FROM 1940 TO 1946 Eric Ambler served in the British army. Enlisting as a private in the artillery, he was discharged a lieutenant colonel.

During much of his service he worked with film. He led a combat filming unit in Italy, became assistant director of army cinematography in the British War Office, and ended up in charge of all training, morale, and educational films for the army.

After his discharge he wrote screenplays for British films. By 1957 his prestige was such that MGM invited him to Hollywood to write the script for the Marlon Brando version of *Mutiny on the Bounty*. For several years Ambler had been living well, but now —the terms were $100,000 down and $3,000 a week.

But by 1950, an Eric Ambler novel had not appeared in a decade. The world was changing politically, and so was Ambler. Eventually, he told Clive James, "When you cleared the Nazis away, all those other shits were still there. But the thing that started my whole MOVE toward disillusionment," he added, "was probably Yugoslavia. One could see that the Russian attitude to Yugoslavia was monstrous."

The trial and execution of Nickola Petkov, on charges of plotting to overthrow the Bulgarian government, got Ambler started on *Judgement on Deltchev*, published in 1951. Its central subject is that process by which a government destroys the reputation of a popular political leader, "Yordan Deltchev," and having done so, arrives at a position where it can safely treat him as a criminal. It is, in other words, about the use of power to manipulate events and opinions.

Judgement on Deltchev was a novel, but not a thrilling one. "I tried to find a new idiom," Ambler explained. "I knew that whatever I did, people would say, 'Aha, it isn't as good as *Dimitrios.*' "

Among the disappointed was Raymond Chandler. "It is not so much that Ambler has let himself get too intellectual as that he has let it become apparent that he was being intellectual," Chandler wrote a friend.

But Ambler, like any artist, was feeling his way. Writing film scripts was his job; writing novels, his personal adventure.

With *Mutiny on the Bounty,* he had the problem of making the role of Fletcher Christian, to be played by Brando, as interesting as the role of Bligh. For a while he thought he had the answer; he discovered that Bligh and Christian had known each other before meeting on the *Bounty.* The studio, however, would not permit the use of this new material. Its executives reasoned that the public was used to the lie and would not accept facts.

But in his novels Ambler was boss. From the start his idea had been to intellectualize the thriller, that "dirty word." He had "decided to intellectualize it, insofar as I was able."

Over the years this remained his basic idea. He regarded the writing of books with a background of power politics and political intrigue as a reasonable method of examining society.

"Even the worst spy novel accepts the essential shiftiness of experience in a way that many other novels do not," the critic R.H.W. Dillard has written. "And of course, the best spy novels are not really about spies and spying at all, but about the world in which spies and spying move, that real world in which we all exist."[2]

In 1953 Ambler published *The Schirmer Inheritance.* Violence did not appear until the story was more than half over. Some people were puzzled.

"The entertainer in my line of country has had a perplexing ten years," Ambler told a reporter. "He has seen his cops changing hats with his robbers and his wildest fantasies transmuted into the most leaden facts. Who can blame him if he attempts to shift his ground a little and put a foot—well, say a toe then—into the novelist's field."

Much of Ambler's energy, during his California period, went into writing for films. In the 1950s he is credited with eleven screenplays, while writing only four novels under his own name.* Of these novels *State of Siege,* which was titled *The Night-Comers* in England, and *Passage of Arms* are outstanding.

In 1958, in San Francisco, Ambler married Joan Harrison. She was a screenwriter who had co-authored some of Alfred Hitchcock's most famous hits, including *Jamaica Inn, Rebecca, Foreign Correspondent, Suspicion,* and *Saboteur.*

This was Ambler's second marriage. In 1939 he had married Louise Smith Crombie, an artist from New Jersey, whom he met in Paris. They were divorced in 1957.

In 1961 a brushfire destroyed Ambler's home in Bel Air. Well into a new book, he lost it to the flames. He struck back spiritedly against disaster and scored with *The Light of Day.* It was successful as a novel and became the even-more-successful film *Topkopi.* "I did it very quickly, and enjoyed myself, felt much better, really," he said of the book years later.

In 1968 Ambler and his wife left California and settled in Switzerland in an apartment overlooking Lake Geneva and the Alps. There he began his third, and most rewarding, period as a writer.

---

*In the late forties Ambler had eased back into novel writing by collaborating with Charles Rodda, a screenwriter. Using the pen name Eliot Reed, Ambler and Rodda turned out four novels of intrigue. The first was published in 1950.

III

AMONG WRITERS OF CRIMINAL FICTION, Eric Ambler is exceptionally involved with the politics of the twentieth century. He has been engaged since the era of Hitler, has weathered Fascism and Communism, and in his most recent novels, has written about guerrilla terrorists, the technology of espionage, and the needs of multinational corporations.

Future historians should find him valuable. Not only is he criminal fiction's most knowledgeable and most elegant storyteller; he is exceptionally aware of those who are, to use Max Weber's phrase, "relentless in viewing the realities of life."

The education that began with Holmes moved forward in Paris where Ambler read Nietzsche and learned to appreciate the importance of the will to power. "Power is a great thing, you know," a character in *Judgement on Deltchev* says. "To be able to move and control great affairs . . . that is the greatest of all pleasures. You feel it in the stomach."

This awareness enlarges Ambler's world and releases him from many of criminal fiction's limitations. Corruption does not interest him. There are very few cops in his novels, and none of them come pounding on the door at three thirty in the morning.

More important, his criminals are interesting. Most of Hammett's crooks are not very bright; Moriarty seems the only thinking thief in Doyle; Simenon's criminals are people caught by circumstances; and Chandler's crooks resemble Hammett's. But Ambler's thieves are intelligent; not so much criminals as problem solvers dominated by the will to power.

In *Background to Danger*, published when he was twenty-eight, Ambler wrote of the "struggle between the free human spirit and the stupid, fumbling brutish forces of the primeval swamp." Fourteen years later, in *Judgement on Deltchev*, he continued to view power politics idealistically.

But by 1956, when he reached the age of forty-eight, the world looked different, and so did its inhabitants. In one of his "Lizzie Borden Memorial Lectures," collected in *The Ability to Kill*, Ambler declared, "Ladies and Gentlemen, our Anglo-Saxon culture is built on studious denials of the existence within us of the primitive. The revelation that there is, after all, an ape beneath the velvet is perennially fascinating."

In *Passage of Arms,* written in 1959, he approached the problem of the real nature of man from another angle and backed away from one of his pre-World War II conceptions.

"Nowadays we don't hear the phrase 'merchants of death' very much," one character observes. "It's all very sad. The idea that the act of selling arms somehow tricked people into making wars they didn't want never really stood up to close inspection, did it? But it was good to have a fine, top-hatted bogeyman to put all the blame on. The trouble is we've learned a thing or two since nineteen thirty-nine. Now we can't even blame the politicians— not with much conviction, anyway. The real bogeyman crawled out of the mud with our ancestors millions of years ago."

Since then Ambler has moved his fiction into territory that is extremely deceptive and intensely relative. This is particularly true of the novels written in Switzerland. Earlier ones, such as *Passage of Arms* and *State of Siege,* are good reads, but they could have been written before, or soon after, World War II.

It is Ambler's three most recent novels, published in 1969, 1972, and 1974, that most accurately reflect the world that many Americans were oblivious of prior to events such as the Bay of Pigs.

The first of these novels is *The Intercom Conspiracy.*

Eric Ambler has always had a taste for the baroque, and *The Intercom Conspiracy* is concerned with juicy events in the world of espionage at a time when the role of espionage has grown dramatically. "You talk about the atomic age," a character in Colin Wilson's *The Black Room* says, "but historians will talk about the age of espionage. This is a new epoch in human history."

Years before, in *Dimitrios,* a master spy named Grodek provided Charles Latimer with some basic information: "There are roughly twenty-seven independent states in Europe. Each has an army and an air force and most of them have some sort of navy as well. For its own security, each of these armies, air forces and navies must know what each corresponding force in each of the other twenty-six countries is doing—what its strength is, what its efficiency is, what secret preparations it is making. That means spies—armies of them."

But by 1969 and *The Intercom Conspiracy,* this situation had changed. Europe was no longer made up of twenty-seven independent states. It consisted of those nations allied to the United States and those allied to Russia.

Dimitrios Makropoulos was a primitive. His first problem was to stay alive; his second, to become rich and powerful. It was all very simple. But Colonel Jost and Colonel Brand, the ranking problem solvers in *The Intercom Conspiracy,* are exotics—peacocks, where Dimitrios was a crow. Professional soldiers, they have become the intelligence chiefs of their respective governments, which are allied to the United States. "They came to power in the early nineteen fifties," Ambler writes of Jost and Brand, "and established themselves in the NATO intelligence community during the bitter cold-war years of that decade."

In their time, in their own countries, both colonels have had immense power. By 1964, however, the situation has changed, and Jost and Brand have become careerists with a grievance.

"Tension between the United States and the Soviet Union had eased considerably," Ambler explains, and "it was becoming increasingly evident that their importance in the NATO scheme of things, already diminished, was likely to become little more than parochial."

But this is only one element in the colonels' predicament. Their positions in intelligence have been costly in terms of their careers. Their jobs are dead ends. Both are such specialists that they can't be moved; and if they can't be moved, they can't be promoted.

"Attempts by both of them to have the establishments of their directorates upgraded had invariably failed," Ambler writes. "These men had not endeared themselves to higher authority."

Over the years, since the founding of NATO, the intelligence chiefs have met four times a year in three-day sessions, and Jost and Brand have become comrades. Both colonels fought in the resistance during the German occupation, both are, by nature and experience, guerrilla fighters, and both recognize the inherent clumsiness of the U.S. and Russian giants.

Gradually, they have realized that each of them is willing to score off either or both of the giants if it can be done safely. The problem is—how?

———

One year after they have acknowledged their mutual situations, a NATO intelligence conference is held in Rome. In the evening, over dinner, Jost tells Brand about an old man who lived in Mexico and forged stamps (not a crime in Mexico) so accurately that a group of international stamp dealers was forced to buy him out.

"A secret negotiating committee went down to Mexico to meet the old man," Jost says. "They not only bought his plates and dies and equipment, they also persuaded him to sign an agreement, enforceable in a Mexican court, that he will retire for good." Jost also explains that on at least two other occasions, stamp dealers have had to buy out forgers because of their "nuisance value."

Brand grasps Jost's intent, and the two opportunists return to their hotel and spend hours considering methods by which the nuisance-value factor can be exploited. Months later, Brand requests a secret meeting. He is sick and must retire in three months. It is now or never, and he has discovered a situation made for Jost and himself.

Paper mills—"the term used to describe," Ambler writes, "the innumerable political warfare and propaganda groups engaged in feeding misinformation to the international news gathering agencies. Some paper mills had government subsidies, others were financed by emigré organizations and separatist movements; a few of the smaller, more furtive paper mills—those, for instance, which specialized in the manufacture of false intelligence documents—were run for profit."*

———

*In *The Light of Day,* which Ambler wrote in 1962, Arthur Abdel Simpson occasionally recalls the mottoes of his father, a British soldier. One motto is, "Bullshit baffles brains," an apt description of the function of paper mills.

Brand has learned that because of the death of its founder, the international weekly newsletter *Intercom* is for sale. Working through a dummy office, the two colonels purchase *Intercom* and begin to publish, in weekly installments, a series of military secrets of both NATO and Warsaw Pact nations.

The CIA, KGB, and British and West German intelligence organizations are appalled. After the Colonels' fifth issue of *Intercom,* an unidentified party purchases the newsletter for one million Swiss francs. Jost and Brand split the profits and retire. Brand crawls into his sickbed, Jost settles in the sun on Majorca.

But their retirement does not finish the story told in *The Intercom Conspiracy.*

Charles Latimer, the mystery writer who appeared in *Dimitrios,* is also a character in *The Intercom Conspiracy.* He too lives on Majorca, and Jost becomes his neighbor.

In 1975 Ambler told Joel Hopkins that he considered his primary theme to be loss of innocence. "Of course, it's a very large theme," Ambler explained. "But I suppose it always depends on the degree of innocence and the quality of innocence which is lost. But thematically—loss of innocence. It's the only thing I've ever written."

The fact is that, in *Dimitrios,* Latimer—Ambler's principal innocent—was instrumental in destroying Ambler's prime example of the individual who is "relentless in viewing the realities of life." Over the years Ambler may have decided that such a situation was unrealistic.

At any rate, Latimer is back, and the reader gradually learns that he has not grown, he is as much of a lightweight as ever. The weeks he spent sniffing through Dimitrios's past have meant little to him; he is unable to make any connection between that world and himself. Nor does relativity or the will to power have any meaning for Latimer. He continues to dwell in the tidy, uncomplicated, monochrome world that readers find in his books.

Yet he remains a clever man, who has picked up rumors about the *Intercom* affair; he has discovered, or come remarkably close to discovering, the perpetrators' identities. He is the only person who could possibly finger Jost and Brand, and he does not appreciate the dangers of his position. He has gone to his neighbor, Jost, and teased him about the situation. He has announced that he is writing a book about the *Intercom* incident. Notice of this has been published in an international journal to the book trade.

Colonel Brand eventually learns all this. He leaves his sickbed long enough to arrange certain matters. Latimer vanishes —without trace. His remains, Ambler suggests, lie buried under cement at a highway construction site, somewhere between Ferney-Voltaire and Strasbourg.

————

The story of the colonels and the solution to their problem is a flamboyant tale, but Ambler, in telling it, has done just about everything he can to mute that quality.

The book is not a thriller. Jost and Brand are not the main characters.

That role is filled by Theodore Carter, a journalist with a drinking problem. He has been the editor of *Intercom* under both its founder and the colonels. He is also the typical Ambler hero, the innocent caught up in desperate matters through no fault of his own. Not only is he the editor of a "paper mill," he is its lone employee, and he does not know the true identity of his new employers.*

As the exceedingly sensitive secrets are revealed in the pages of *Intercom,* Carter is repeatedly assaulted by agents of the various espionage establishments.

But he is not a Latimer. He learns from his experience and comes out of it a better man. Ambler is specific here. When the colonels' takeover began, Carter was a tired man who disliked both his job and himself. Someone tells him at the end of the novel,

————

*In Ambler's Switzerland novels, it is especially noticeable that, like Sherlock Holmes, the problem solvers have no real interest in victims or villains as people and are only concerned with solving the problem at hand. Detection can be "as a-moral as geometry," Hugh Kenner pointed out in *James Joyce.* "Whenever they become components in a problem, human beings become numbered points, devoid of rights and autonomy. . . . To Watson's horrified protest at his quasi-seduction of a housemaid with information to give, Holmes calmly replies, 'You must play your cards as best you can.' "

"I detect a new confidence in you . . . you have come to terms with yourself."

———

In *The Schirmer Inheritance,* published in 1953, Ambler refers to "the regrettable tendency of reality to assume the shape and proportions of melodrama."

It is a tendency that civilization seems to nurture. After Abraham Lincoln was murdered thieves plotted to seize his corpse for ransom. A whore reported them, and they were nabbed by the Pinkertons. In the 1970s a citizen's chances of being held hostage in some far-fetched melodrama—of losing an ear, being kidnapped and buried in a box, or somehow robbing, at gunpoint and on camera, a bank owned by the father of your best friend, seem disagreeably good.

Michael Howell, the hero of *The Levanter,* the novel that followed *The Intercom Conspiracy,* is one victim of this tendency. Michael, who is in his early thirties, was trained in England as an engineer, and is the wealthy managing director of the Agence Howell, a sales and importing empire founded by his grandfather. The main office is in Beirut, but Michael spends much of his time in Damascus, where the branch office is managed by his mistress, Teresa.

But like the world in which he lives, Michael Howell is more complicated than he seems, for "with a Lebanese-Armenian grandmother and a Cypriot mother, I am no more than fractionally English," he explains. "Ethnically . . . I could be described as 'Eastern Mediterranean' . . . I prefer . . . 'Levantine mongrel.' Mongrels . . . tend to adapt . . . they are among the most likely to survive."

———

Opposed to Michael Howell is Salah Ghaled, leader of a band of Arab guerrillas and a man with a problem that requires a solution.

Salah Ghaled was a student in Cairo when the first Arab-Israeli war began. He fought bravely in the army that the Jews humiliated. His response to defeat was to create his own guerrilla group, the Palestine Action Force, otherwise known as the PAF.

"Far out fanatics," one journalist said of them. "By hatred out of illusion."

As *The Levanter* begins Salah Ghaled is in his forties and has become a maverick, dangerous to both Jews and Arabs. If an Arab leader even hinted of the possibility of a peaceful settlement with Israel, Ghaled or others like him would slit the hinter's throat. He and his PAF have gone underground in Syria, and he has concentrated on solving his gravest problem: the fact that although he is well known in the Middle East, he has no identity internationally.

To correct this flaw he has conceived a complicated deed. On the night of July 3, a few hours before Israel's greatest national holiday, he will attack Tel Aviv. The attack will come in two forms: rockets will be launched from a ship at sea while, simultaneously, a large number of previously positioned bombs will explode throughout the city.

"If the operations were even partially successful," Ambler writes, "Ghaled could count on international headlines. The smiles of other Palestine leaders might be forced, and their congratulations less than wholehearted, but smiles there would be and congratulations too. The PAF would have become a force to reckon with politically."

As *The Levanter* begins, Ghaled's weapon is incomplete. Three large tasks lie ahead of him.

He has more than a hundred Russian rockets, but the Russians have withheld essential parts which he must somehow manufacture.

He must also construct the bombs that will go off simultaneously in Tel Aviv.

Since the rockets are to be fired from a ship ten kilometers out to sea, he must invent a way to screen the ship from Israeli radar.

With the help of a captain in the Syrian Internal Security Service, PAF infiltrates the Green Circle battery plant, an Agence Howell subsidiary in Damascus. Soon afterward, because Ghaled requires the services of a trained engineer, his men seize Michael Howell and his girl friend, Teresa.

At gunpoint, Ghaled forces Howell and Teresa to take the

oath of allegiance to PAF. He then demands that his prisoners sign faked confessions which state that they have broken Syrian laws by working for the Zionist secret service and have conspired to make bombs to blow up the house of a Palestinian patriot.

With some assistance from the Israeli authorities, whom he contacts at great risk, Howell eventually succeeds in wrecking the project and killing Ghaled. How he does so is not important here. What is important is that Michael comes out of the affair with a problem that is not really solvable.

It seems that during the trial of the PAF guerrillas, captured by the Israeli navy aboard an Agence Howell freighter, the existence of PAF and its scheme for attacking Tel Aviv are totally ignored. The charge against the PAF guerrillas is reduced to piracy.

Meanwhile, some of the small bombs planted in Tel Aviv have been discovered. Disguised as dry batteries, they carry the Green Circle label, and it contains the phrase, "Made in Syria."

The Syrian government, anxious to disassociate itself with Green Circle and Agence Howell, releases the confessions that Michael and Teresa have signed, and the newspapers leap into the story.

"The Arab press, hysterical as ever, tore into him with everything they had," Ambler wrote, "and they had plenty. Here was this Howell, a rich businessman whose family had battened for years on poor Arab countries, revealed as an Israeli provocateur and spy."

And so, in *The Levanter,* Michael Howell is involved in an exceptional situation that he handles courageously.

But because the Israeli government refuses to acknowledge the complete details of the threat to Tel Aviv, and Michael's role in destroying it, the newspaper-reading public is confused.

At first, when dealing with the press, Michael denies everything. But when the story breaks in Europe, he attempts to explain the situation to reporters.

His troubles immediately multiply. Michael is a brave man, devious and diplomatic, but he is also a great one for shaking his finger in his listener's face. He simply has no talent for dealing with the press. When a reporter asks him for "a brief, simple recital of the facts of the case," Michael turns out a hundred-page statement that weighs two pounds.

That the world is complicated, that society is not the simple affair we like to imagine it is, has long been an Ambler theme. Because, in a complicated situation, Michael lacks the ability to present matters simply, in a way that reporters can pass along, he is his own worst enemy. He will spend the rest of his life under a cloud; a victim, in a small way, of the fact that people in the mass have no taste for complications.

Sometimes it seems as if Eric Ambler's most exceptional ability is his gift of prescience. The strife in his first novel, *The Dark Frontier,* centered around an atom bomb. This, in 1936.

"With some scientific education and access to academic journals," he explained many years later, "I read about the early work of Rutherford . . . and understood its implications. The atomic bomb that I deduced was a one-man invention. The difficulties of producing substances like enriched uranium . . . were factors I was able to ignore because I was unaware of their existence."

And in 1939, after the publication of *Cause for Alarm,* a British Foreign Office official, disturbed by Ambler's use of certain escape routes between Yugoslavia and Italy, requested an explanation. Ambler replied that he had worked out the routes for himself after studying various small-scale maps.*

But the true extraordinariness of Ambler's abilities as an anticipator did not become evident until years later, after the move to Switzerland.

As noted, *The Levanter* is concerned with Arab-Israeli relations, and centers around a dramatic Arab plot that would create world headlines. The book was published on June 21, 1972.

---

*Ambler, it appears, has always denied any association with any intelligence service. *The Intercom Conspiracy* is extremely critical of the value of espionage. In *Who's Who in Spy Fiction,* Donald McCormick wrote that Ambler "has been far and away the most accurate of all modern spy fiction writers right down to the smallest detail. . . . The detail is faultless, yet Ambler, as far as anyone knows, was never employed by the Secret Service or any similar organization."

On September 5, 1972, an Arab terrorist gang murdered eleven Israeli athletes at the Olympic Games in Munich.

In New York alone, during the weeks that followed, *The Levanter* sold 35,000 copies in hardback.[3]

Ambler's next novel, *Dr. Frigo,* came out in 1974. It contained, as will be seen, an interesting amount of comment on the use, by North American corporations, of enormous bribes as a weapon in international business. A few months later the actual use of such bribes to secure international business contracts became, for the *first time,* headline news in the United States, which did not hurt the sales of *Dr. Frigo.**

In matters tied to criminal themes, coincidence is viewed skeptically.

It seems reasonable to inquire, How does Ambler do it?

In 1977, when an interviewer asked about his prescience, Ambler acknowledged, "I do have an unhappy knack."

Otherwise, it seems that the only explanation Ambler has ever offered is, "I've always been quite good at making things circumstantial. Having a scientific training I'm often able to draw a whole animal from the evidence of a few bones."

This, of course, is also the situation of Sherlock Holmes, who once declared, "The ideal reasoner would, when he had . . . been shown a single fact in all its bearings, deduce from it not only the chain of events which lead up to it, but also the results which would follow from it."

Conan Doyle, a biographer has pointed out, was "dominated

---

*Conan Doyle also possessed a talent for the *coup de théâtre.*

As Charles Higham wrote in *The Adventures of Conan Doyle,* Doyle's " 'A Scandal in Bohemia,' with its echoes of scandal involving a German-speaking prince, as well as recent events in Vienna, was aimed directly at the public taste."

Doyle began this story in April 1891, and finished it in early June, at a time when the Prince of Wales—"a German speaking prince"—was caught up in an enormous British scandal revolving around a gentleman accused of cheating at baccarat.

Higham also points out that "The Adventure of the Bruce-Partington Plans" was founded on an actual scandal involving the theft of the Irish Crown Jewels. Doyle changed the item stolen to submarine plans, doing so at a time when the subject of submarine warfare was rarely mentioned. "Since presumably he was not . . . gifted with second sight," Higham wrote, "it must be deduced that his friendship with Edward VII, and with the new Prime Minister, Asquith, gave him access to privileged material."

by a desire to investigate and explain." He and Eric Ambler have much in common.

Like Holmes-Doyle, like Maigret-Simenon, like Hammett and Chandler, Eric Ambler exemplifies the unmasking trend, "the systematic search," as Ellenberger wrote, "for deception and self-deception and the uncovering of the underlying truth."

Eric Ambler can be regarded as a sort of latter-day Holmes who uses the methods of his old tutor not so much to solve the case as to investigate and dramatize the world as it is known to him, "a world which he believed his readers would have no inkling of," Greil Marcus observed.

Ambler's ability as an anticipator seems less mysterious when he is specifically compared to Holmes.

The fact that Holmes, rationality's most imposing figurehead, has scientific training is known throughout the world. The original meeting between Holmes and Watson took place in the laboratory at St. Bartholomew's Hospital at a time when Holmes had just solved a chemistry problem involving bloodstains.

Ambler's scientific training began in grammar school. Later he won a four-year scholarship to study electrical engineering at Northampton Polytechnic. According to Oscar Levant, Ambler scored 100 percent in the chemistry section of the examination. After two years at the polytechnic, he dropped out and found a job as an apprentice engineer.

Holmes, the world's foremost consulting detective, solved his first case in 1874 and retired in 1903. In 1912, at the request of the prime minister, he came out of retirement to hunt down Von Bork, an effort that required two years. All told, and not including the nine years between 1903 and 1912, the great sleuth spent thirty-one years in the field.

Ambler is also affected by the fact that he is preeminent in his field. He has been writing thrillers since 1935, has been recognized as a master since the publication of *Dimitrios* in 1939, and is still active in 1978. Not counting the ten-year interval, 1940 to 1950, when he wrote no novels, Ambler has been on the job for thirty-three years and has, in fact, surpassed his tutor. Between them, it is Ambler who is the veteran.

Holmes is well connected. His name is known in very important places, and he has received a token of regard from, it is surmised, Victoria herself.

Ambler, for a time, was attached to Churchill's staff and had his contacts with the great man. In addition, Ambler did important work in connection with Anglo-American relations and was well thought of by American officials. The record is very clear here. On October 15, 1945, for his services in preparing the documentary film *United States,* Lieutenant Colonel Eric Clifford Ambler was awarded the American Bronze Star for "outstanding success in the promotion of the highest type of relationship," his citation read, "between the armed forces of Great Britain and the United States."

Holmes filed news clippings about international crimes. When no case was on hand, he would review this material.

Ambler may also have such a file, but much of his information appears to come from other people. "What is evident from an Ambler interview," Joel Hopkins wrote, "is that personal experience, friendships, acquaintances and a prodigious memory all make for . . . an Ambler novel."

Ambler's friends include journalists, diplomats, politicians, television reporters, soldiers, retired spies, and others connected to twentieth-century politics.

Judgement on Deltchev concerned the destruction of the reputation of a popular politician, who happened to suffer from diabetes, and was based on actual events. "A French diplomat who sat through the whole sad farce," Ambler has explained, "told me how they withheld the insulin."

The Schirmer Inheritance involved a problem of historical identity going back to the Napoleonic era. "There was a woman I knew in Paris," Ambler told Joel Hopkins, "who was a very, very skillful interpreter. . . . She had researched the Napoleonic War records."

Holmes is theatrical, amazing, and grand, so uncommon in all that he does that the phrase "common sense" does not seem appropriate for him.

Ambler, however, wears "common sense" gracefully. This

becomes clear when the few available interviews with him and the equally rare statements of his friends are examined.

Oscar Levant, in *The Unimportance of Being Oscar,* wrote, "Eric Ambler . . . told me that he had once visited a sanitarium devoted to therapy for practically incurable criminals. One of the patients was a murderer who explained patiently to Ambler that he had been framed. He had not plunged the sword into the man's skull. He had merely been withdrawing it when someone came in. 'He *was* crazy,' Eric said authoritatively. 'You don't plunge a sword into a man's skull. You look for a soft spot.' "[4]

Ambler and a British reporter, Bruce Page, once had a friendly argument about "deficiencies in the respectable imagination." Later, in the *Sunday Times* (February 22, 1970), Page described one of the points that Ambler had made. "In 1944 . . . it was his duty," Page wrote of Ambler, "to scour newly liberated Italian villages for evidence of atrocities committed by the departing SS. He was in company with some American officers. 'In each village you would ask for the local anti-fascisti [Ambler explained], and usually they sent you to the priest. I recall one priest who was especially excited by our arrival.' " The priest's actions convinced some members of the party that the man was crazy. " 'It had not occurred to those men,' says Ambler—with a faint assumption of wonder—'to think that perhaps a real anti-Fascist in an Italian village of that time would *have* to be mad.' "

And finally, in an interview in the September 9, 1974, *Publishers Weekly,* a reporter wrote of Ambler, "Violence in any form distresses him, and he regards a lot of fictional violence as phony. 'What nobody seems to observe is that the human hand is about as substantial as a bunch of chicken bones. Punching someone else on the jaw might not hurt the other person much, but it could maim *you* for life.' "

In his way, Ambler appears to be as rational as Holmes. "And it was Ambler, paradoxically the one man who had not been mixed up in the Intelligence game," Donald McCormick wrote, "who . . . produced the most factual, authentic spy stories of the century. He achieved this simply by patient, meticulous attention to detail, by checking and cross-checking on his facts."

It seems reasonable to believe that Ambler's position as criminal fiction's "Great Anticipator" is founded on a combination of factors including a first-class mind, scientific training, superior information, excellent connections, and common sense. He is, indeed, a *sleuth.*

"The early representatives of our genus . . . knew how to hunt big game—an enterprise which implies a high order of social organization," the scientist René Dubos has observed.

Other scholars have commented on the enormous step forward taken by the human species when weapons with long handles were invented, and it was not necessary to fight quite so close to the beast.

Today, just as the size of the prey has increased to an interesting extent, so has the elaborateness of our social organization. In Eric Ambler's *Dr. Frigo,* the beast is oil and the weapons used in the hunt have a length and intricacy that are fascinating.

Although it has long been known that the Coroza Islands, themselves the possession of an unnamed coffee republic, contain oil, the deposits lay so deep that the cost of tapping them has been prohibitive. But by 1972, or thereabouts, the price of a barrel of crude oil has risen to a point where it has become practical to drill for the Coroza oil, and a group of multinational corporations, known jointly as the Consortium, has decided to do so.

Because it will be spending billions of dollars to extract the oil, the Consortium requires that the government of the coffee republic be able to control the population while the oil is being extracted.

But the government of the coffee republic lacks such authority. For years its political leaders have been devoted to the interests of the great coffee plantations and have paid little attention to the needs of the citizens, most of whom are Indians, so superstitious and primitive that they are known as "animals with names." The population, accordingly, is restless, and there is some urban guerrilla activity, most of which is led by a former student now known as El Lobo.

Such being the situation, representatives of the Consortium go to their friends in the intelligence community, and the problem ends up in the lap of the French secret service, the Service de Documentation Extérieure, commonly known as S-dec.

And so, in the third of Ambler's Switzerland novels, the problem solver is not an individual but an organization.

Because of its clumsy handling of an affair involving Ben Barka, a Moroccan leftist opposition leader and distinguished mathematician living in exile in Paris and Geneva, S-dec has recently been reorganized by the French army.

"They need a brilliant coup that will help them with their new image," a character in *Dr. Frigo* says of S-dec. "Once that is established . . . they will look like a responsible and efficient secret service again."

S-dec, accordingly, goes to work on the problem in the coffee republic. Guerrilla activity in the capital city soon increases to a point that not even the controlled press and radio can ignore. In six weeks six wealthy persons or corporation executives are kidnapped for ransom. The corpses of two victims, whose family or employer refused to pay, are dumped in front of the military barracks.

Obviously, the government sponsored by the coffee planters is no longer competent to rule.

Meanwhile, S-dec has decided on the man it wants to head the new government. He is Manuel Villegas, a politician who was forced to flee the coffee republic when the government formed by the plantation owners took power.

As the story begins in *Dr. Frigo,* Manuel Villegas and his party are on the island of Saint-Paul-Les-Alizés in the French Antilles. They are waiting for the proper moment to fly to the coffee republic and assume power.

A few days before the coup occurs, the three most important "weapons" in the upheaval are flown into the island for a conference with Manuel Villegas. They are:

Father Bartholomé: a maverick "worker's priest" of about sixty. Besides being supplied with money by S-dec, he profits from a protection racket that he has organized in the barrios of the capital city—pay or be bombed. He is capable of bringing the poor people into the streets in mobs.

Dr. Tomás: the present Minister of Education. He is responsible for the only social improvement made during the last few years in the coffee republic—the creation of a fairly good public-school system. He can bring the high school and university students into the streets.

El Lobo: the twenty-eight-year-old guerrilla chieftain.

Any sort of government that Manuel Villegas and his team can establish is acceptable to S-dec and the Consortium, providing it is stable and not out-and-out communist. "Accepting the need for change," a knowledgeable character in *Dr. Frigo* says, "we come to terms with those who can make it stick and if that means coming to terms with something further left of center than we like, so be it."*

_____

Ernesto Castillo, the central figure in *Dr. Frigo,* is a native of the coffee republic. His father, a liberal lawyer and politician, was assassinated just before the present government seized power.

Ernesto himself is a doctor on the staff of the French government hospital at St. Paul-Les-Alizés. Since Manuel Villegas was an associate of Ernesto's father's, S-dec arranges for Ernesto to be appointed Villegas's personal physician.

Soon after he has reluctantly accepted this appointment, Ernesto meets Robert L. Rossier, whose business card identifies him as a Senior Assessor with the ATP-Globe Insurance Company of Montreal. Rossier is in some way connected to American intelligence, and in *Dr. Frigo* he has the same function as the "nice"

*Since early in World War II, what is essentially problem solving has been known as Operational Research, itself loosely based on Sherlock Holmes's methods. According to the authors of *The Origins and Development of Operational Research in the Royal Air Force,* "one can say that the famous detective would have been a first class Operational Researcher."

Operational Research has been described by Sir Charles Goodeve as "a scientific method of providing executive departments with a quantitative basis for decisions regarding the operations under their control." Operational Research is conducted, not by an individual, but by a mixed team of representatives of various disciplines. Its object is not so much to find the ultimate truth as to achieve a workably good answer to a problem.

communists in Ambler's first novels. He is there to read the clues to the hero, cue him in on the newest techniques in big-time problem solving.

As Rossier sees it, factors like patriotism and emotionalism are old-fashioned. Rationalism is in complete control. The "new style coup" is built around "the deal made in advance"; a token demonstration of bravery, a minimum of strife, "no victimization and the special plane to destination of choice."

Ernesto asks about casualties.

Corpses are bad, Rossier acknowledges. "A couple of palace guards who haven't been told the score in advance, okay," he says. "The assistant chief of police whom nobody likes anyway, also okay. But that's it. Bloodless if possible. Virtually bloodless will do."

Nevertheless, certain problems remain. There is the question of the correct way to handle, post-coup, people like El Lobo. Terrorism—assassinations and bombs—can become a habit, Rossier points out. He thinks that the solution is to have El Presidente give El Lobo "a post in which he can make himself rich."

And it is money, Rossier continues, that is going to be El Presidente's biggest problem. "Money that *he* can control, I'm talking about. He personally," Rossier specifies.

Yet even here there is a solution and part of Rossier's task is to get Ernesto to pass certain information on to Manuel Villegas: the news, specifically, that Rossier's clients have already allocated five million dollars—"a floater"—for El Presidente's private, personal fund. "I'd say he'd be glad to hear that particular piece of good news," Rossier observes.

Dr. Frigo is an instance of the interference of an industrial combine in the affairs of a so-called sovereign power.

Although the coffee republic will become richer because of the oil, this will mean very little to the average citizen.

In the final pages of the book Ambler presents a conversation between Ernesto and a priest. The priest believes that the greatest need of the coffee republic is a better medical program. But even here he sees huge problems.

"Yet are endemic diseases wholly evil?" the priest asks. When you rid yourself of disease, the healthy population doubles, he says, and so does the economic problem.

Ernesto agrees, and the priest points out that healthy people want interesting jobs and become angry when none are available. "Then they turn to the El Lobos," the priest says. "Oil will make no more work than coffee. Just bank balances. In good years the coffee has done that too."

Both the priest and Ernesto agree that neither of them, individually, has a solution to this problem. They further agree that neither the church nor politics has a solution. This, it would appear, is an acknowledgment that none of the ideas which Ambler placed his hopes on when he was a young man really work. If so, it is made without bitterness.

Of the three novels that Ambler has written in Switzerland, *Dr. Frigo* is the one in which he is most involved with his characters.

As the story begins Ernesto, thirty-one, views life in terms of black and white. With strangers, he is somewhat stiff and easily offended. He can also be pompous and arrogant. Indeed, he is a rather chilly person, and his nickname at the hospital, Dr. Frigo, means frozen meat.

During the thirty-four days in which the action of the novel takes place, Ernesto is, to use a phrase of Ralph Harper's, "lifted out of private life and into a life of international dimensions."

For Ernesto it is an adventure of the spirit.

He has been connected to large events, and he has realized his limitations. He has learned that the world is a far more complicated place than he thought it was, and he has discovered how difficult it is to accomplish anything in it.

He has also acquired a much more respectful appreciation of his father, whom he had previously regarded as an incompetent politician. It has been a chastening experience.

As the novel ends Ernesto is waiting for a plane to take him back to Saint-Paul-Les-Alizés, the hospital, and his girl friend. As he waits he sums up his situation in a manner that is very attractive. He then tops his summation with a joke, and it is a very good joke, so that, in the final sentence, Dr. Frigo comes through warm and human.

Dr. Frigo is the novel in which Ambler attained the goal he set out for so many years ago—to "intellectualize the thriller," the novel of intrigue. In the United States the copy on the dust jacket of the book declared that he was "writing at the height of his powers," and most critics agreed.*

Dr. Frigo is a novel that can be reread with pleasure. "A novel of intrigue and a comedy of a high and conspicuously intelligent order," the reviewer in *The New Yorker* said. The reader closes it, finally, with an awareness that someone has been able to penetrate deeply into the confusion of our times, study it, identify various portions of it, then return and present an elegant report in which he comments, as an adult and as an artist, on the human situation.

In the United States R.H.W. Dillard and Paxton Davis, scholars associated with Hollins College, have been observing Ambler for years. In one essay on Ambler, Davis spoke of the "continuous fable of international politics he has been writing since 1937."[5]

This fable is the story of Ambler's education as a writer.

In *Background to Danger,* written in 1937, Ambler used the phrase "ghastly simplicity." One part of his contribution as a writer has been to recognize this ghastly simplicity and communicate it. In *Dr. Frigo* he tells an anecdote about a resort hotel

---

*In 1975, at its annual banquet in New York, the Mystery Writers of America gave Ambler its Grand Master award, with special reference to *Dr. Frigo.* The tribute read in part:

"To be working at the top of one's form at the time of receiving the Grand Master nomination has to be highly gratifying. This circumstance may, to some extent, seem a deprivation to the rest of us: we must forego a sentimental journey. '*A Coffin for Dimitrios,*' we would say, 'they don't write books like that anymore.' But Eric Ambler does.

"Which is not to suggest that he borrows even a nuance from himself. In common between *Coffin* and Mr. Ambler's latest book, *Dr. Frigo,* almost solely, is the author's way with reluctant heroes, the bystanders sucked into history."

The same organization had, in 1964, awarded him its Edgar Allan Poe trophy.

In England Ambler has twice won the Gold Dagger presented by the Crime Writers Association. The first was for *Passage of Arms,* the second for *The Levanter.*

on the beach of an island in the French Antilles.

Because swimming in the sea is "a recognized way of committing suicide," the hotel requires a pool. "The Ajoupa swimming pool, for instance," Ambler writes, "looks splendid in the hotel's brochure because the photograph was taken during the dry season. What is not explained is that the landscape architect, more familiar with the French Riviera than the French Antilles, sited the pool at the foot of a slope artificially created by bulldozers. So, every time it rains heavily a torrent of mud pours over or around the retaining wall into the pool area. The cost of providing adequate drainage is currently estimated at a million francs. Management has responded to the challenge so far by removing the warning signs about the dangers of sea bathing and giving out-of-season visitors free rum-punch vouchers redeemable only at the Beach Bar. Casualties to date have been light and caused mainly by sea-urchin spines and jelly fish."

We live in a world where, as Loren Eiseley has noted, the human species, until recently, never looked forward to anything more than the next day's hunting.

It is a world, as Ralph Harper has written, "full of wretched faces, cruelty, and meaninglessness, and some thriller writers show that world to us, and we are actually grateful to them, for we would rather know the truth about ourselves than be entertained by a boy's dream or an adolescent's sensations."[6]

When he was a boy, Eric Ambler's desire was to be an educated man. Today he is, and with elegance and wit he is passing his knowledge on to others. The reader, indebted, remembers Holmes and is grateful for his kindness to young Ambler.

— PHILIP MARLOWE —
Raymond Chandler

You must remember that Marlowe is not a real
person. He is a creature of fantasy. He is in a false
position because I put him there.

Raymond Chandler Speaking

I

WHEN THIS OLD FRIEND has been examined and reappraised, he comes out as, above all else, honest—intensely, fanatically honest. He is the man most politicians only pretend to be; he is "Honest Phil."

Not that he, personally, has ever claimed such an identity. Raymond Chandler, who invented him, has advised that Marlowe is as he is "by instinct, by inevitability, without thought of it, and certainly without saying it."

And so, on those occasions when Marlowe talks about himself, he restricts himself to statements such as: "I'm a licensed private investigator and have been for quite a while. I'm a lone wolf . . . getting middle aged, and not rich. I've been in jail more than once and I don't do divorce business. I like liquor and women and chess and a few other things. The cops don't like me too well, but I know a couple I get along with."

Character that he is, fictional all the way, Marlowe might as well be flesh and blood, for he has most of our problems.

He inhabits a world where very little works right. It is a place where people sneer at his profession, where affluent gangsters advise him that he is small-time. On occasion, when he is working on a case, he has the special problem of resisting the advances of his client's daughters. When he is not working a case, however, he has the problems of any loner, and knows it.

"When I get knocked off in a dark alley sometime, if it happens, as it could to anyone in my business, and to plenty of people in any business or no business at all these days, nobody will feel that the bottom has dropped out of his or her life."

But these and other difficulties are merely portions of Philip Marlowe's own special problem: his compulsion, unvoiced but always there, to be a decent human being.

One part of his strategy for protecting himself is resistance to money. Never once, in any of his cases, does Marlowe attempt to make a deal. He works like hell, but he does not hustle.

When one prospective client inquires, "What are your charges?" Marlowe replies, "I get twenty-five dollars a day and expenses—when I'm lucky." When a woman complains that his fee is too high, he quietly disagrees. "I take big risks, sometimes quite big risks, and I don't work all the time. No, I don't think twenty-five dollars a day is too much."

Money that might be improperly earned, Marlowe resists totally.

In *The Big Sleep* he is hired by General Guy Sternwood, a multimillionaire widower who has lost control of his beautiful daughters, Vivian and Carmen. Marlowe's first task is to recover some nude photographs which Carmen posed for. After bringing this off he receives $500.

He continues his investigation of the general's daughters and ends up in the middle of a situation that the general did not ask him to investigate. When his client points out this fact, Marlowe volunteers to return the $500. The general says no and tells Marlowe he will pay an additional $1,000 if Marlowe can find Rusty Regan, Vivian's missing husband.

Through hard work Marlowe learns that Rusty was murdered by Carmen Sternwood. He withholds this information, however, because he wants to protect "what little pride a broken and sick old man has left in his blood, in the thought that his blood is not poison."

By withholding the information Marlowe forfeits the $1,000. When he tells Vivian Sternwood Regan the fate of her husband, she offers him $15,000 to forget what he knows. He declines and insists that Vivian have Carmen put away where she cannot kill anyone.

In *The Little Sister* he returns the twenty-dollar fee that he had previously accepted from Orfamay Quest.

Marlowe's scrupulousness about money is noticeable in all his adventures, but especially in *The Long Goodbye*. One of the themes in this novel is the feeling of fraternity that Marlowe slowly develops toward Terry Lennox, a World War II veteran uncertainly married to the daughter of a California tycoon.

One morning at four o'clock, Terry shows up at Marlowe's house and asks Marlowe to drive him to Mexico. Marlowe agrees and on the return trip learns that Terry's wife has been murdered and that Terry is the prime suspect.

A few days later Marlowe receives a letter, mailed from Mexico, containing a $5,000 bill. With this exotic banknote—"My portrait of Madison," Marlowe calls it—as a cushion, he takes on a series of small cases and charges the clients, all of whom are poor, either very little or nothing at all.

As *The Long Goodbye* continues, Marlowe—still holding on-to his banknote—becomes involved with Roger Wade, a best-selling novelist whose drinking problem has been enlarged by his suspicion that his wife, Eileen, murdered Sylvia Lennox. Eventually, Eileen Wade kills her husband, then commits suicide.

As the book ends Terry Lennox returns to Marlowe's house. Marlowe insists that he take back the $5,000 bill. It has too much blood on it, Marlowe says. If Terry had told him the truth about the death of Sylvia, Marlowe continues, he would have been able to save the life of Roger Wade, whom he describes as "just a human being with blood and brains and emotions. He knew what happened and he tried pretty hard to live with it."

Philip Marlowe is not a fool, but he is a fanatic. "So little of us is pure and undiluted," Chandler once wrote. Honest Phil is the great exception, and determined to remain so.

In *The Big Sleep* Vivian Sternwood Regan gambles at Eddie Mars's Cypress Club and wins $32,000. She puts this sum in her purse and leaves the casino.

Before she is off the grounds, a holdup man (actually one of Eddie Mars's boys) tries to rob her. But Marlowe has been observing in the background and has the thief covered.

Vivian thinks this is good work. She indicates her willingness to reward Marlowe with her body. He insists that this is not part of his job. "The first time I met you I told you I was a detective," he tells her. "Get it through your lovely head. I work at it, lady. I don't play at it."

After he has escorted Vivian and her $32,000 to safety, he returns to his apartment and finds Carmen Sternwood naked in his bed. He rejects her, and she curses him.

That she does so does not disturb him, but that she does it in his own bedroom is alarming because, as he explains, "this was the room I had to live in. It was everything that was mine, that had any association for me, any past, anything that took the place of a family. Not much: a few books, pictures, radio, chessmen, old letters, stuff like that. Nothing. Such as they were they had all my memories."

The thumb-sucking Carmen's invasion of his privacy is too much for Marlowe. He gives Carmen three minutes to get dressed and get out. She does the job in two.

Marlowe opens the windows to get rid of her scent. Then— "I put my empty glass down and tore the bed to pieces savagely."

———

That Philip Marlowe has so far repudiated $21,020 ($15,000, Vivian Sternwood Regan; $5,000, Terry Lennox; $1,000, General Sternwood; and $20, Orfamay Quest) does not mean he is ignorant of the facts of life. Nor does it mean he is a radical.

Philip Marlowe does not talk about it much, but he has a very definite appreciation of the way things are and have long been established. He proves this on the opening page of *The Big Sleep*.

"I was wearing my powder blue suit with dark blue shirt, tie, and display handkerchief, black brogues, black wool socks with dark blue clocks on them," he says. "I was neat, clean, shaved and sober, and I didn't care who knew it. I was everything the well-dressed private detective ought to be. I was calling on four million dollars."

But if Marlowe accepts the way things are, he does not applaud, is frequently irreverent, and on occasion enjoys the little weaknesses of the mighty.

In *Farewell, My Lovely* events lead him to the mansion of Merwin Lockridge Grayle, who owns a chain of radio stations and is the permissive husband of a young wife who likes to show a lot of leg. Soon after Marlowe's arrival, Mrs. Grayle turns to her husband and suggests that his presence is not needed.

Here is Marlowe's memory of the tycoon's response: "Mr. Grayle stood up and said he was very glad to have met me and that he would go to his room and lie down for a while. He didn't feel very well. He hoped that I would excuse him. He was so polite I wanted to carry him out of the room just to show my appreciation."

The fact is, however, that although Marlowe recognizes propriety, its restrictions and restraints plague him, and his relations with authority are bad. This has probably been the case ever since that brief time—before he was fired for insubordination—when Marlowe was, if not a cop, then at least an investigator working for the District Attorney of Los Angeles County.

In the novels of Raymond Chandler the basic problem of the police is best described by Captain Al Weber of the Bay City Police Department.

"Police business is a hell of a problem," he says in *The Lady in the Lake*. "It's a good deal like politics. It asks for the highest type of man, and there's nothing in it to attract the highest type of man. So we have to work with what we got."

In *The Big Sleep* Captain Al Gregory, LAPD, puts it another way. "I'm a copper," he tells Marlowe. "Just a plain ordinary copper. Reasonably honest. As honest as you'd expect a man to be in a world where it's out of style. That's mainly why I asked you to come in this morning. I'd like you to believe that. I'd like to see the flashy well-dressed mugs like Eddie Mars spoiling their manicures in the rock quarry at Folsom, alongside of the poor little slum-bred guys that got knocked over in their first caper and never had a break since. That's what I'd like. You and me both lived too long to think I'm likely to see it happen. Not in this town, not in any town half this size, in any part of the wise, green, and beautiful U.S.A. We just don't run our country that way."

The trouble with Philip Marlowe, from the cops' point of view, is that he considers the interests of his clients more important than the interests of the police, and so withholds information. More than once he is warned, as Lt. Randall of the LAPD puts it, that "little by little you will build up a body of hostility in this department that will make it damn hard for you to do any work."

But Marlowe is very aware of the failings of the police, aware that in the mass, they are not much more competent than newspaper reporters, television repairmen, or garage mechanics. He is also aware of the power of money, the influence of position. His attitude is that until the police change for the better, and decidedly, he has the right to protect his client by withholding information.

In *The High Window,* at the end of a discussion about a historical Los Angeles crime—the Cassidy case, Marlowe calls it —he tells two LAPD detectives, "Until you guys own your own souls you don't own mine. Until you guys can be trusted every time and always, in all times and conditions, to seek the truth out and find it and let the chips fall where they may—until that time comes, I have a right to listen to my conscience, and protect my client the best way I can."

For most of his career Marlowe manages to retain some sympathy for the police. In *The Little Sister* two LAPD detectives are described as having "the look of men who are poor and yet proud of their power, watching always for ways to make it felt." He adds, "What would you expect them to be? Civilization had no meaning for them. All they saw of it was the failures, the dirt, the aberrations and the disgust."

But by the time of *The Long Goodbye,* Marlowe has been on

the job for some fifteen years and has lost almost all of whatever sympathy he once had for cops. When a brace of LAPD plain-clothesmen arrive at his house, he observes, "You don't shake hands with cops. That close is too close."

Soon after the interview begins, Marlowe is slugged by one of the cops, then taken down to headquarters, where he is slugged by Captain Gregorius, head of homicide. Marlowe receives additional attention when Gregorius walks over and plants himself toe to toe in front of Marlowe.

"He put his big hard hands in his pockets. He rocked on his heels.

" 'Never laid a glove on him,' he said under his breath, as if talking to himself. His eyes were remote and expressionless. His mouth worked convulsively.

"Then he spat in my face.

"He stepped back. 'That will be all, thank you.'

"He turned and went back to the window. Green opened the door again.

"I went through it reaching for my handkerchief."*

The trouble here is caused, once again, by Marlowe's insistence on withholding information, an act that both puzzles and irritates the cops. "And for that amount of money (twenty-five dollars a day and expenses) you are willing to get yourself in dutch with half the law enforcement in this country?" one detective asks him, early in his career.

Marlowe replies, "I don't like it, but what the hell can I do. I'm on a case. I'm selling what I have to sell to make a living. What little guts and intelligence the Lord gave me and a willingness to get pushed around in order to protect a client."

---

*Six months later, according to Chandler, Gregorius was indicted for perjury in another matter and resigned from the LAPD. He then retired to his ranch in Wyoming, where he was kicked to death by a stallion.

II

LOS ANGELES HAS ALWAYS been a hard place: tough, rowdy, and mean. When the Spanish founded the original settlement, the first building they put up was the jail.

By 1870 Los Angeles had been American for twenty years and was "the toughest town in the nation." Bars, gambling halls, and brothels ran full blast seven days a week. The Protestant ministers simply locked their doors and left town.

The great flat metropolis of today was made out of virtually nothing. There was no important harbor, no good river, no water supply. The only card Los Angeles had was climate. Its pioneer nabobs, Yankees for the most part, were exceptionally rational and skillful manipulators; masters of chicanery, repression, and the merchandising of sunshine.

In the beginning the troublemaker was the Mexican. Lynchings were frequent, and if the victim wasn't Mexican, he was Chinese.

When the American workingman arrived, it turned out that he favored socialism. From 1907 through most of 1909, a near state of war existed between management and labor. This ended on October 1, 1909, when bombs exploded in the offices of the Los Angeles *Times.* Twenty people died. In court a union organizer admitted that he had planted the bombs.

The public was furious; the socialist possibility collapsed; and a right-wing coalition seized the city. "Red" squads were formed, liberal teachers and ministers fired, textbooks censored, and minority citizens arrested arbitrarily.

The Chamber of Commerce began to describe Los Angeles as the White Spot of America, meaning that it was free of such problems as radicalism, vice, and crime.

Meanwhile, for years, churchgoing Christians from the Midwest had been pouring off the trains. The Chamber of Commerce boasted that Los Angeles had more churches than any other city of comparable size. Religion was an important industry, the repressed population an easy target for quacks.

In the Los Angeles that Raymond Chandler knew, from 1919 to 1946, the thieves were as busy as the divines. Crime was controlled, most of the time, by a syndicate of gamblers, vice mongers, and lawyers with names like Charley Crawford, Rusty Williams, Charles Addison, Stanley Page, and Guy "Slats" MacAfee, a one-time member of the LAPD vice squad.

When Jimmy Richardson, city editor of the Los Angeles *Examiner,* published his autobiography, *For the Life of Me,* he recalled, "The syndicate owned the police department. I knew all the boys in the syndicate. They had been around for a long time, and they really had the town organized. They had it so well organized that when Scarface Al Capone came out from Chicago to look the town over with the thought of taking charge himself, he was rousted out of his hotel room and put on the train back to Chicago. And the boys who did the rousting and who told Al to get out and stay out were cops owned body and soul by the syndicate."

Things began to change around 1938, when the ostensible ruler of Los Angeles was its mayor, Frank Shaw.

At the time, George Creel wrote in *Collier's,* the City of the Angels contained "600 brothels, 300 gambling houses running full blast, 1800 bookies doing business openly, and 23,000 'one armed bandits' . . . all of these evil activities operated under the direction of a 'syndicate' that owned the city by outright purchase. Out of an annual take estimated at $20,000,000 the heads furnished campaign funds for the election of complacent officials or else gave key men a 'cut.' "

Trouble—the devil himself—entered this scene disguised as a citizen named Clifford Clinton, the son of a Salvation Army couple who had spent years in China. Creel wrote that "this bustling young proprietor of a profitable cafeteria system" was "calling his establishment the Golden Rule, and serving organ music and hymns along with the meals."

Sometime in 1937 Clifford Clinton became a member of the county grand jury, acquired accurate information on crime in Los Angeles, and began to name names. Bombs soon exploded in various homes, including Clinton's. Every victim, it turned out, was a critic of the Shaw administration.

Eventually, Earle Kynette, Chief of the Intelligence Bureau of the LAPD, was arrested, prosecuted, and found guilty of the bombings. "Captain Kynette's Intelligence Bureau was utilized for only two purposes," the prosecution charged. "One was to attack anyone who had the temerity to run for mayor in opposition to Frank Shaw, and the other was to silence anyone who raised his voice to cry out that there was vice and corruption in the city."

Clinton organized a recall movement which succeeded in removing Frank Shaw from office. It then elected its own candidate, Fletcher Bowron.

————

Soon after Mayor Bowron had been sworn in, he conferred with Jimmy Richardson of the *Examiner,* and pointed out that in spite of all the shouting about police protection of vice and gambling, his administration did not have the evidence to back up its assertions. What was needed, the mayor and the editor agreed, was someone who was willing to talk.

Tony Cornero (*a.k.a.* Anthony Cornero Stralla) was a stubby man who wore a ten-gallon hat and walked with a rolling gait. During Prohibition he had made a fortune operating a fleet of speedboats off the California coast, and the newspapers had named him King of Western Rumrunners. Now he was the owner of a profitable gambling ship, the *Rex,* anchored three miles off the shore of Santa Monica.*

"But trouble was brewing for Tony," Jimmy Richardson wrote. "Federal and State officials were seeking a way to put him out of business. Tony insisted his ship was operating outside the territorial waters of the United States. He claimed immunity under maritime law. . . . Tony hated the syndicate for a valid reason. The syndicate had always barred him from operation in Los Angeles. If he opened a gambling spot it would be knocked

*Chandler made use of the *Rex* in *Farewell, My Lovely.* At the time there were four gambling ships operating off the California coast, two off San Diego and two off Santa Monica. The *Rex,* the only one belonging to Cornero, was the biggest and the focus of attention.

over by police raiders immediately. . . . And Tony was smart enough to know just how the syndicate ran its business and who they owned in the police department."

Jimmy Richardson arranged a midnight meeting at the mayor's home, above Hollywood Bowl. Only three people attended, the mayor, Richardson, and Cornero, who laid out the syndicate's entire operation and provided a list of twenty-six LAPD officers on the syndicate's payroll.

Mayor Bowron then hired an ex-FBI agent to check up on the twenty-six cops, all of whom ranked high in the department. They soon resigned and were followed by the chief.

A neighborhood newspaper then broke a story about the midnight meeting at the mayor's house and charged that in return for his information, Cornero had been given the gambling concession in Los Angeles. Mayor Bowron, forced to demonstrate that he was not protecting Cornero, demanded that Earl Warren, Attorney General of California, raid the *Rex.*

When deputies attempted to board, they were repelled with fire hoses. The *Rex* was then blockaded by a flotilla of vessels owned by the State of California. Cornero organized a publicity campaign based on the patriotic line "Don't give up the ship" but after ten days surrendered.

The Bowron administration then turned its attention to other criminal problems. As George Creel wrote in *Collier's,* "all gambling establishments have been wiped out," and "likewise the slot machine, and the Syndicate admits to liquidation."*

Over the years the LAPD has had many harsh things said about it, and by others besides Raymond Chandler.

In 1931 Ernest Hopkins wrote in *Our Lawless Police,* "Very

*But in the meantime a different sort of criminal, the eastern mobster, had penetrated Los Angeles. Bugsy Siegal was the most flamboyant. Arrested on charges of murder, he was sent to the Los Angeles County Jail. Its house physician was an old pal, so that during his first forty-nine days in the can, Siegal made eighteen visits to his dentist. These visits were made at night, with Siegal chauffeured by a deputy sheriff. On one of them a photographer from the *Examiner* caught Siegal and actress Wendy Barrie in a Wilshire Boulevard restaurant. Raymond Chandler used this situation, the hoodlum out on the town when he was supposedly in jail, in *The Little Sister.*

early, the Los Angeles police ceased to distinguish between the economic dissenter and the criminal. This line of activity, kept alive by hysterical propaganda . . . passed through successive stages: assistance in strike breaking, espionage upon labor-union organizers . . . the 'Bolshevik' scare . . . false arrest, brutality with arrest, unlawful detention, incommunicado, and the third degree, with the relative incompetence at skillful or lawful detective work which these imply, tended to last as basic police conditions."

Things did not really begin to improve until 1951 when William H. Parker, a tough, dedicated, and paternalistic cop, became chief. Under Parker the first task of the police was to police themselves. The Internal Affairs Division, therefore, became the most powerful section of the LAPD. Neither cops on the take nor any deviation from good police practice was tolerated.

Parker also directed an intense drive to develop the professional outlook of his men. Procedures were improved, better-educated men were recruited, and salaries were raised.

By 1965, Jonathan Rubenstein noted in *City Police,* the LAPD was "the most mobile force in the country and widely regarded as the most professional." In 1968, in *The Police Establishment,* William W. Turner described the LAPD as "a crack unit of 5,161 sworn personnel . . . with a nationwide reputation for law enforcement. Its pay scale is one of the highest in the country." In 1976, in the San Francisco *Chronicle* for December 25, Charles Gain, chief of the SFPD, described the LAPD as "the best overall police organization in the country."*

In 1970 the LAPD found itself in a situation which no other police department had ever confronted before. It had acquired, whether it liked it or not, a voice exceptionally capable of presenting the cop's side of the argument.

But it was not the voice of the Chief of Police, or his media-conscious assistants. It was the voice of the low man on the totem pole, the street cop, the patrolman, in the black and white,

*For a negative view of the LAPD, with special reference to its intelligence units, see Louis Tackwood's *The Glasshouse Tapes,* published by Avon in 1973.

as found in the books of Joseph Wambaugh, LAPD.

Wambaugh's first two novels, *The New Centurions* and *The Blue Knight*, were published in 1970 and 1972. *The Onion Field*, his first book of nonfiction, came out in 1973. In 1975, after resigning his sergeantcy in the LAPD, he published what is so far his finest novel, *The Choirboys*.

Holmes, Maigret, Spade, and Marlowe are able to solve their problems, but in Wambaugh's LAPD many of the problems faced by the cops are as yet unsolvable.

In London, in 1829, the police problem was to take control of the streets and end the tremendous disorder. In Wambaugh's Los Angeles of the 1970's the police problem is not control of the streets and not crime—the mafia, Commies, hippies, blacks. It is the many citizens of the huge city who are unable to cope with the troubles they have met in life and are, accordingly, a problem to the rest of the population, whose representatives, armed and uniformed, are the cops.

"See boys, there's just a million problems in this world that there ain't no solution to and the cops get most of these kind," a veteran advises in *The Choirboys*.

The ugly inadequacies, the primitiveness of the metropolis, are familiar to Philip Marlowe. In *Farewell, My Lovely* he says bitterly, "The eighty-five cent dinner tasted like a discarded mailbag, and was served to me by a waiter who looked as if he would slug me for a quarter,"—things are so bad that Marlowe can only make a joke of it—"cut my throat for six bits," he continues, "and bury me at sea in a barrel of concrete for a dollar and a half, plus sales tax."

Wambaugh's cops endure in a similar environment, but it is not 1940 or thereabouts; it is 1975 and the problems of living in Los Angeles have not changed, they have only grown, like the smog that Marlowe hardly knew.

In *The Choirboys* the police are confronted by a shocking series of grotesqueries. Included are:

Oscar Mabley. Fifty-eight years old, white, unmarried, lives alone, unemployed. Likes to paint his car red, "did it with paint and brush and did it perhaps once a month. The policemen who knew him said his fifteen-year-old Ford outweighed a Cadillac limousine, so thick were the coats of peeling red enamel." The cops are called in because he has attempted to paint a lady's face and hair red. When they arrive at Oscar's he, naked, steps out from behind a chair. Except for his teeth and his eyeballs, he is completely red.

Lena Rivers. An alcoholic divorcée with four kids. Her youngest, the son of a sailor who has deserted her, spends his first six years with his grandmother. When the grandmother dies Lena is forced to take back her son. Because of her feelings about the father, Lena carries the "naked, screaming child through the house by a pair of pliers clamped to his penis."

Such problems are confronted regularly by the police in *The Choirboys,* and their cumulative effect is dangerous.

Officer Baxter Slate says that "the physical dangers of police work are grossly overrated," but that "the emotional dangers make it the most hazardous job on earth."

He makes this statement because of the lessons he learned while working juvenile. "I mean that the mother of a sexually molested child," he says, "will not leave nor truly protect the child from the father as long as the man has a good job. . . . I mean that weak and inept parents will always refuse to surrender their neglected children to the authorities because they want to atone for failure with previous children and the cycle inevitably repeats itself."

For Baxter Slate, who is the intellectual in *The Choirboys,* "the weakness of the human race is stupefying." Speaking as a cop he says, "The very best, most optimistic hope we can cling to is that we're tic birds who ride the rhino's back and eat the parasites out of the flesh and keep the beasts from disease and hope we're not parasites too."

In *The Choirboys* the LAPD is presented as bureaucratic to an extent that might even have surprised Edgar Allan Poe.

In the first few pages the reader learns that Deputy Chief Lynch is not happy about the way Commander Moss's secretary is answering the telephone. The correct procedure for answering the telephone, written by Lynch himself, goes "Good morning, Wilshire Watch Commander's Office, Officer Fernwood speaking. May I help you?"

Lynch asks Moss to straighten out his secretary. "I've had reports," Lynch explains, "she didn't say good morning twice last week when my adjutant called."

Out in the streets the brass are policing the cops just like the cops are policing the citizens. During one of his weekly nights on the street, Lieutenant "Hardass" Grimsely catches "eight officers with their hats off, one smoking in public, and three others drinking coffee which proved to be gratuitously received."

As for the war on crime, what police supervisors really want from their men, Wambaugh says, is to have them "respond promptly to radio calls, write one moving traffic violation a day and stop at least three people daily for field interrogations."

One of the few instances of successful problem solving in *The Choirboys* involves Sergeant Dominic Scuzzi of the vice squad. Since citizens complain about degenerate acts in public rest rooms, the duties of the vice squad include monitoring men's toilets by observing through small screens and two-way mirrors. Sergeant Scuzzi has a unique solution to the problem of the proper response toward the man who misbehaves when alone in a public toilet.

" 'I shoot him. With this,' Scuzzi said, pulling a pink plastic water pistol from the pocket of his baggy gabardines. 'I just shoot him through the screen where I'm peeking. First it confuses him, then it scares him soon's he realizes where it's coming from. See, I don't add to his thrill by bracing him or any of that shit. . . . Remember, guilt and punishment and stuff from his kiddy days is partly the reason he has to do all this in a public place. So I just shoot him with my gun. Pretty soon he yells, "Who're you? You store security? You a cop?" . . . I just shoot him again. It's humiliating. It degrades himself in a way he can't stand . . . he can't take the humiliation I give him. I'm saying with my water gun that his little act ain't worth more than a few squirts of water. *That* he can't stand.' "

One hundred years or so ago Antoine Claude, head of the Paris police, wrote, "I can only compare a police prefect to the director of a hospital. Like him he sees of humanity little but its wounds and afflictions."

In *The Choirboys* a cop asks, "Why's a cop need an education anyway? No more than a trash collector. . . . That's all we do, clean up garbage."

And in *Stories Cops Only Tell Each Other*, NYPD veteran Gene Radano wrote, "Being a cop gives you a look at life through its asshole."

III

AMONG PROBLEM SOLVERS considered here, Philip Marlowe is the most handicapped.

Raymond Chandler described him as "the best man in his world and a good enough one in any world." Chandler made his creation scrupulously honest, a man in revolt against a corrupt society, a man whose attitudes toward money and sex are spectacularly different from the man on the street's—the cop's—attitude toward these basic and conversational desires.

And then Chandler drove his point home by making Marlowe a failure. The politics of honesty are the politics of failure.

"Of course Marlowe is a failure," Raymond Chandler once acknowledged. "He is a failure because he hasn't any money. A man who without physical handicaps cannot make a decent living is always a failure and usually a moral failure. But a lot of very good men have been failures because their particular talents did not suit their time and place.—In the long run I guess we are all failures or we wouldn't have the kind of world we have."

With lack of funds as Marlowe's basic position, the rest follows logically. He operates alone in a seedy, unsatisfactory world with resources others would consider unacceptable.

In *Farewell, My Lovely* events require him to slip aboard the gambling ships that lie off Bay City. Because he has just been bounced around by the cops, he checks into a waterfront hotel to rest before going out to the boats.

At nightfall he awakens. "I got to my feet and threw cold water on my face. After a little while I felt a little better, but very little. I needed a drink. I needed a lot of life insurance. I needed a vacation. I needed a house in the country. What I had was a coat, a hat and a gun. I put them on and went out of the room."

Wherever Marlowe goes, things are about the same, including his office. "The pebbled glass door is lettered in flaked black paint: Philip Marlowe—Investigations. It is a reasonably shabby door at the end of a reasonably shabby corridor in the sort of building that was new about the year the all-tile bathroom became the basis of civilization."

Quite often Marlowe gets socked in the jaw. In *The Lady in the Lake* he spends part of an afternoon being slapped around by the villainous Sergeant Degarmo of the Bay City Police. By early evening, a warm, open-windowed evening in Southern California, Marlowe is back in his office. He has tried to accomplish something; he has failed and taken a licking. Now he attempts to repair his psyche.

He takes a couple of drinks and tries to get his mind off his troubles by studying the contents of a note that a Miss Fromsett, who works for a perfume company, has pushed under his door. But the drinks are not much help, so he puts the bottle away and rinses the glass.

"When I had done that I washed my hands and bathed my face in cold water and looked at it. The flush was gone from the left cheek, but it looked a little swollen. Not very much, but enough to make me tighten up again. I brushed my hair and looked at the grey in it. There was getting to be plenty of grey in it. The face under the hair had a sick look. I didn't like the face at all.

"I went back to the desk and read Miss Fromsett's note again. I smoothed it out on the glass and sniffed it, smoothed it out some more and folded it and put it in my pocket.

"I sat very still and listened to the evening grow quiet outside the open window. And very slowly I grew quiet with it."

———

But he does solve problems.

Sherlock Holmes once observed that he "had the good fortune to bring peace to many troubled souls." Marlowe can say the same thing.

Although he is never in a position to do anyone a fantastic amount of good, he is able to do a reasonable amount of good for people who, generally speaking, are competent to handle their own lives but have suddenly been overwhelmed by an emergency. In every instance, his clients benefit from knowing P. Marlowe.

In *The Big Sleep* he protects General Sternwood from learning too much about his daughters. Instead of turning Carmen Sternwood over to the cops, Marlowe simply insists that Vivian Sternwood put her sister away. "Someplace far off from here where they will keep guns and fancy drinks away from her," he says. "Hell, she might even get herself cured, you know. It's been done."

In *Farewell, My Lovely* his efforts enable the New York police to pick up an international con man who has been operating in Bay City.

He is also responsible for a big shake-up in the Bay City police. The chief resigns, several detectives are reduced to acting patrolmen, and a likeable young man named Red Norgaard, who had helped Marlowe with the problem of getting aboard the gambling ships, gets back his job on the Bay City force.

In *The High Window* Marlowe establishes that Merle Davis is innocent of murder. For eight years the high-strung Merle has been dominated by a Pasadena widow named Murdock, who has her convinced that she pushed Mrs. Murdock's first husband out of a skyscraper window.

Marlowe discovers that it was actually Mrs. Murdock who did the pushing. At first, Merle refuses to believe him.

"You were made to think you had pushed him," Marlowe explains. "It was done with care, deliberation and the sort of quiet ruthlessness you only find in a certain kind of woman dealing with another woman. . . . You were just a scapegoat for her. If you want to come out of this pallid sub-emotional life you have been living, you have got to realize and believe what I am telling you. I know it's tough."

Marlowe then drives Merle from Pasadena to Wichita to be with her parents.

In addition to helping Merle, Marlowe makes life easier for another person: he accepts the statement of Mrs. Murdock's son, Leslie, that his shooting of a blackmailer was accidental.

And it is worth noting that, in this case, a nice thing happens to Marlowe, who has had to go exceptionally far out on the limb to protect his client. At the end of the book Lt. Breeze, LAPD, tells Marlowe that he himself once worked on the Cassidy case, which Marlowe had cited earlier as a specific instance of the purchase of "justice" by money.

"On account of the Cassidy case, and the way it made me feel," Breeze explains, "I sometimes give a guy a break he could perhaps not really deserve. A little something paid back out of the dirty millions to a working stiff—like me—or like you. Be good."

In *The Little Sister* Marlowe protects the screen starlet Mavis Weld at a time when her rising career is threatened by a scandal for which she is not responsible. And in *The Lady in the Lake* Marlowe manages to protect the interests of his client, Derace Kingsley, a business executive. In doing so he creates a situation in which the main villain, a Bay City cop, kills himself.

Raymond Chandler, without being especially accurate, once called *The Maltese Falcon* "the record of a man's devotion to a friend."

Such is the theme of *The Long Goodbye,* in which Marlowe eventually realizes that Terry Lennox is unworthy of friendship or fraternity. But before he realizes this, Marlowe works hard to uncover evidence to demonstrate that Lennox could not possibly have killed his wife, Sylvia, as had been formally charged by the district attorney.

––––––

Nevertheless, in any consideration of Marlowe as problem solver, certain difficulties do arise. At the end of each case he still has to contend with the problem of living in the world as it is known to him. He never solves his own problems, only those of others. And the question is, How?

Holmes cracked his cases by deduction, Maigret through sympathy for the victim, Spade by guts and common sense. But it sometimes seems as if Marlowe only solves his cases because custom demands that he do so.

Raymond Chandler was more interested in moral drama than in who killed whom. In *The Dangerous Edge* Gavin Lambert wrote, "For Wilkie Collins the main objective was never the solution but the experience of the mystery." The same can be said of Chandler. It was the events along the way, rather than the arrival, that interested him. In most of his novels the identification of the villain is the result of a chain of events that appears to be rational but is actually irrational.

Like Hammett, Chandler was a graduate of *Black Mask,* in which the scene outranked the plot. "With me a plot . . . is an organic thing," Chandler once explained. "It grows and often it overgrows. I am continually finding myself with scenes that I won't discard and don't want to fit in. So that my plot problem invariably winds up as a desperate attempt to justify a lot of material that, for me at least, has come alive and insists on staying alive."*

Philip Marlowe solves his clients' problems because he sympathizes with them as people and wants to get them out of trouble, because he takes unusual risks, and because he is on the case virtually 100 percent of the time.

Like Spade, he is an experienced detective. He started out as an insurance investigator, moved on to the office of the Los

*When *The Big Sleep* was made into a movie, Howard Hawks directed. Later, talking to Richard Schickel, then gathering material for his *The Men Who Made the Movies,* Hawks explained, "During the making of *The Big Sleep* I found out, for the first time, that you don't have to be too logical. You really should just make good scenes. You follow one scene with another and stop worrying about hooking them together. . . . Once during the picture Bogart said, 'Who killed this fellow?' And I said, 'Well, it probably was . . . I don't know.' So we sent a wire to . . . Raymond Chandler and asked him and he told us the name of the fellow. And I wired him back, and I said, 'He was down at the beach when that happened. It couldn't be done that way.' So nobody knew who killed that bird. It didn't hurt the picture."

Angeles County district attorney, then set up on his own.

But when all is said and done, the emotional and passionate Marlowe plays no part in the evolution of sleuthing and makes no contribution to what Ellenberger called "the unmasking trend." He is not so much a detective as he is a weapon, a weapon wielded by an ironic moralist against what he regards as a botched and violent civilization.*

When Conan Doyle invented Holmes in 1881 or thereabouts, he created a transcendent, totally successful figure who, for the most part, represented what crime buff John Patterson has called "the staid, comfortable, secure society of the pre-1914 period . . . the sober gentility and crude optimism of an earlier and more complacent generation."

Representatives of that privileged world were still on deck in 1919 when Raymond Chandler appeared in San Francisco. He was American born, but British educated, and had recently endured two years as an enlisted man in the Gordon Highlanders.

In San Francisco, working temporarily in a branch of a British bank, Chandler came across those whom he later described as "the kind of English who don't live in England, don't want to live in England, but bloody well wave their Chinese affectations of manner and accent in front of your nose as if it was some kind of rare incense instead of a distillation of cheap suburban snobbery

---

*Among recent books about real-life private detectives, one of the best is *Blye, Private Eye*, by Nicholas Pileggi. As it ends the author makes a point of contrasting Blye's life with Marlowe's. The difference is dramatic. Blye is presented as a master of red tape, a man with an exceptional ability to pull information out of bureaucratic channels, such as the Bureau of Motor Vehicles.

In *The Private Police*, by James S. Kakalik and Sorrel Wildhorn, the authors point out, "While the mass-media image of a 'private eye' is romantic and exciting, the reality is quite different. The private investigator usually is an information-gatherer, and often the information gathered has little to do with either prevention of crime or apprehension of criminals. However, some of the private investigators' activities are crime related. In terms of relative frequency, the primary activities of investigators are preemployment background checks on personnel, background checks of insurance and credit applicants, plainclothes undercover work to detect employee dishonesty, and pilferage or customer shoplifting in retail stores, and investigation of insurance or workingmen's compensation claims."

All of which is still not the complete story. With problem solvers such as the Texan, Jay J. Armes, working out of El Paso, the melodrama continues.

which is just as ludicrous in England as it is here."

In the lexicon of Raymond Chandler, "sham" is a key word. So is "phony."

Marlowe talks with "a disgust for sham," and Chandler himself points out, "P. Marlowe and I do not despise the upper classes because they take baths and have money; we despise them because they are phony."

The fact that phony people, with their "Chinese affectations of manner and accent," were—in spite of the efforts of Hammett and others—still dominant in criminal fiction in the thirties, disgusted Raymond Chandler.

He complained zestfully about "the same careful groupings of suspects, the same utterly incomprehensible trick of how somebody stabbed Mrs. Pettington Postelwaid III with the solid platinum poniard just as she flatted on the top note of the 'Bell Song' from *Lakme* in the presence of fifteen ill-assorted guests" and "the same moody silence next day as they sit around sipping Singapore slings and sneering at each other while the flatfeet crawl to and fro under the Persian rugs with their derby hats on."

What Chandler wanted, when he began to write in 1932, was someone he could have some fun with. Someone who was not phony.

Someone who lived in the real world of corrupt and grotesque Los Angeles, loathed it, and was as exasperated by it as Chandler himself.

"I think Mr. Chandler is interested in writing, not detective stories, but serious studies of the criminal milieu, the Great Wrong Place," W. H. Auden observed; "his powerful but extremely depressing books should be judged, not as escape literature, but as works of art."

And so Raymond Chandler created his weapon—Philip Marlowe, the honest man in the corrupt world.

"It is the agent of social justice," Chesterton said, "who is the original and poetic figure, while the burglars and footpads are merely old cosmic conservatives, happy in the immemorial respectability of apes and wolves." This is a brilliant anticipation of

Marlowe. "The personification of an attitude," Chandler called him; "the exaggeration of a possibility."

———

But there is one world in which P. Marlowe looks very bad, and that is the world of Mendy Menendez, a Sunset Strip hood and affluence buff who knows for sure that crime does pay, and adores, loves, respects every minute of the good deal civilization is for him.

One morning, in *The Long Goodbye,* Marlowe arrives at his office and finds Mendy and a couple of his boys waiting out in the hall. Marlowe unlocks his door and Mendy—"a guy who owned the place where he happened to be"—walks in, looks around, and is unimpressed.

"You're a piker," he tells Marlowe. "A Peanut grifter . . . you got no guts . . . no connections . . . you throw out a phony attitude . . . Tarzan on a bright red scooter."

He stares at Marlowe with "bird-bright eyes," then demands, "You know who I am?"

Marlowe attempts a pair of jocular identifications, then Mendy decides it's time to provide his own ID.

"I'm a big bad man, Marlowe. I make lots of dough. I got to make lots of dough to juice the guys I got to juice. I got a place in Bel-Air . . . a platinum-blond wife . . . two kids in private schools . . . I got a butler, two maids, a chauffeur, not counting the monkey who walks behind me. Everywhere I go I'm a darling. The best of everything, the best food, the best drinks, the best hotel suites. I got a place in Florida . . . seagoing with a crew of five . . . Bentley, two Cadillacs . . . Chrysler station wagon . . . MG for my boy. . . . What you got?"

Not much, Marlowe acknowledges. He has a house—doesn't have to share it with anyone—a few bucks in the bank, and a grand or so in bonds.

Mendy asks him what's the most he's ever made on one case. Marlowe says "Eight-fifty" and Mendy sneers, "Jesus, how cheap can a guy get?"

Here, in as gloriously comic a situation as exists in criminal fiction, Chandler has reversed his field and is laughing at Marlowe —"Tarzan on a bright red scooter."

All the masters of criminal fiction are amusing and witty, but Chandler's humor is the fiercest.

"My kind of writing demands a certain amount of dash and high spirits—the word is gusto, a quality lacking in modern writing," he once observed.*

At its best, Chandler's joy is wild and negative and purely American, and much more of an experience than simply intellectual fun. It blasts out of the guts as something fiercely negative, is then seized by the mind and zestfully restyled into pure fun.

Time after time, with joy and gusto, Chandler accomplishes what he praised Hammett for doing—"He wrote scenes that seemed never to have been written before."

What other hood or villain ever had a line like Mendy's "Everywhere I go I'm a darling"?

Chandler once wrote, "The realist in murder writes of a world in which gangsters rule nations and almost rule cities, in which hotels and apartments and celebrated restaurants are owned by men who made their money out of brothels, in which a screen star can be the finger man for a mob, and the nice man down the hall is boss of the numbers racket; a world where a judge with a cellar full of bootleg liquor can send a man to jail for having a pint in his pocket . . . where no man can walk down a dark street in safety because law and order are things we talk about but refrain from practicing."

But Chandler's world of the "realist in murder" offers the reader only one portion of a larger reality.

In *Farewell, My Lovely* a client asks Marlowe if there is any money in being a private detective.

"There's not much money in it," Marlowe replies. "There's a lot of grief. But there's a lot of fun too." He then adds, "And there's always the chance of a big case."

It is regrettable that Raymond Chandler never gave Philip

---

*Evelyn Waugh defined gusto as zest for the variety and absurdity of life.

Marlowe a chance to work on "a big case"; a case, that is, which would allow Marlowe to recognize that the world is a far more remarkable place than he thinks it is.

The fact is, "a big case" means big people, major characters whose roles are enlarged by the peculiarities of their situation in society.

In *Conan Doyle* Hesketh Pearson wrote, "Chesterton once remarked that if Dickens had written the Holmes stories he would have made every character as vivid as Holmes. We may reply that if Dickens had done so he would have ruined the stories, which depend for their effect on the radiance of the central character and the relative glimmer of the satellites."

Like Holmes, Marlowe must dominate, which Chandler understood from the start. He insisted that Marlowe be "The best man in his world . . . everything."

But until the final novel, *Playback,* Chandler refused to allow Marlowe to stray from "his world," which is why, in the adventures of Philip Marlowe, all cops are crooks and all rich men, fools. Anyone whose worldly situation tops Marlowe's has got to be bad, for only because they are contemptible and phony can Marlowe be heroic.

It should be recognized, therefore, that in getting murder "as far as possible from Emily Post's idea of how a well-bred debutante gnaws a chicken wing," Raymond Chandler presented a reality that is not much more satisfactory than the one it replaced. The world we live in is a far more romantic place than the world of the realist in murder. It is a world in which magical things do happen.

It is, among other things, a world where a forty-four-year-old business executive, Raymond Chandler, an accountant who has lost his job, can abandon his corporate habits and, turning his attention to words, slowly create what Ross Macdonald has described as "an overheard democratic prose which is one of the most effective narrative instruments in our . . . literature."

With this prose Chandler did wonderful things and had, at times, immense fun.

In *The Long Goodbye* Marlowe has an interview with Harlan

Porter, one of the wealthiest men in California, and a man who does not enjoy having Marlowe poke around in the affairs of his family.

Afterward, Porter's daughter Linda asks Marlowe how he liked her father. "Fine," Marlowe says. "He explained civilization to me. I mean how it looks to him. . . . He's going to let it go on for a little while longer. But it had better be careful and not interfere with his private life. If it does, he's apt to make a phone call to God and cancel the order."

An honest man in a corrupt world is a good act, put together for excellent reasons, but it must be acknowledged that its creator did with it just about everything possible. In 1978 it is dated.

Philip Marlowe is a thirties and forties character touched lightly by the fifties. He comes out of the economically depressed yet wisecracking thirties and fades away during the Senator McCarthy period. He cannot successfully be removed from this parochial era.

If Raymond Chandler had begun to write in the sixties or seventies, his attention would have focused on a far more complex and sophisticated scene. In *The Big Sleep* a book dealer runs a circulating library of pornographic books out of his back room. In the seventies, in neighborhood drugstores, skin magazines peddle pubic hair. The criminal reality of the last two decades—assassinations, Watergate, kidnapping, terrorist bands—is far more bizarre than anything Chandler ever portrayed; it is Technicolor contrasted with primitive old black-and-white.

In 1969 an oil company had the problem of informing certain of its executives about the results of its test drilling in Alaska. To make sure that these executives would not be able to use microphones and transmitters to relay the news, the oil company hired a San Francisco detective named Ralph Bertsche.

After the executives had assembled, they were required to undress and stand around in their underwear while Bertsche searched their luggage. Dressed again, they climbed aboard a chartered Canadian National Railways train that Bertsche had already combed for bugs.

"The next five days for the oil men were spent in a communications limbo," John Schwada wrote in *San Francisco* magazine; "no *Wall Street Journal* or ticker-tape reached them, and they sent none, as they shuttled between Calgary and Edmonton on that train. As the Canadian landscape whooshed by, the cloistered executives talked of oil and money. When the train stopped for provisions, and was surrounded by guards, only Bertsche debarked."

As the train rolled back and forth, back and forth, between Calgary and Edmonton, the local newspapers became curious. The explanation was simple. It is difficult to bug a moving train.

To be any kind of character today, Marlowe would probably need a considerable amount of special information, technical knowledge of one sort or another. He would also have to abandon the gloriously exaggerated simplicities of the idealistic, redeeming knight and become more of a hunter/seeker. He might even have to join up with the rest of the race, those who are not so much corrupt, whatever that means ("Changed from a state of uprightness, correctness, truth, [etc.], to a bad state; depraved"—*Webster's New Collegiate,* 1956) as they are complicated and, accordingly, shifty characters who, scientists say, are wired for hunting and on a primitive model.

IV

RAYMOND CHANDLER DID NOT mind making fun of himself. "Yes, I am exactly like the characters in my books," he wrote one inquirer. "I am very tough and have been known to break a Vienna roll with my bare hands. . . . I do not regard myself as a dead shot, but I am a pretty dangerous man with a wet towel. But all in all I think my favorite weapon is a twenty-dollar bill."

In his prime he was five feet eleven inches tall, and weighed one hundred and seventy-five pounds. The humorist H. Allen Smith, who knew him when they were both screenwriters, wrote, "I had expected to find a hulking guy with a flat nose and football shaped biceps. He turned out to be the last man in the world I would have picked as the author of his books. He is a mild mannered guy of medium size with black wavy hair and a sensitive face. He looks like a poet is supposed to look." The actor José Ferrer knew Chandler briefly, and remembered that he was "wearing a nondescript tweed jacket and gray flannels, seemed cheerful . . . and was so far from the Philip Marlowe tough guy image that I was bewildered."

He was born in Chicago on July 23, 1888. His mother, Florence Dart Thorton, was one of eight daughters in a Protestant family in Waterford, Ireland. His father, Maurice Chandler, a Quaker from Philadelphia, turned out to be a periodic drunk. After six years of marriage, his wife divorced him and sailed for Ireland with her son.

There, for some time, Raymond Chandler was the only male in a houseful of women: "he was thrown into a matriarchal household," Patricia Highsmith has pointed out sympathetically, "and thus saw women as the source of stability as well as love objects."

Eventually, a wealthy uncle sent him to England to study at Dulwich College. His mother accompanied him and remained with him while he studied as a "day boy" from 1896 to 1905.

He then spent a year studying in France and Germany, and afterward returned to England to write. By the time he was twenty-three, he had published twenty-seven poems, seven essays, and a handful of reviews. He was a young man on the fringes of literary London, but it was always the fringes, and in 1912 he joined his mother in California.

Eventually, sometime after World War I had begun, he went to Canada and enlisted in the Gordon Highlanders. A few months later, in France, he won a battlefield promotion to sergeant.

Of writers considered in this book, Raymond Chandler is the only one to have led infantry attacks against direct machine-gun fire; the only one to have been in a squad pinned down by a barrage of eleven-inch German high-explosive shells, a situation from which he emerged the sole survivor.

In 1918 he was transferred to the Royal Flying Corps. Discharged in 1919, he returned to Los Angeles and his only parent.

By nature Chandler was exceptionally bright. In Los Angeles he needed only six weeks to complete an accounting course that normally took two years. "I have the type of mind," he eventually wrote, "that can become a pretty good second rate anything, and without much effort."

He was hired as an accountant by the Dabney Oil Syndicate, soon became its auditor, and was then appointed vice president with a salary of $1,000 a month.

"Chandler handled all the paperwork for the company," Frank MacShane wrote in *The Life of Raymond Chandler*. "The office people . . . were astonished at the ease with which he dictated letters of three or four pages on complicated negotiations which were a delight to read as prose."

When his mother died in 1924, Chandler, thirty-six, almost immediately married Pearl Eugenia Hurlburt, commonly known as Cissie. It was his first marriage, her third, and she was older by seventeen years.

In her time she had been a doll, a knock-out beauty. In New York she had studied to be a concert pianist, and it is possible that she was the model for a nude painting that hung in a major Manhattan hotel. Chandler had a set of nude photos that had been taken when she was young.

At the time of the marriage, Chandler's drinking was limited to weekend cocktails. He enjoyed playing tennis with others from the Dabney office, and he loved to fly, as a passenger.

Gradually things changed. He became involved with the secretaries at the office, took an apartment for one of them, and spent his weekends with her.

"They would have such binges," MacShane wrote, "that she simply was unable to turn up for work on Monday." Chandler would not show up until Wednesday, if then. "His colleagues tried to cover for him," MacShane reported, "but he would be away for weeks at a time."

J. B. Dabney, Chandler's employer, was finally informed of the situation. He gave Chandler one warning, then fired him. It was 1932, and the Great Depression had begun, but Chandler, instead of moving toward the breadlines, stepped into his car and traveled.

"Wandering up and down the Pacific Coast in an automobile," he explained years later, "I began to read pulp magazines, because they were cheap enough to throw away and because I never had at any time any taste for the kind of thing known as women's magazines. This was in the great days of *Black Mask* and it struck me that some of the writing was pretty forceful and honest, even though it had its crude aspects. I decided that this might be a good way to try to learn to write fiction and get paid a small amount of money at the same time. I spent five months over an 18,000-word novelette and sold it for $180."*

Between then and 1939 Chandler published some fifteen short stories in the pulps. His first novel, *The Big Sleep,* was published in 1939. His second, *Farewell, My Lovely,* came out in 1940. It was followed by *The High Window,* 1942; *The Lady in the Lake,* 1943; *The Little Sister,* 1949; *The Long Goodbye,* 1953; and *Playback,* 1958.

Raymond Chandler was exceptionally romantic. To be emotionally involved was most important to him. A doctor described him as "one of the most highly strung and emotional people" he had ever met.

At the same time, alcohol did not provide the relaxation that Chandler required. Chandler's mind operated on a subconscious level "which alcohol can't reach," the doctor explained; "it merely irritates the emotions it can reach."

He continued to have various affairs with younger women. At one time, while working as a film writer, he set up housekeeping with someone from the studio.

Yet he seems to have adored Cissie, then in her seventies. "I never really thought of what I wrote as anything more than a fire for Cissie to warm her hands on," he wrote a friend. "She didn't even much like what I wrote."

*This was *Blackmailers Don't Shoot,* published in *Black Mask* in December 1933. Of it, Chandler later wrote Erle Stanley Gardner, "I made an extremely detailed synopsis of your story, and from that rewrote it and . . . then compared what I had with yours, and then went back and rewrote it some more, and so on."

Besides being a romantic, he was antisocial. Picasso once remarked that "every poet and every artist is an anti-social being. He's not that way because he wants to be; he can't be any other . . . if he really is an artist it is his nature not to want to be admitted."[1]

With Cissie, before moving to La Jolla, Chandler lived in unpretentious houses in middle-class neighborhoods. Nevertheless, he was prosperous. As a screenwriter he began at $750 a week and finished at $4,000, plus a share of the profits. He drove a gray green Packard convertible. John Houseman, a friend, described the car as "monumental."

At the studios the atmosphere was convivial. "For the first time in a decade," MacShane wrote, "he was involved in intellectual conversations as a normal part of his daily life."

One scriptwriter told MacShane that Chandler "loved to talk and argue about anything, and he usually dominated, though never with arrogance—but with an ironic humor."

Later, in La Jolla, where he and Cissie lived in a white house overlooking the Pacific, they seldom socialized. During these years his income from royalties ranged from $15,000 to $25,000 a year.

In the afternoons, MacShane reported, Chandler would go to the grocery store, then drop in at the office of his lawyer or his accountant. "These errands constituted his social life, or were a substitute for one. . . . He enjoyed chatting with shopkeepers, garage men, and postal clerks. He seemed to prefer their company to that of his own sort. He enjoyed the anonymity of his life."

Toward the end of his life, Chandler visited England several times. While there, he spent part of his time playing darts with the warehousemen who worked for his English publisher.

He was also the guest of honor at a luncheon given by Ian Fleming. It was, it appears, a typical society luncheon. "Chandler was a man shy of houses and 'entertaining,' " Fleming wrote. "I am pretty sure he hated the whole thing."

———

During much of the time when Chandler was writing *The Long Goodbye,* his wife was very ill. She died December 12, 1954, aged eighty-three. For thirty years, her grieving husband said, she had been the beat of his heart, "the music heard faintly at the edge of sound."

A few weeks later Chandler's cat also died. With no one left to bestow his affection on, his misery was total.

"He desperately needed another woman in his life," Patricia Highsmith has observed. "He was lost without a female figure or figurehead."

He made a gesture toward suicide, firing off two shots that ended in the ceiling of his shower stall. The police put him in the psycho ward of the county hospital. Neil Morgan, a columnist for the San Diego *Evening Tribune,* moved him into a private sanitarium.

After a partial recovery Chandler sold his home: house and every stick of furniture. For the next few years he traveled between England, Europe, and America.

Chandler "was lost without women," Ian Fleming recalled, "and . . . was never without some good looking companion to mother him and try to curb his drinking."

———

In 1958 he published *Playback,* his last novel.

It is 190 pages long, and 142 of them pass before Marlowe runs into his first cop, the duty officer in the station at Esmeralda, a La Jolla-like resort near San Diego. Right behind the duty officer comes Esmeralda's number-one cop, Captain Alessandre, a decent fellow who treats Marlowe as if he were also decent.

Leaving the station, Marlowe is puzzled. "I wasn't too used to cops who treated me as if I had a right to live," he muses.

It is a far cry from *The Long Goodbye.* There, Marlowe's final line had been, "I never saw any of them again—except the cops. No way has yet been invented to say goodbye to them."*

---

*Chandler had a tendency to ease up on the fuzz as soon as he got Marlowe out of the metropolis. In *The Lady in the Lake* Chandler presented Jim Patton, deputy sheriff and constable of a mountain village, as an able officer and a decent fellow.

Doyle and Hammett might have found the implication here suspect. In "The Copper Beeches" Holmes's advice to Watson is that "the lowest and vilest alleys in London do not present a more dreadful record of sin than does the smiling and beautiful countryside." Hammett, writing of his experiences with the Pinkertons, noted, "Going from the larger cities into the remote rural communities, one finds a steadily decreasing percentage of crimes that have to do with money and a proportionate increase in the frequency of sex as a criminal motive."

But his new, pleasant relationship with the cops is only one of the changes in Philip Marlowe's situation. The fact is, the dame-spurning fanatic has been replaced by a stranger who sleeps with every attractive woman he meets.

In only one way does he remain the old Marlowe. He returns $450 to a client who appears to be dissatisfied with his services.*

In February 1959, Chandler was elected president of the Mystery Writers of America. In March, already ill, he flew to New York to attend a cocktail party in his honor. Two days later, he flew back to La Jolla. He died there on March 26, 1959, a victim of bronchial pneumonia.

———

"I'm only a man," Simenon wrote.

This was Chandler's trouble too. When judged by bureaucracy's staid, gustoless prejudices, he seems almost as undesirable as Edgar Allan Poe, who was thrown out of West Point at the end of his plebe year, married his first cousin when she was still thirteen and—shattered by her death—died one day after being found drunk in a Baltimore gutter. Along the way, he invented the detective story and the spy story and wrote some poems with lines like:

> To the glory that was Greece
> And the grandeur that was Rome.

Raymond Chandler contributed seven novels, six of which are classics of criminal fiction, and made poetry out of the tawdry side of Southern California.

"His vision was clear and his prose matched it," Lawrence Clark Powell wrote. "Through his transparent language we see landscape and life in exact register, without the slightest blur."

For Charles McCabe, columnist on the San Francisco *Chronicle,* Chandler's novels are "marvelous, like a landscape with an always pleasing effect although each detail seems new with each

---

*Marlowe later agrees to take $250 of this money back. Accordingly, he actually spurns only $200 in *Playback.* This brings the grand total to, at the minimum, $21,220 spurned in a lifetime. In *Playback* he also refuses a $5,000-bribe offered by a hotel owner. Marlowe recognizes that this money is an indirect bribe from a man who has committed two criminal acts. If Marlowe had accepted it, he would have been an accessory after the fact. Thus, this $5,000 does not count as money righteously spurned by Honest Phil.

viewing. I can read a Chandler novel, and come back to it in a year and it's as though I have never seen it. The whole thing is as stylized as a sonnet and as forgettable."

Both Poe and Chandler were magicians, as much so as Blackstone or Houdini.

———

Dulwich College, attended by Chandler for nine years, was a solid and honorable example of the English public school. "Not quite on a level with Eton or Harrow from a social point of view," Chandler advised a friend, "but very good educationally."

In *The Life of Raymond Chandler,* Frank MacShane reported that the headmaster there taught his students that a man of honor was a person "capable of understanding that which was good; capable of subordinating the poorer part of his nature to the higher part."

It was a concept that Chandler never forgot. Proud of his English public-school background, he regarded himself as a man of honor. This was evident on several occasions—most gloriously, during a Hollywood adventure.

In 1945 Paramount Pictures had an urgent need to make a film starring its most valuable box-office draw, Alan Ladd, who in three months would be entering the army. Meanwhile, Chandler was having trouble with the manuscript of a novel, *The Blue Dahlia,* and was thinking of turning it into a screenplay. The result was that Paramount bought the novel and hired Chandler to write the script. Halfway through the assignment, he found himself in trouble.

Originally, his villain had been a war hero, an enlisted man in the navy. Now the Navy Department refused to cooperate on any project that portrayed a war hero as a murderer.

A new solution to the question of who killed who was required, this at a time when the picture was in front of the camera and the camera was gaining on the script. Soon only seven pages of script remained, and the director needed thirty more.

Paramount's chief executives went behind the back of John Houseman, producer of the picture, and talked to Chandler in a manner that dismayed him and caused him to conclude that he could not finish the script. After thinking things over for a day, however, he changed his mind somewhat.

He went to Houseman, also the product of an English public school, and explained that, while he could not possibly continue to work on the script at the studio, he could finish it at home, drunk.

At the time Chandler had been on the wagon for quite a while and knew that what he was suggesting was dangerous. The advantage, he told Houseman, was that "alcohol gave him an energy and self-assurance that he could achieve in no other way."

Years later, in a memoir published in *Harper's* and later reprinted in the book *The Blue Dahlia,* Houseman wrote, "He did not minimize the hazards: he pointed out that his plan, if adopted, would call for deep faith on my part and supreme courage on his, since he would in effect be completing the script at the risk of his life."

It wasn't the drinking that was dangerous, he explained, since he had a doctor who gave him such massive injections of glucose that he could last for weeks with no solid food at all. It was the sobering up process that was perilous, "the terrible strain," Houseman wrote, "of his return to normal living."

Chandler then presented Houseman with a list of his basic requirements. These were:

"A. Two Cadillac limousines, to stand day and night outside the house with drivers available for:

    1. Fetching the doctor (Ray's or Cissie's or both).

    2. Taking script pages to and from the studio.

    3. Driving the maid to market.

"B. Six secretaries—in relays of two—to be in constant attendance and readiness at all times for dictation, typing, and other possible emergencies.

"C. A direct line open at all times, to my office by day and the studio switchboard at night."

Unofficially, the heads of Paramount accepted Chandler's proposal and cars and secretaries were soon in position. Houseman's account continues:

During those last eight days of shooting Chandler did not draw one sober breath, nor did one speck of solid food pass his lips ... his doctor came twice a day to give him intravenous injections. The rest of the time, except when he was asleep ... Ray was never without a glass in his hand. He did not drink much. Having reached the euphoria that he needed, he continued to consume just enough bourbon and water to maintain him in that condition. He worked about a third of the time. Between eight and ten every evening he sat in Cissie's room and they listened to the Gas Company's program of classical music on the radio. The rest of the time was spent in a light sleep from which he woke in full possession of his faculties and picked up exactly where he had stopped. ... He continued until he felt himself drowsy again, then dropped back comfortably into sleep while the girl went to the next room, typed the pages, and left them on the table beside him to be reread and corrected when he woke up. As his last line in the script Ray wrote in pencil: "Did somebody say something about a drink of bourbon?"

A month passed before Chandler recovered.

"During his convalescence," Houseman wrote, "he lay neatly dressed in fresh pajamas under a silk robe; when I came to see him he would extend a white and trembling hand, and acknowledge my gratitude with the modest smile of a gravely wounded hero who had shown courage far beyond the call of duty."

He had taken a bit of a beating but he was recuperating now, getting stronger every day. And along the way he had managed to save the situation for another product of an English public school. It was the sort of thing he would have expected of any gentleman.

Philip Marlowe is as he is because, for Raymond Chandler, the whole world couldn't be like "the eighty-five cent dinner [that] tasted like a discarded mailbag." There had to be something better than that. Something better, also, than the monumental gray green Packard convertible, something better than the house overlooking the Pacific at La Jolla.

And so he created Philip Marlowe. Chesterton's remark is worth repeating. "It is the agent of social justice who is the original and poetic figure, while the burglars and footpads are merely old cosmic conservatives, happy in the immemorial respectability of apes and wolves."

There had to be something romantic, something superior.

It could be a private eye: "down these mean streets a man must go who is not himself mean, who is neither tarnished nor afraid. He is the hero; he is everything. . . . He must be, to use a rather weathered phrase, a man of honor."

It could also be an English public-school man who was willing to risk his life to help another English public-school man.

"I accepted his proposal," Houseman wrote. "Ray now became extremely happy and exhilarated."

In his essay, "The Shape of Crimes to Come," Frank D. McSherry refers to a science-fiction novel, *The Adventures of Wyndham Smith,* by S. Fowler Wright. To McSherry the book suggests "that a society that has solved all its problems may well be in trouble just as deep as one with too many problems."

In the novel an experiment places Wyndham Smith in a distant future where there is no war, no poverty, and no crime. The irony, McSherry points out, is that the people, with all their problems solved, "have nothing left to do and are bored to death. The government council decides that the only logical solution to the quandary is mass suicide. The people agree and . . ."

But that is not the problem here.

NOTES

Sherlock Holmes—Conan Doyle

[1] Daniel Hoffman, *Poe Poe Poe Poe Poe Poe Poe*, p. 121.
[2] Lionel Tiger and Robin Fox, *The Imperial Animal*, p. 21.
[3] Duncan Chappell and Marilyn Walsh, " 'No Questions Asked': A Consideration of the History of Criminal Receiving." This paper was presented at the conference, "Present Day Implications of the History of Violence and Other Crime," held at the State University of New York College at Brockport on February 19, 1972, and reprinted in "An Analysis of Criminal Redistribution Systems and their Economic Impact on Small Business," a Staff Report, prepared for the Select Committee on Small Business, United States Senate (Government Printing Office, stock number 5270–01628), p. 22.
[4] Gerald Howson, *Thief-Taker General*, p. 37.
[5] " 'No Questions Asked,' " p. 28.
[6] Charles Reith, *The Blind Eye of History*, p. 144.
[7] *Ibid.*, p. 157.
[8] Henri F. Ellenberger, *The Discovery of the Unconscious*, p. 537.

Jules Maigret—Georges Simenon

[1] Blake Ehrlich, *Paris on the Seine*, p. 83.
[2] Sanche de Gramont, *The French*, p. 217.
[3] Loren Eiseley, *The Invisible Pyramid*, p. 146.
[4] Letter to Author, October 29, 1975.
[5] Lionel Trilling, *Sincerity and Authenticity*, p. 58.

222

Sam Spade—Dashiell Hammett

[1] From Allan Pinkerton's *General Principles and Rules of Pinkerton National Police Agency,* as quoted in Wayne G. Broehl, Jr., *The Molly Maguires,* p. 135.

[2] *Ibid.,* p. 136.

[3] *Ibid.,* p. 142.

[4] *Ibid.,* p. 141.

[5] Steven Marcus, in the Introduction to Dashiell Hammett's *The Continental Op,* p. xix.

[6] Ron Goulart, *An Informal History of the Pulp Magazines* (New York: Ace Books, 1973), p. 185.

Eric Ambler

[1] Joel Hopkins, "An Interview with Eric Ambler," in the *Journal of Popular Culture* (Fall, 1975), p. 286.

[2] R.H.W. Dillard, "The Great Game," in *Bookletter* (September 16, 1974), p. 8.

[3] Clive James, "Eric Ambler," in the London magazine, *New Review* (September, 1974), p. 69.

[4] Oscar Levant, *The Unimportance of Being Oscar* (New York: Putnam, 1968), p. 176.

[5] Paxton Davis, "The World We Live In: The Novels of Eric Ambler," *The Hollins Critic,* published by Hollins College (February, 1971), p. 11.

[6] Ralph Harper, *The World of the Thriller,* p. 47.

Philip Marlowe—Raymond Chandler

[1] Francoise Gilot, *Life with Picasso* (New York: McGraw-Hill, 1964), p. 197.

SELECTED BIBLIOGRAPHY

Sherlock Holmes—Conan Doyle

Baring-Gould, William S. *Sherlock Holmes of Baker Street.* New York: Clarkson N. Potter, 1962.

Carr, John Dickson. *The Life of Sir Arthur Conan Doyle.* New York: Harper & Row, 1949.

Doyle, Arthur Conan. *Memories and Adventures.* Garden City, N.Y.: Doubleday, 1924.

Harrison, Michael. *In the Footsteps of Sherlock Holmes.* New York: Drake, 1972.

Higham, Charles. *The Adventures of Conan Doyle.* New York: Norton, 1976.

Nordon, Pierre. *Conan Doyle: a Biography.* New York: Holt, Rinehart & Winston, 1967.

Pearson, Hesketh. *Conan Doyle.* New York: Walker, 1961.

Starett, Vincent. *The Private Life of Sherlock Holmes.* New York: Macmillan, 1933.

Jules Maigret—Georges Simenon

Brophy, Brigid. *Don't Never Forget.* New York: Holt, Rinehart & Winston, 1966.

Collins, Carvel. "Simenon," in *Writers at Work: The Paris Review Interviews,* ed. Malcolm Cowley. First Series. New York: Viking, 1958.

Galligan, Edward L. "Simenon's Mosaic of Small Novels." *South Atlantic Quarterly,* Autumn, 1967.

Lambert, Gavin. *The Dangerous Edge.* New York: Grossman, 1976.

Raymond, John. *Simenon in Court.* New York: Harcourt Brace Jovanovich, 1969.

Sam Spade—Dashiell Hammett

Bazelon, David. *Nothing but a Fine Tooth Comb.* New York: Simon & Schuster, 1970.

Chandler, Raymond. *The Simple Art of Murder.* Boston: Houghton Mifflin, 1950.

Edenbaum, Robert I. "The Poetics of the Private Eye: The Novels of Dashiell Hammett," in *Tough Guy Writers of the Thirties,* ed. David Madden. Carbondale: Southern Illinois University Press, 1968.

Ephron, Nora. "Lillian Hellman Walking, Talking, Cooking, Writing, Walking." *New York Times Book Review,* September 23, 1973.

Fechheimer, David. "Interview with Mrs. Hammett," *City of San Francisco,* November 4, 1975.

Gide, André. *Imaginary Interviews.* New York: Pantheon, 1944.

Gores, Joe. *Hammett.* New York: Putnam, 1975.

Hammett, Dashiell. Introduction to *The Maltese Falcon.* New York: Modern Library, 1934.

Harper, Ralph. *The World of the Thriller.* Baltimore: Johns Hopkins University Press, 1974.

Hellman, Lillian. *Four Plays,* Introduction. New York: Modern Library, 1942.

————. *Scoundrel Time.* Boston: Little Brown, 1976.

————. *An Unfinished Woman.* Boston: Little Brown, 1969.

Macdonald, Ross. *On Crime Writing.* Santa Barbara, Cal.: Capra Press, 1973.

Malin, Irving. "Focus on *The Maltese Falcon:* The Metaphysical Falcon," in *Tough Guy Writers of the Thirties,* ed. David Madden. Carbondale: Southern Illinois University Press, 1968.

Marcus, Steven. Introduction to *The Continental Op,* by Dashiell Hammett. New York: Random House, 1974.

Nolan, William F. *Dashiell Hammett: a Casebook.* Santa Barbara, Cal.: McNally & Loftin, 1969.

Ruehlmann, William. *Saint With A Gun.* New York: New York University Press, 1974.

Sanderson, Elizabeth. "Ex-Detective Hammett." *Bookman,* Jan. 1932.

Pat Garrett

Metz, Leon C. *Pat Garrett: The Story of a Western Lawman.* Norman, Okla.: University of Oklahoma Press, 1975.

O'Connor, Richard. *Pat Garrett.* Garden City, N.Y.: Doubleday, 1960.

Prassel, Frank R. *The Western Peace Officer.* Norman, Okla.: University of Oklahoma Press, 1972.

Sonnichsen, C. L. *Tularosa.* New York: Devin-Adair, 1963.

Eric Ambler

Ambler, Eric. *The Ability to Kill.* London: Bodley Head, 1963.

————. Introduction to *The Adventures of Sherlock Holmes,* by Arthur Conan Doyle. London: Jonathan Cape, 1974.

Ambrosetti, Ronald. "The World of Eric Ambler: From Detective to Spy," in *Dimensions of Detective Criticism,* ed. Larry N. Landrum, Pat Browne and Ray B. Browne. Bowling Green, Ohio: Bowling Green University Popular Press, 1976.

Davis, Paxton. "The World We Live In: The Novels of Eric Ambler." *The Hollins Critic,* February, 1971.

Dillard, R.H.W. "The Great Game." *Bookletter,* September 16, 1974.

Hopkins, Joel. "An Interview with Eric Ambler." *Journal of Popular Culture,* Fall, 1975.

James, Clive. "Eric Ambler." *New Review,* September, 1974.

Lambert, Gavin. *The Dangerous Edge.* New York: Grossman, 1975.

McCormick, Donald. *Who's Who in Spy Fiction.* New York: Taplinger, 1977.

Marcus, Greil. "The Thriller Memorandum, Part II." *Rolling Stone,* March 25, 1976.

Philip Marlowe—Raymond Chandler

Durham, Philip. *Down These Mean Streets a Man Must Go: Raymond Chandler's Knight.* Chapel Hill, N.C.: University of North Carolina Press, 1963.

Gross, Miriam, ed. *The World of Raymond Chandler.* New York: A & W, 1978.

MacShane, Frank. *The Life of Raymond Chandler.* New York: Dutton, 1976.

Ruehlmann, William. *Saint With a Gun.* New York: New York University Press, 1974.

Ruhm, Herbert. "Raymond Chandler—From Bloomsbury to the Jungle —and Beyond," in *Tough Guy Writers of the Thirties,* ed. David Madden. Carbondale: Southern Illinois University Press, 1968.

Symons, Julian. "The Case of Raymond Chandler." *New York Times Book Review,* December 23, 1973.

General

Armes, Jay J. *Jay J. Armes, Investigator,* ed. Frederick Nolan. New York: Macmillan, 1976.

Astor, David. *The New York Cops.* New York: Scribner, 1971.

Astor, Mary. *A Life on Film.* New York: Delacorte, 1971.

Auden, W. H. "The Guilty Vicarage," in *The Dyer's Hand and Other Essays.* New York: Knopf, 1956.

Barzun, Jacques. *The Energies of Art.* New York: Harper & Row, 1956.

Belin, Jean. *Secrets of the Sûreté.* New York: Putnam, 1950.

Broehl, Wayne G., Jr. *The Molly Maguires.* Cambridge, Mass: Harvard University Press, 1964.

Chesney, Kellow. *The Anti-Society.* Boston: Gambit, 1970.

Chesterton, G. K. "A Defense of Detective Stories," in *The Defendant,* ed. R. Brimley Johnson. London, 1902.

Chevalier, Louis. *Laboring Classes and Dangerous Classes.* New York: Fertig, 1973.

Cobb, Belton. *The First Detectives.* London: Faber, 1957.

Creel, George. "Unholy City." *Collier's,* September 2, 1939.

Daley, Robert. "Inside the Criminal-Informant Business." *New York,* March 24, 1975.

de Gramont, Sanche. *The French.* New York: Putnam, 1969.

Edwards, Samuel. *The Vidocq Dossier.* Boston: Houghton Mifflin, 1977.

Ehrlich, Blake. *Paris on the Seine.* New York: Atheneum, 1962.

Eiseley, Loren. *The Invisible Pyramid.* New York: Scribner, 1970.

Ellenberger, Henri F. *The Discovery of the Unconscious.* New York: Basic Books, 1970.

Green, Martin. *Children in the Sun.* New York: Basic Books, 1976.

Grella, George. "Murder and Manners: The Formal Detective Novel," *Dimensions of Detective Criticism,* ed. Larry N. Landrum, Pat Browne, and Ray B. Browne. Bowling Green, Ohio: Bowling Green University Popular Press, 1976.

Heppenstall, Rayner. *Bluebeard and After.* London: Peter Owen, 1973.

————. *French Crime in the Romantic Age.* London: Hamish Hamilton, 1970.

Hibbert, Christopher. *The Roots of Evil.* Boston: Little Brown, 1963.

Higgins, George V. "The Private Eye as Illegal Hero." *Esquire,* December, 1972.

Hoffman, Daniel. *Poe Poe Poe Poe Poe Poe Poe.* Garden City, N.Y.: Doubleday, 1972.

Hopkins, Ernest J. *Our Lawless Police.* New York: Viking, 1931.

Horan, James, and Howard Swiggert. *The Pinkerton Story.* New York: Putnam's, 1951.

Horan, James. *The Pinkertons: The Detective Dynasty That Made History.* New York: Crown, 1968.

Howson, Gerald. *Thief-Taker General.* London: Hutchinson, 1970.

Klockars, Carl B. *The Professional Fence.* New York: Free Press, 1974.

Leakey, Richard, and Roger Lewin. *Origins.* New York: Dutton, 1977.

McWilliams, Carey. *Southern California Country.* New York: Duell, Sloan & Pearce, 1946.

McWilliams, Wilson C. *The Idea of Fraternity in America.* Berkeley: University of California Press, 1973.

Maugham, Somerset. "The Decline and Fall of the Detective Story," in *The Vagrant Mood.* Garden City, N.Y.: Doubleday, 1953.

Morn, Frank Thomas. "Allan Pinkerton," in *Pioneers in Policing,* ed. P. J. Stead. Montclair, N.J.: Patterson Smith, 1977.

Murch, A. E. *The Development of the Detective Novel.* New York: Philosophical Library, 1958.

Ousby, Ian. *Bloodhounds of Heaven.* Cambridge, Mass.: Harvard University Press, 1976.

Patterson, John. "A Cosmic View of the Private Eye." *Saturday Review,* August 22, 1953.

Phillips, John, and Anne Hollander. "Lillian Hellman," in *Writers at Work: The Paris Review Interviews,* ed. Malcolm Cowley. Third Series. New York: Viking, 1967.

Reith, Charles. *The Blind Eye of History.* Montclair, N.J.: Patterson Smith, 1975.

Richardson, James H. *For the Life of Me.* New York: Putnam, 1954.

Rubenstein, Jonathan. *City Police.* New York: Farrar, Straus & Giroux, 1973.

Rumbelow, Donald. *I Spy Blue.* New York: St. Martins, 1972.

Snow, C. P. Introduction to *The Casebook of Sherlock Holmes.* London: Jonathan Cape, 1974.

Stead, P. J., ed. *Pioneers in Policing.* Montclair, N.J.: Patterson Smith, 1977.

_____. *The Police of Paris.* London: Staples Press, 1957.

_____. *Vidocq: A Biography.* London: Staples Press, 1953.

Stein, Aaron Marc. "The Mystery Story in Cultural Perspective," in *The Mystery Story,* ed. John Ball. New York: Publishers, Inc., 1976.

Symons, Julian. *Mortal Consequences.* New York: Harper & Row, 1972.

Tiger, Lionel, and Robin Fox. *The Imperial Animal.* New York: Holt, Rinehart, & Winston, 1971.

Trilling, Lionel. *Sincerity and Authenticity.* Cambridge, Mass: Harvard University Press, 1972.

Turner, William W. *The Police Establishment.* New York: Putnam's, 1968.

Vidocq, François. *The Personal Memoirs of the First Great Detective.* Trans. and ed. Edwin Gile Rich. Cambridge, Mass.: Riverside Press, 1935.

Wilson, James Q. *Thinking About Crime.* New York: Basic Books, 1975.